SPELLBOUND

DAVID MᶜKAIN

SPELLBOUND

GROWING UP IN GOD'S COUNTRY

The University of Georgia Press/Athens & London

1988 by the University of Georgia Press
Athens, Georgia 30602
All rights reserved
Designed by Louise M. Jones
Set in Trump Mediaeval
Typeset by The Composing Room of Michigan, Inc.
Printed and bound by Thomson-Shore
The paper in this book meets the guidelines for
permanence and durability of the Committee on
Production Guidelines for Book Longevity of the Council
on Library Resources.

Printed in the United States of America
92 91 90 89 88   5 4 3 2 1

Library of Congress Cataloging in Publication Data

McKain, David W.
Spellbound: growing up in God's country.

1. McKain, David W.—Biography—Youth. 2. Poets,
American—20th century—Biography. 3. Pennsylvania—
Social life and customs. I. Title.
PS3563.A3133Z475 1988   811'.54 [B]   88-4721
ISBN 0-8203-1048-4 (alk. paper)

British Library Cataloging in Publication Data available

Winner of the
Associated Writing Programs Award
for Creative Nonfiction

For Walter and Elizabeth McKain
and in memory of Charles and Ida McKain

Troubles overcome are good to tell.

Contents

PART TWO

Acknowledgments

I would like to thank those friends, acquaintances, and strangers who helped me scout down sources, dig up forgotten photographs, and shift commas and who generally offered their support and encouragement. They are Philip Zaeder, Kelly Wise, Marion Vernon, Marta Troy, Jack Troy, Jay Taylor, Jane Stack, Dave Smith, Ted Sizer, Fred Shuey, Jean St. Pierre, Betty Robinson, Michael Robertson, Marty Robacker, Hilary Reeves, Harvey Phillips, Kevin O'Connor, Jean Mitchell, Megan McKain, Joshua McKain, Gerald Long, David Knight, Nancy Holmes, Mary Hill, Donald Hall, Fehmi Hakim, Lee Gutkind, John Gould, Peter Gilbert, Margaret Gibson, Ruth Daily, Jim Daily, Jim Coleman, Joe Cleary, Malcolm Call, and Nelson Aldrich.

Both Phillips Academy at Andover and the University of Connecticut provided me with time off from teaching duties to write this book. From 1984 to 1987 I was fortunate to serve as writer-in-residence at Phillips Academy under a grant given to the school by Roger F. Murray, and for this I am most grateful.

SPELLBOUND

Part One

CHAPTER I

God's Country

The shocks chatter over the frost heaves as I bounce west on Route 6 through north-central Pennsylvania, through state forest and game lands, through what people out there call God's Country. A few logging roads spill out onto the highway, trailing mud and skidmarks on the blacktop. The trucks, like animals, leave their droppings, their tracks. I shift down behind a silver oil pumper crawling up a hill, an eighteen wheeler spewing diesel smoke into the mountain haze. Nearly noon, a mist hangs below the ridge, obscuring the crown. Bursts of sunshine slant through the fog—gold, faint, like gunsmoke. Then *crack:* a cloudburst releases every scent in the forest. The rain lasts for a minute, gentle, spattering, even while the sun is shining. The forest remains thick with oak and frostgrape, hemlock and redvine, thicker as the leaves glisten. But already the ferns gather dust, and spore and seed scatter inside a slant of yellow light. I still can't see the top of the ridge. The mountain seems to rise up forever, my spirits with it.

Potter County Recreation has painted tall blue letters the color of sky on a billboard near Pine Creek: "Welcome to God's Country." The sign welcomes barkpeelers, trap shooters, rattlesnake hunters, campers, deer hunters, hikers, fishermen, trappers, and people like me, heading back home. I lift my eyes to watch a hawk circle against the sky, riding an updraft.

During the heat of the summer the dogs whimper, the mosquitoes whine. Then the epithet "God's Country" seems appropriate because no one else but God could live here. There is only stillness. The very shape and touch of the air change its clarity and heft. The air turns to steam.

"You need gills just to breathe," my mother used to complain, collapsing on the couch and stirring the air with a fan from the First Baptist Church of Bradford. Tuckered out at the end of the day, she would ask, "Is it God's Country or has God forsaken it? That's what I'd like to know." Then quickly she would jump up off the couch and fan away her words as well as the heat. "Mercy," she would laugh, "I don't mean that."

Amid the loonlike cries of the bedridden, Beth and Miss Doubleday traipse up and down the long corridor of the Mystic Manor Convalescent Home in rumpled nightclothes, my mother between them. Arm in arm, the three of them glide for a few steps, then jangle to a stop in exaggerated unison. "Oh my, yes!" Beth slurs emphatically. "Well," Miss Doubleday responds, "I do hope so. For both of you. I sincerely hope so." She clasps her long thin fingers in front of her chin and speaks in perfect Oxonian English. My mother nods encouragingly. "Both of you have what it takes to bring us back!" Beth, heavily drugged, begins to teeter but is saved from falling by my mother's arm around her waist. They steady themselves, then lose their balance, laughing at their own bewilderment.

New friends, they wear each other's clothes and support one another. A handsome woman, Beth is in her late sixties, about my mother's age. She wears scuffed brown Oxfords and a pleated Pendleton skirt under her nightgown. She has the husky voice of a woman who once enjoyed whiskey sours and cigarettes. She might have sailed at one time, played golf or tennis. Tall and graceful, Miss Doubleday must be close to eighty. She holds the hem of her housecoat as though crossing a stage, her arm extended and bent slightly at the elbow, her wrist upturned. She is beautiful, with the bones of a sparrow. My mother looks like a retired schoolmarm from the Allegheny Mountains. Without a permanent, her hair is combed straight back over her ears like an Indian, her face drawn and haggard like that of an old woman staring vacantly into a WPA camera—Appalachian Still Life: 1937. There is a sadness and strength in her face lacking in the other women.

The CAT scans show a sinking of the cerebral cortex, a kind of saddleback in the middle of her brain. I call the declivity on the X-rays the "valley" of her life. She might enjoy that; the image puts her up on a ridgetop surveying God's Country. When I look at her, I think of myself. The odds are one out of five that one day I'll lose my mind as well. The odds are slightly better in Russian roulette: one out of six. It's nearly a family tradition. Wearing only a housecoat, my mother's mother waltzed downtown in the moonlight to gather flowers just as my mother did. I remember my mother crying when, at three in the morning, the police brought Grandma back—tears for herself. She shook her head. "In a few years I'm going to be just like Grandma. You mark my words." Her words are marked, but most everything else she ever said or knew is filed away in the snarled circuitry of her brain, deep in the base of the nucleus of what doctors call "the neurofibrillary tangle."

On mornings when I stop in to see her before teaching school, I sneak in the back door so I can sit at the foot of her bed and watch her sleep. Still and dark, the room fills me with a kind of suspicion, as though I shouldn't be there, as though I might get caught. Somewhere I read that fear is an emotion we use to distract ourselves from knowing the truth, a kind of deliberate confusion we create to protect ourselves from whatever it is we don't have the strength to face.

"Ida! Ida!" the nurse is shouting, "David is here! David! Isn't that nice?"

The nurses exaggerate every syllable as though my mother

is hard of hearing or speaks a foreign tongue. On good days she nods, battling through the aphasia to say, "Good. We, we, we . . . yayaya . . . oh." Once she said, "Oh dead deat dat . . . ," adding, "no," her face clouding over from a misfiring "known only to God Almighty," as she would have put it. But most of the time she does not speak at all. The talking falls to me, and I am not used to making small talk in her presence. There never used to be any need to explain or entertain. I brush her hair back over her ear with my fingers and smile. Through all these years I had always respected her from a distance, but now the distance has closed. I try to show my love by touching her, the way I would reach out to touch a child.

I tell her about the slightest change in the weather and praise her hair. She always had an eye for the strained, and for an instant I expect her to push me away and laugh at my feeble attempt at conversation. "Go on, you big galoot," she would playfully chide. "I've got better things to do than listen to your nonsense all day!" One day a few months ago, when I realized she could no longer live alone, I told her I loved her. She turned and looked at me hard for several seconds as though she hadn't quite heard. "Well," she finally said, "I would certainly hope so." But now she is silent. She smells of urine. The smell penetrates deep into the foam rubber pad and is absorbed into the pores of the mattress.

She frightens easily, without provocation. Mickey, her favorite nurse, comes in to feed her. Mickey does not shout as though she were deaf. Mickey talks easily as she feeds her, spooning in the oatmeal. Then, abruptly, my mother falls forward and jerks up her knees, batting the air, rocking in fits and starts, her eyes blinking in terror. "God bless you," I say, but it is not a sneeze: the spasm lasts ten minutes. Mickey shakes her head; she is sorry for me, sorry I have to see this. When the seizure stops, she gently washes my mother's face and hands with a damp washcloth, assuring her that everything is all right.

"She'll do that," she explains. "Something up there misfires." Mickey speaks slowly to calm everyone down, herself included. "Did I tell you about the two aides? The first time they saw her like that? They were giving her a shower, and all of a sudden Ida raised her hands and covered her face to protect herself. Just like she did a minute ago. I tell you. The aides were nearly hysterical. They came running out to the desk to complain. They thought somebody on another shift had been beating her. If you haven't seen her do it before it sure looks that way. One of the doctors called it fear-reflex. It's like she was afraid someone was going to hit her." I remember earlier beatings. I remember my father standing over her, raising his fist.

For years she called me "Willy" or "Billy," nicknames for her younger brother; but I didn't think much of it, not until I called one Sunday and she put down the receiver to check the fire under the potatoes and didn't come back. I couldn't get through the busy signal until the next morning. A month or so later there were reports that she was beginning to lose control in her classroom. Luckily, the superintendent of schools appointed her to an administrative post, covering for her until she reached retirement. When I thanked him for it, he just smiled. "Oh, well," he said, "we don't think of it that way." He didn't say how he did think of it; he didn't have to. But friends could only cover for her for so long. Once a neighbor called and said she was standing on the sidewalk when he got home from work, "looking lost." I had seen her that way before, pacing in small circles, moving her lips as though she were murmuring a prayer. When he followed her upstairs, the place was full of gas, ready to explode. For awhile we pretended that all she needed was a different stove, so we ordered a new one with an electric pilot, but the stove wasn't the problem.

More than a neighbor, Strut Bauer came every day. He mowed the patch of grass by the steps, walked her downtown to appointments, picked up her prescriptions, shopped for her, and promptly at five o'clock came to prepare her supper. "Make sure," he put it, "she'll have one balanced meal a day." Her diet was balanced, but she was not. He could not be there all day. Once, the temperature eighty, she put on three layers of clothes and wandered four miles to the new mall on the other side of town. Inside the mall she rested by the fountain, content to gaze at the stream of shoppers, the sweat dripping from her chin. Mr. Cleveland, the neighbor who discovered gas in the apartment, sat down on the wet stone beside her, struck up an easy conversation, and brought her home.

Strut suffered through all of this more than anyone. They had been friends ever since my father left. After work, still in his matching khaki workclothes and carrying his lunch pail, he would walk across town to tighten the hinges on our front door or change a washer in our sink, but everybody in town knew he came to visit my mother. On warm summer nights the two of them sat out on the glider watching lightning bugs, talking softly. I overheard them talking whether I wanted to or not: the apartment was small. Then, one night, I heard them whispering about marriage. "I know, Ida," he said patiently and apologetically. He spoke slowly, pausing for a long time between words. "I feel the same way . . . but, well . . . I don't want to find myself leaning on you. That's all."

Strut worked for the Dresser Manufacturing Company dispensing cotter pins and stove bolts to the men who ran the machines—a stock room operator. The next morning my mother explained that he did not want to get married because his retirement money would be less, he thought, than hers. She laughed and shook her head. "Ah, men," she said. "Amen!" But I think she was proud of him. His real name was Estrata, meaning "general" in Spanish. They never did get married, but she entered his name in Parker's blue ink on the records page of the family Bible: "E. C. Bauer, born in Titusville, Pa., January 19, 1903."

Now I am returning home, through years and God's Country, with double-strength trash bags to clear out her apartment. Maple seedlings sprout in the sagging gutters. The window trim of my mother's apartment needs to be scraped and painted, the panes reglazed. She had lived on the third floor where an electric Christmas candle still stands in the window; a shingle dangles from the roof. The old women in the houses on either side live alone. The bushes have grown up in front of Mrs. O'Dell's porch; scraps of paper cling to the lower branches, a yellow newspaper rots on the bottom step. Mrs. O'Dell is sitting behind her curtain in the living room. I see the curtain move but I resist the urge to wave. Yellow cats stretch in the sun beside the porch, their spray baking in the heat. Stink weed grows on the steep bank on the hill across the street. The smell of crude oil hangs in the air year-round, heaviest now in August. I take a deep breath.

Nearly a month of mail has been jammed through the slot in the front door: bills, fliers, magazines, and newspapers. I put the newspapers and magazines on the bottom of the stack and climb the stairs. The apartment is stuffy; I glance at a bouquet of plastic flowers on the dining room table and throw open the window. A jug of water from Kennedy Springs sits on the refrigerator shelf, but I let the water run in the sink. I have been drinking Bradford water all my life, and I refuse to accept the fact that the water is contaminated. "Oh, yes," Strut warned. "They call it the Giardia. You can get stomach cramps and diarrhea. You can even die." But I refill my glass at the tap with a certain pride. I grew up in this town; I feel immune.

I look around the apartment to see what I should take back to Connecticut. Everything I take back must fit into the car in this one trip. My mother would want Strut to have first choice, and I set aside a few things he might like: two mixing bowls, a brass coffee grinder, the vacuum cleaner. The piano, the books, and maybe even the organ will go to the Tuna Valley Free Methodist Church. The television set and some of the pictures on the wall will go to Margaret DeGolier down the street. Most everything else will be turned over to Mrs. Adams, a woman Strut has recommended to run the yard sale. The objects in the living room have lost whatever life they gather from being around people. After a month of not having the air stirred around them, they sit there forlorn, abandoned. I go back into the kitchen for another glass of water, noticing a soapstone carving of Robert Burns's cottage over the sink, an old tin match holder over the stove, and a plaque over the toaster that says, "In Everything Give Thanks." The message has hung over the kitchen table for as long as I can remember.

I take it down so I won't forget it, tapping it with my finger to see if it is metal or ceramic. It is made to look like hammered bronze, but it is ceramic—the size of a postcard. I sit down and pull my chair close to the table so I won't drop it. If my parents were here they would not let me touch it; it was, to them, as holy as an icon—even though they did not believe in icons. The letters on the plaque stand out and fill the entire space inside the border. In cursive, the letters are Gothic, molded as Scripture: "In Everything Give Thanks." An artificial burst of gold leaf with pink flowers and mint leaves entwines the letters, like the illustrations in a medieval manuscript.

Whenever, as a child, I looked up over my spoon, I looked at the sign. The message announced the strategy of our lives. Sometimes my father pointed to it with the tip of his fork and said that, if I followed it all of my days, it would make me "brave." It was, he said, "the foundation of our spiritual lives. Our very faith." To be forever grateful filled the mind with joy and thanksgiving, hardly leaving space for suffering and want. "Thessalonians," my father said. "In everything give thanks: for this is the will of God in Christ Jesus concerning you." He emphasized the will of God by speaking slowly, keeping time by raising and lowering his voice on every syllable. Our reward would come later—on Judgment Day. "That's the only day that matters," he argued, "for it is harder for a rich man to enter the kingdom of heaven than it is for a camel to pass through the eye of a needle." This was my father's favorite parable—a way of judging Bradford's rich without feeling mean spirited. Our poverty seemed to assure us easy access.

When I recall the past, I think about the town of Bradford as much as I think about my parents. The streets were paved with red brick and lined with maple and elm, and I roamed within its protective indifference from one end of town to the other. The demands on my parents' lives to pay the rent gave me freedom. Out of necessity, they turned me over to the streets and the hills—the most wonderfully lax set of parents a boy could know. The strongest rebuke I ever received came from Miss Pike, my teacher in the third grade. On the back of one of my report cards she wrote, "David wanders about the room and leaves at will." I was, I suppose, intensely haphazard, one of those kids with a vacant look that comes from daydreaming and having his head shaved for ringworm.

Bradford was the cultural and economic center of the upper Alleghenies, the largest and most important city in the world. What other town could compete: Derrick City, Cyclone, Custer City, Rew, Big Shanty, Lewis Run, Burning Well, Turtlepoint? The banner across the top of the *Bradford Era* boasted that the town was "The Oil Metropolis of the World," and I grew up with a huge provincial pride, unaware that the boundary between the town and the hills existed only on the "Welcome" signs posted by the Lions and Elks. The town, actually, was just a dot in the mountains, but to me it was like another person, and each day I went out to meet it, to be in its company.

All through my school years I used to walk from Amm Street to West Branch, out South Bradford and out East Main, counting and memorizing the numbers, eager to enter the inventory into my ledger back home. There were three blacksmiths, five ice cream makers, five billiard parlors, and eighteen cigar stores; there were twenty candy shops, twenty-four toy stores, three movie theaters, twenty-six barber shops, four newspapers, two bath parlors, eleven tailors, five explosive manufacturers, seventy grocery stores, and two pet shops—my father's (McKain's Pet Shop) and the Bradford Pet Supply.

Now, like an old man, the town has shrunk, and Strut, like a symbol of the town, stands in front of my mother's apartment waiting to wave good-bye. To see me off, he wears a white belt and Southern Baptist white shoes to match his white hair, cropped short like the Marine he wishes he might have been. His eyes are red, his face twisted. I know it is difficult for him to cry. He has lived in Bradford nearly all his life. Seven years ago he had a quadruple bypass, and at leave-takings his eyes mist over. We have filled the two-dozen trash bags and, four deep, set them out neatly by the curb. I am bringing back two wired kitchen chairs, some sheet music, three box-framed portraits of the women on my mother's side, some pots and pans, a photograph of my mother in a turquoise kimono, Robert Burns's cottage, and the plaque, "In Everything Give Thanks." The car is jammed.

I start the engine and pull out quickly, tooting the horn and returning Strut's wave casually, pretending, in the habit of the place, that everything is fine, that my mother in her madness will someday return home, and that Strut is not weeping. For the time being nothing more can be done, although I know that the moment is incomplete. I turn on the radio loud and raise my voice over it, as though singing at the top of my lungs might help. I promise to remember Strut standing there; I promise to remember what it was like growing up in God's Country. I promise to remember.

CHAPTER 2

Roots

U ntil I started kindergarten God was my best friend.
There was no one else around to play with. I hunted
in the backyard for snakes under rocks and trapped
bees inside the soft, loose petals of the hollyhocks. I
climbed trees and tied rope from one branch to another to
make a hammock, but whatever I did, I did it alone or with
God. Dad had moved to Elmo to live by himself because of
Grandma, or at least that was what I was told. Grandma
would not let him have pop bottles in the house because she
belonged to the Woman's Christian Temperance Union, and
bottles of any kind reminded her of the evils of alcohol. She
didn't believe in smoking either, and once, when she caught
him lighting a Camel on her front porch, she chased him off
with a wet towel, waving it over her head like a bullwhip.
From the story I heard, Dad just kept walking all the way to
Elmo.

Elmo, Mom said, was a disgrace, but it was there that my
father first hand-painted a sign that proclaimed, "McKain's
Pet Shop." Somewhere on Route 854 between Elk City and
Fern, he tried to sell lovebirds and angel fish to anyone happening by, but I learned to count to ten by keeping track of
the number of cars that passed on a busy summer day. The
front porch of the house leaned toward the road, a sign of
decay my father took advantage of by displaying the birds so
they could be seen at an angle from the road. The landlords,
the MacIntyres, lived next door. With no electricity, the rent

was cheap. In addition to the lovebirds and a few small fish, he kept a dog named King, a Chow Chow watchdog chained to the outhouse.

On the few occasions that I visited him, we slept on mattresses on the living room floor because, in the back of the house, the morning sun would wake us. He brought the birds in off the porch at night, and they flicked out seed that ticked onto the linoleum floor like a clock gone haywire. My mother refused "to put one foot inside the door of the awful place." The house was rather crude, but she made it worse than it was because she was still upset that he had lost his church.

My father lost his church in 1937, the year I was born, but he used the title of reverend for the rest of his life. "Hi," he greeted strangers cheerfully, shaking hands with a strong grip and smiling, "I'm Reverend McKain." The title of reverend was magical, transforming him into a man who commanded respect—a man who inspired reverence. Respect and reverence were important for my father, especially after he was forced to retire from the ministry at the age of thirty-six. All the time I knew him he was a minister without a church, a shepherd without a flock. According to *Methodism in Western Pennsylvania*, he had been "admitted on trial to the church in 1930" and forced to retire because of "ill health" seven years later. According to my mother, a more accurate source, "ill health" meant that the church had lost patience with his frequent letters to the *Pittsburgh Press* and the *Buffalo Evening News* lambasting Roosevelt, "that Jew in the White House."

His churches were remote. The year I was born he had been preaching in Valier, an outpost so small it was never recorded on the Official Transportation Map of the State of Pennsylvania. On the banks of the Mahoning Creek, it had a feedstore, a filling station, a general store, and a church—the First Methodist. "If you can't find Valier," my mother joked, "look for Panic, Stump Creek, or Desire." While his church was in

Valier, we had lived in Punxsutawney, the town where I was born. "Punxsutawney," my mother teased, "the Indians named it that. They called the rotten wood of a blowdown *punk*. And then those little flies that buzz and hum over it? They called them *punkies*. And there you have it. Where the punkies live. The home of the gnat."

An expressive woman, she blew air through her nose when she mentioned the place, a burst of bravado and good cheer. "But," she added seriously, "we've lived in worse. A whole lot worse." And then she would drag out the names of the other places where my father had preached: Parker's Landing, Forestville, and Riceville. "One-horse towns if I ever saw one."

When she married my father on March 2, 1934, the day of her twenty-first birthday, she married a bright, handsome, serious young minister who was thirteen years older than she was, an older man to revere and look up to. Her own father, Reverend William Crawford, had died the year before, but she did not connect her strong need to find a replacement until it was too late. Three years after she married, my father was kicked out of the church. She was then the mother of two children. By this time in their marriage my father was having a hard time hiding his spells, an affliction which made him dangerous as well as angry. He tried to sell tropical fish in Punxsy for awhile, but he never made enough to earn a living.

Before my father lost his church, he baptized me in the kitchen sink. "Imagine that!" Mother railed. "The kitchen sink! The faucet leaked so bad we couldn't get rid of the silverfish, the cockroaches, and those things with all the legs? Centipedes? And there you were, getting baptized!" My father had worn a green velvet smoking jacket for the occasion and parted his thick black hair down the middle. In a black and white snapshot taken on the same day, he was standing under a clothesline in the backyard, his hair slicked down with Jeris, his face a ghostly white. "Yes, it was green!" my mother said as though the color had been chosen to deliberately offend her. "A green smoking jacket! A God-awful velvet green smoking jacket!"

Shortly after I was baptized, my mother, my sister Joanne, and I moved to Clarion to live with Grandma Crawford while my mother looked for work and took courses at the Clarion Normal School. It wasn't too much longer that my father, disgruntled, moved down the road to Elmo.

By contrast with the house in Elmo, Grandma Crawford's house in Clarion was something of a showpiece. Standing in the center of a perfect acre, it was approached by a long and wide slate sidewalk. Grandma made sure the lawn was trimmed, the hedges clipped, and the earth around the border flowers black and rich with used coffee grounds. I walked the full acre among fruit trees and flowers as though strolling through the Garden of Eden. Flagstone paths led to all manner of earthly delights: to the brass sundial or the silver ball, to a rabbit hole or a robin's nest, to the birdbath or the bench, to apples, pears, plums, or cherries, to peppermint leaves or sweet currants—and all of it, every leaf and every blade of grass, all of it was framed by Grandma's red-berry hedge.

The massive square house in the middle of this plot had fourteen rooms with French windows in the front which ran from floor to ceiling. My grandfather had the house built to his specifications from investments he had made in motion pictures and Florida real estate. Whether coal miner or preacher, he had saved scrupulously all his life. He wanted the house to please his wife and to help them both forget the poverty from which they had sprung. Now that he was "gone," Grandma's word, it was her house, and her vegetables grew all the way to the alley that ran alongside the tracks of the Clarion and Franklin Railroad. The railroad line ended right there in our backyard. I played at the depot nearly every day, climbing in and out of the boxcars and sitting inside the caboose with the men when it rained. If the sun melted the ice in a layover refrigerator car, the yardman loaded me down with full-size watermelons; one day I made three trips home before my mother stopped me at the back door with a lecture on greed. At bedtime, by lifting myself up on one elbow and looking out my bedroom window, I learned to read by sounding out the names of the railroads on the sides of the freight cars. The Great Northern had a white circle with a battering ram inside. But my lucky car, which I saw only twice, was the Santa Fe. It was painted gold, the color of the sun, my favorite color.

The names of faraway places on the rolling stock in the yard soon became familiar. In Clarion, my entire world was familiar; family was everywhere. I had relatives in four out of the five houses on the block where we lived, most of them, like my grandfather, immigrants from Scotland. Uncle Jim Harvey lived next door in a red brick house with fancy dadoes and scrollwork in the green trim along the rake of the roof and around the windows. He was the first in the family to build on East Main Street. Uncle Jim Harvey—we ran all three of his names together when we spoke of him—had been a coal miner. He had yellowish white hair and sat most of the day slumped by the window. I saw him wave when I gathered the good apples that dropped from his trees across the hedge into our yard; my mother called them windfalls.

The Sedaris family lived on the other side of Grandma's house, and their daughter taught me to count to one hundred. She tried to teach me the Jew's harp too, but when I tried to pluck it, the metal frame set my decaying teeth on edge. The Sedarises owned the restaurant across the street from the Clarion County courthouse called "The College Grill." My father said it was the best restaurant in town, but we didn't eat there because liquor was served. Aunt Mills lived next door to the Sedarises, and next to her, the Borrowmans, my Uncle Tom and Aunt Gertrude. I did not understand much of what they said for they spoke in broad

Scots. "Never call it a brogue," my mother warned, "and it's not exactly a burr either. But when he gets 'is engine goin, ken ye ketch a wee bit a whirr in it?"

William Anderson Crawford, my grandfather, was born in Cumbernauld, Scotland, and at the age of fourteen sailed steerage alone for America to find work. At Ellis Island he asked directions to the coal mines, setting off on foot for Pennsylvania. He stayed for a time in Snow Shoe, then wound up around Stump Creek, where he was later joined by ten brothers and sisters. Together with three or four of his brothers, he opened up a groundhog mine in the backyard, working the coal with a mule.

Had it not been for a circuit rider on horseback who saw spiritual promise in the young man, I don't know how long he would have stayed a miner. Without my grandfather's knowledge, the itinerant preacher raised enough money among his five congregations to send him to college. He graduated from Bucknell in 1895 at the age of twenty-seven, and shortly thereafter he was ordained into the Baptist church. He died several years before I was born, but Mom and Grandma spoke as though he were alive; they still considered his opinion, reminding each other of his likes and dislikes. My mother saved a record of his life in a brown leather volume called "Treasured Memories," courtesy of the Jenkins Funeral Home. Among the newspaper clippings, poems, photographs, and names of the nine reverends who officiated at the service and the four hundred "Friends Who Called," an obituary in the *Clarion Democrat* said, "Reverend Crawford was a thorough biblical scholar. . . . His sermons were of a clear expository character . . . revealing God's beneficent purposes for man. He was also very clear and forceful in the delivery of the Gospel. . . . It has been remarked . . . that the sermon he delivered on a baccalaureate occasion was one of the ablest, and best, and most inspiring ever delivered on such an occasion in town." I knew only that he had been a rich baritone, was kind, and had favored my mother with boundless love—perhaps, judging from her expectations in marrying my father, with too much love. Grandpa's photograph hung in an oval frame over the mantel in the music room: a life-size picture Grandma had touched up with peach watercolors and wash, giving him color.

Grandma, by far the most powerful person in my world, altered the lives of the living as well as the dead. According to the *History of the Pennsylvania Woman's Christian Temperance Union*, she hung the picture of Frances E. Willard, WCTU world leader, in every public and private school in Clarion County, installed two water fountains in Clarion High School, and, in New Bethlehem, placed an especially large fountain with a plaque which read: "For Man, For Horse, For Dog." At East Brady, along the banks of the Allegheny River, Grandma and her friends sponsored a dramatic presentation on the evils of alcohol called "Tell the World About Ethyl." She also helped raise funds for the hanging of lanterns at office headquarters in order "to lighten the way." She and others provided Scientific Temperance Instruction in the schools, donating copies of "Father Penn and John Barleycorn" to every high school in the county. As recognition of the importance of her work, Grandma's photograph appears in the frontmatter of the *History.* She is wearing a dark blue tulle dress and rimless glasses, looking every bit as formidable as she did when she took the pulpit to speak out against those who misused the Sabbath. The *History* also states that she led a successful campaign to close down the Garby, the only theater in town that tried to show movies on Sunday.

Grandma's vegetables grew in straight lines and stood at attention, spaced evenly according to the notches in the long stick she dragged behind during planting, marking the exact and proper distance between each seed. She wore a sunbonnet patched with a piece of calico cut from an old lavender apron, too old to be mended. At the end of each row she stuck an empty seed packet on top of a piece of lath, each length of wood cut evenly, propped vertically in the middle of a pyramid of grey pebbles and matching stones. She weeded at sunup on her hands and knees so that each row was a smooth furrow of shale-colored earth, turning lighter behind her as she kneeled in the warming sun.

On Grape Day no one else could pick but Grandma. The arbor ran from the back porch across the yard almost to the garden, a sturdy archway of beams and latticework supported by ten black iron poles sunk in concrete. Grandma climbed to the top of the stepladder herself, snipping each cluster with special pruning scissors, the ones with a brass spring she kept locked in a private drawer.

"Blood of Christ," she announced solemnly, handing a cluster down as though it was made of glass. My mother stood at the foot of the ladder putting grapes into one of three bushel baskets, according to quality and Grandma's instructions: the basket of grapes for jam: the basket of grapes for ordinary juice; and the basket of grapes for Communion, these the most perfect grapes of all. After the grapes were picked, we lugged them into the laundry room and cranked them through the wringer, the juice dripping into one of two soapstone tubs. Covered by unsized muslin as thin as gauze, they soaked overnight. The next day Grandma added a five-pound bag of sugar to each tub, stirring the juice with the bottom half of an old wooden oar, paddling through the brew like a woman lost at sea. Then the juice sat there and worked a few days until, ladle by ladle, they strained it through cheesecloth into half-gallon jars, the clearest marked "F.B.C." for the First Baptist Church.

At the end of the summer, she dried, pickled, canned, and stored enough vegetables in the root cellar to last beyond winter into spring, her larder buckling the whitewashed shelves in the basement. I never did learn how she managed to obtain sugar and other wartime scarcities. Ration stamps were hard to come by.

CHAPTER 3

Spinning

asoline was in short supply as well as sugar, and my mother said she didn't like to ask anyone to drive us to Elmo to see my father while there was a war going on. Besides, she was still busy studying for her teaching certificate at the Normal School, and I didn't like to go to Elmo anyway. King growled and snapped, flinging himself into the air on the end of his chain as I tried to sneak by to the outhouse. It did not help that my father beat him with a stick and then talked softly to him, explaining that all three of us were pals. King, I knew, would bite me if he could; that was why he was chained to the outhouse. At least these were some of the excuses we used for not going to Elmo. The truth was that my mother seemed happier when my father was away, and that made me happier as well. He frightened both of us. Mom was afraid of his temper, but I was more afraid of what he would do to himself than anything he might do to me. Sometimes he frowned before his eyes glazed over, and the next thing he crashed to the ground like a horse that had been shot. Even worse, when he woke up he acted as though nothing had happened. The pretense was the worst part. "I just had a spill," he would say, forcing a smile through the pain. "I just slipped on a wet spot." He wiped up his own blood smiling, and he smiled when he washed his wounds at the sink.

One morning I jumped out of bed, flew down the hall, and slammed the bathroom door all in one breathless thrashing

of arms and legs, seeking a place to hide. The sun glared
through the east window against the white walls and on the
white tiled floor so that the porcelain sink burned in the
blazing light and the water ran blue and gold from the nickel
spigot. On fire with the promise of morning, the bathroom
was always brilliant. I hid there when dark thoughts clouded
my mind. I woke from a dream I could not shake. I splashed
cold water on my face and looked out across the backyards of
the Sedarises, the Millses, and the Borrowmans, but still the
dream would not go away.

Another child had been in the house, a sister who had
loved and comforted me, her eyes laughing, her breath like
warm milk. In the dream I had been sitting inside a wooden
pen while she stood outside and clapped her hands. Con-
tented, I had gazed and babbled into her soft round face, occasionally tossing a teething ring out onto the floor so she
could pick it up and pretend to scold. She weaved and
bobbed and clapped her hands. Then, abruptly, the room
emptied. I woke up, wondering where she had gone and who
she was. My hands smelled like oilcloth when I woke, the
smell of the rubber ring.

I ran down the front stairs instead of taking the dark back
stairs, tearing through the house and the front parlor where
my playpen had been and where I had bounced my rubber
teething ring to the floor. I ran so hard I glanced at the pearl-
tipped buttons in the hall, but I didn't stop to push them on
and off as I usually did. Instead of strings dangling from the
middle of the ceiling, Gramdma had pearl-tipped buttons
everywhere, and I pushed them every morning as a kind of
ritual. But the dream would not go away. I ran to the kitchen
and waited until my mother turned around from the stove.
She said good morning and smiled as she always did, trying
to make me feel as though I had come back from a night's
adventure to begin a new day. By the way she looked at me, I
realized she knew about my dream. She walked toward me

the way she would approach a wounded bird trembling under the hedge, moving slowly, wiping her hands on her apron and smiling, talking in a soft voice. "Did you have a bad dream?" she asked, her knees creaking as she squatted down on the floor in front of me.

Frightened, I tried to tell her about the dream, but I could not make sense of it. Nothing terrified me like the things inside my mind I could not reach out and touch. I had been told I had had a sister, and on the mantel stood a framed photograph, but the photograph was like others of places and people far away. Grandma had tinted the picture with artificial pastels, giving us rosy cheeks and pink arms, but I did not remember sitting in the studio or holding the bright blue ball in front of the camera. I did not remember anything about Joanne either except the warm milk on her breath from the dream. And yet, in my mind, she was still there, leaning over the side of the playpen, clapping her hands.

Mom coaxed me into the parlor where we sat on the sofa. "Yes," she said, "that's your sister, Joanne." In the picture Joanne was three and I was one. She was wearing a yellow dress, her hair a henna red; Mom said girls with red hair should not wear pink or red dresses, but Grandma colored her cheeks pink. I was holding the blue ball. We sat for a while in silence, and then Mom told me the story.

"I bet you don't remember when that picture was taken, do you? Joanne was three and a half. You were a little over a year. She came up after supper . . . not long after the picture was taken. She came up after supper and said she couldn't help with the dishes. And that wasn't like her. She liked to help with the dishes. She liked to run the Bissel, make the beds, do anything to help her mother."

Mom stopped talking and straightened the doily on the arm of the sofa. She caught her breath.

"You might as well know now as ever. Joanne. She said she

couldn't help with the dishes because she couldn't catch her breath. She said she wanted to go to bed early. An hour later she died.

"There wasn't anything anybody could do. Your father wasn't home. He was in an airplane. The plane had just left the airport in Pittsburgh for Rochester, Minnesota. He was flying out to the Mayo Clinic to take tests to see why he had spells. They gave him the message on the plane.

"But Joanne wasn't afraid. At first I didn't believe her. I called Dr. Fitzpatrick right away, but I didn't think anybody could be that sick. But she was. She walked up the steps to bed. Right up overhead to the guest room. Grandma and I put her up there so we could build a fire to keep her warm. We tucked her in and she smiled. As peaceful as she could be, she said, 'Mommy, I am going to die.' She told me not to worry because God was taking her away to Heaven to live with Him.

"Dr. Fitzpatrick stood at the foot of the bed with me and Grandma. There was nothing he could do. The mountain roads were all ice and the nearest hospital was Butler. Joanne lay there in peace . . . she smiled and looked up at us but she couldn't . . . she couldn't breathe!"

Mom's voice rose and cracked, growing faint until it faded altogether. She looked out toward the dining room for a moment, then cleared her throat and closed the curtain behind the sofa.

Shaking her head sadly, she said, "Your poor father, your poor father. They told him just after the plane left the ground in Pittsburgh. He thought there was some mistake. He couldn't believe it. He refused . . . Do you know? He thought it was you. You were the scrawny one. Joanne was healthy. Just look at her picture! See her rosy cheeks! Oh, how he loved her. He called her Ticky, and he loved her more than anyone else on earth."

Her voice trailed off as we gazed across the room at the picture on the mantel. Joanne hugged me, laughing as much as she smiled. I knew Dad hadn't gotten over her death. Once while they were arguing he had called Mom a killer; he said if he had been there, he would have carried her to the hospital through the snow. He said he would cut off his right arm if he could bring her back.

I felt relieved when the story was over: my dream had been true. I had had a sister who had played with me after all, even though she had died. My mother said I no longer needed to be frightened. From then on, when people asked me if I had brothers or sisters, I was to answer yes, I had a sister once but she died. But even with words to say, I was still frightened. I did not want to go away and live with God forever.

When I was four, Dad brought me ten yellow chicks that cheeped and ran with their heads strained forward, their wings tipped up behind them. They were too small to keep outside on the porch, so my mother put them in a cardboard box for me to play with in the back room. Frantic creatures, they quivered with fright when I came near them, making a mess on the floor. I decided to watch from Grandma's step chair, the one she climbed to string her red and green peppers door to door.

I spoke softly to the chicks, with thin grown-up patience, explaining the rules of the new game I had invented. First I drew a purple dot on the gray linoleum with a crayon, a target. If none of the chicks walked across the purple dot, nothing, I warned, would harm them. If, however, they did cross the purple dot, a one-inch steel ball bearing might drop on them—one of the steelies Uncle Tom Borrowman gave me from his shop. I was pleased with the rule; it was as clear and certain as Grandma's rule that I could not leave the backyard or go upstairs when she closed the swinging door to the kitchen. Sitting on top of the step chair I felt grown up, understanding, fair.

When the ball hit the floor it rolled and spun without

bouncing, grinding invisible grit into the linoleum, its weight and power audible. After each drop, I climbed down from the stool, picked it up, and started all over again, zeroing in on the purple dot. The chicks, however, quickly forgot the rules and began to wander carelessly. I had given them fair warning, I thought. Why didn't they listen? They seemed defiant, and when I climbed to the top of the stool, I shouted, "Bombs away!"

The steely caught one of the chicks in the middle of its back and it dropped to its side, dragging itself in a circle, one good leg serving as a pivot. Then the chick managed to right itself, going about its business as though nothing had happened, pecking at the bottom of a buttermilk container, nudging it until it rolled in a half-circle, shooing another chick in its path. For a moment, I lost the wounded chick among the others, then one small bird spun and sat down on its rear end. I climbed off the stool and spoke softly, "Stand up, Little Chick. Stand up," but it would not listen. A soft paste oozed out of its anus and stuck to the floor, holding it back as it tried to walk forward. It teetered for a moment, blinked, then rolled over on its side.

My mother found the dead bird and cradled it in her hand, stroking its head with the tip of her finger. Without speaking, she carried it out of the room. I knew I had broken some basic law, but I did not understand which one or why. The next day my father came to the house and put the remaining nine chicks back into the small cardboard box. My mother was angry. "You should have known better," she said, "David isn't old enough to take care of baby birds."

The words came to me as a stern judgment. She did not mean to be judgmental or stern, but a small bird had died because of me. The worst part of it was that my father handled life day in and day out without ever accidentally killing anything. Once in awhile he had to wring the neck of a sick cat or flush an unwanted litter of kittens down the toilet, but that was putting them out of their misery, putting them to sleep. Dad ministered to small birds and turtles every day; why couldn't I? My mother's words were painfully true: I wasn't old enough to take care of baby birds.

When Grandma's patience wore thin, she closed the swinging door into the dining room from the kitchen and made me stay in the back of the house, back where I had killed the baby chick. There the morning sun warmed the gray walls and woodwork, the gray bins and cabinets, and the gray wooden table and chairs in the kitchen; it also warmed the gray porcelain cast-iron stove and the gray hand pump for water beside the sink. The two rooms off the kitchen were also gray: the sewing room, where she kept the icebox, and the back room, where she hung her handwash when it rained and where, late in the summer, she ripened her peppers, stringing the huge red and green bells on wires that crisscrossed like Christmas decorations from doorway to doorway. Sometimes they called the back room "David's room," especially when they wanted to keep me out from under foot.

There I made up a game: a spinning game to match my confusion. I stood in the middle of the room with my eyes closed, my arm and finger extended, making myself rigid like a spinning arrow in the center of a gameboard. As the room raced by, I peeked at the dark green shade over the window and at each door: the mudroom door, the pantry door, the kitchen door, the laundry door, the bathroom door, and the Poison Door. Wherever I stopped spinning and pointed, I had to open that door, and I moved like a sleep-walker toward it, feeling my way through the dark.

After awhile I got so good at guessing where I was without peeking that I learned to come to a stop wherever I wanted just by the force of the spin. The rules were in my favor: either I had to point exactly at the center of the doorknob or I could spin again. I played for hours, spinning in the middle of the room one way, then spinning the other way so I would not get dizzy and bang into the wall. My mother said I made a fool of myself, spinning out in the back room all day, but she did not make me stop. Sometimes I spun with all my might, my arms whirling frantically, saliva flying from the corner of my mouth, tears running from my eyes.

One morning, wobbly from a spell of spinning, I sighted down my arm beyond the tip of my finger directly to the center of the doorknob of the Poison Door—no denying it. Staggering forward, I obeyed the command, carefully squeezing both hands around the filigreed brass knob, turning it slowly until I could feel the bolt slide away from the latch inside without clicking. Silence was crucial. Sealed off by double-lined velvet drapes, the tunnel of stairs stood darker at the top. I stared up into the black well without blinking, and after a minute or so, I could see the first dim steps and the vague outline of a handrail. I could also make out two mother-of-pearl buttons on the wall, but to switch on the light would have cracked the silence. Without breathing, I got down on my hands and knees. I tested the bottom treads for creak-spots, avoiding the sixth step which, I knew, groaned loudly under the lightest foot.

I had two enemies: the dark spirits of the house and my grandmother. Both enemies were perfectly still in the mid-afternoon, especially the Dark Spirit. I had to creep up the stairs, get through the thick drapes, then pick my way through the mine field in the hall. I also had to swim through another set of velvet drapes and pass by the room where my sister had died. My heart pounding, I held my breath and closed my eyes, pretending I was a blind man. I paused for only a moment on top of the stairs, listening for the footsteps of my grandmother. The banister down the stairs was quicker and quieter, but I risked chafing my bare legs, skin squeaking and crying out. Once down, I still had to work my way through the hall, sneak past the front parlor and the dining room, then worm my way through the swinging kitchen door until, secure, I could collapse back in "my" room and huddle in the corner, sick with fright. But the spinning pleased me, and after I caught my breath I spun again, slowly at first, then gaining speed as my confidence grew. I challenged all the spirits of the house, my arm rigid, my finger pointing toward freedom or the terrifying darkness.

CHAPTER 4

~~~~~~~~~~~~~~~~~~~~~~~~~~~~~~~~~

The Mark

Shortly after the baby bird died my mother signed me up for kindergarten. I was only four at the time, but she said, "Enough is enough. I hear you back there banging into the walls and talking to yourself. You're alone too much. You've got to get out and make friends." The kindergarten teacher, Miss Viola, was strict. During the first week of school she sent home a list of suitable punishments to match our various misbehaviors. Her favorite punishment was to lock a bad boy or a bad girl in a dark closet, the length of the sentence to be determined by the parent. My mother and grandmother had tied me to the grape arbor before, but they would never lock me in a dark closet. "I sent you to kindergarten to learn to make friends," Mother argued, "not to hide your light under a bushel basket."

But I was slow to make friends in school, and one day toward the end of the year, she brought home John Paul Chamberlin and Billy Schneider. John Paul was a tall, gawky kid with thin white hair on his head and black wires that grew out of the moles on his pale, thin arms. He wore thick, round glasses that made his dark bird eyes into tiny beads that darted behind three blurred orbits of curved glass. When his mother blew two times on her whistle, John Paul fumbled for the whistle around his neck and blew back. "Quiet!" he barked harshly, grabbing my arm and cocking his ear toward home. If his mother whistled three times,

tears came to his eyes, and he fell to his knees and pum-
meled the ground as though he had been shot. Two years
older than I was, John Paul owned a microscope and a tele-
scope, but he still had to run home to take a nap.

John Paul told Billy and me what to do, only he had to be
careful how he bossed Billy or he would get socked in the
stomach. John Paul was the brain of our trio, Billy the muscle. Short and stocky with straight black hair, Billy carried a
mumblety-peg knife and played without his shirt on. I may
have had a slight edge on John Paul in strength, but the two
of them teamed up against me whenever we had a fight, so it
didn't matter. They wore holsters at their sides, and John
Paul had a straw cowboy hat tied loosely around his neck.
When he wanted to show off, he worked the lanyard back
and forth, making the hat jump up and down on his head in
time with his bobbing Adam's apple.

Billy and John Paul teased me because I didn't know anything about the Japs and Pearl Harbor and because my grandmother would not let me own or even play with a cap gun.
The only reason they played with me at all was that one
time I had flung an apple off a stick that hit the telephone
wire where the crows sat, scaring the birds into a burst of
black wings and chatter. When they challenged me to do it
again, I knew better. "Why should I?" I said.

Once after supper John Paul knocked at the back door and
asked me to go with them to the depot to throw apples at the
blackbirds. Billy hung back in the shadows of the grape arbor, twisting a twig in his hands. They did not say anything
as we walked through the garden toward the tracks, but
when we got to the end of the railroad line, Billy squatted
down in the twilight and pointed to the tracks.

"Blood," he announced with authority, pointing to red
stains on the silver rails. "You know why?" I shook my head.
" 'Cause there's a man who rides the train at night who kills
kids."

"Not just any kid," John Paul interrupted. "Just kids who

live beside the tracks. And not just one man. There's a whole bunch of them. No one knows who they are. They wear white hoods and white robes."

"Why do they want to kill kids?" I asked.

"They drink their blood," Billy said.

"No, they don't!" John Paul contradicted. "They just kill kids who look a certain way. They just kill kids who are marked!"

Together they were on me. Billy grabbed my arms and John Paul pulled my shirt up over my head so I couldn't see. "See!" John Paul shouted. "He's got the spot!"

"God!" Billy said, "he really does!"

They pushed me away as though I had scarlet fever or polio, and I fell to the ground. The two of them stood back from me with their mouths open. I could feel tears come into my eyes. I started to run.

"Stop!" John Paul whispered fiercely. "See that guy?" A man was sweeping the loading dock of the depot. "That might be the killer. Pretend you don't see him!" I knew the man at the depot; he had given me cookies from a broken shipment and loaded me down with watermelons. He held his broom and looked over at us, continuing to sweep without waving.

I stopped. John Paul put his hand on my shoulder. "Listen," he whispered, "we can help. We can save you." He slapped the gun in his holster. "All you have to do is listen. Do what we say from now on. If you don't the killer will see your mark and you'll be next." Looking at Billy, John Paul closed both eyes and opened one in a kind of squint. He had been practicing winking and had not mastered it, but that did not matter; just trying to wink proved he was older.

"Come on, Billy," John Paul said a little too sweetly. "Let's walk him home."

Billy took me under one arm, John Paul under the other, as though I had been hurt already. Their support made me feel weak and helpless. They slapped their six-shooters against their thighs, the bright silver barrels gleaming in the moon-light.

Safe at home, I kneeled beside my bed to pray; usually I said my prayers in bed, but that night I wanted to make sure God listened. "Dear God," I said, "please save me. Keep the killer away." The next day I ran down alleys and took short-cuts to try to throw the killers off my scent. As I cut across a new backyard for the first time, a German shepherd jumped in front of me. Snarling, it pinned me in the corner of a thick privet fence and tore a hole in my sleeve. I put my head down and covered my eyes, tearing through the prickers.

That evening I called my mother into the bathroom to look at my cuts and bruises. She washed my back and hummed a song. The warm water and the warmth of her voice made me feel sorry for myself all over again.

"Mom," I asked, "what's that mark on my back?"

"What mark?" she wanted to know. "You don't have a mark on your back. Only scratches on your arms and neck." She ran the tip of her finger across my shoulder so that it tickled. I hated being tickled when I was trying to be serious, for I did not know whether to laugh or cry; caught in the middle, I flinched and scowled.

John Paul had been right: only the killer would know the mark. I climbed up onto the slippery edge of the tub so I could look in the mirror over the sink and see for myself. And there it was: a raspberry stain as shapeless as a cloud, ready to burst and spread in all directions.

"Don't you see it?" I cried hysterically, reaching around with my free hand to touch it.

"Oh, that!" Mom said playfully. "That's your birthmark!"

"Does it spread?" I wanted to know. "John Paul told me it would spread and people would call me a nigger."

"A what?" Mom asked sternly. "Don't you ever use that word again. It's 'knee-grow,' and they are just like you and me except their skin is dark."

Finally I told her about the blood on the rails and the men

who rode the trains looking for knee-grows who lived beside the tracks. She laughed. "That's a tall tale if I ever heard one," she said. "Besides, you have never even seen a colored person."

That was true, but in Sunday school I had seen pictures of colored children wearing robes and strange hats as they gathered around Jesus who "suffered them forth." The Sunday school teacher told us that Jesus loved all the children of the world, as though loving a colored child required God's special effort. If that was so, I had felt, I did not want to be colored.

Before saying my prayers that night, Mom sat down on the edge of my bed and taught me to sing "Steal Away" and "Go Down, Moses." She said the slaves sang about stealing away to Jesus because they were not free, and that every time we sang one of the spirituals we were joining them in their struggle for freedom. I listened closely to the words and felt sorry for the slaves, but I also felt sorry for myself. I wanted to believe my mother's explanation of the mark on my back, but John Paul and Billy had been more convincing.

Although I was still under the spell of John Paul and Billy at the end of the summer, I had nearly forgotten about the killers in the white robes and white hoods. I was even looking forward to going to first grade. Then, one night, Mom sat down beside me on the porch swing and stroked my hair. She was acting, I thought, a bit too friendly. She said the early evening shadows under the grape arbor looked like a ring of dancing bears and that, before we knew it, we would be off daylight saving time. On daylight saving time the farmers had less light in the morning to milk their cows. She slouched on the porch swing and pulled my head to her shoulder.

"It's a beautiful world," she observed softly. "Do you see the red sky? It's a beautiful world, and you are a new person in it." She rocked us back and forth slowly with her foot.

"Are you happy?" she asked.

"Yes," I answered, but I was not happy with her question.

"Good. I know you are a happy person." A minute of silence passed before she spoke again. "We are going to move soon. To a town called Bradford. Have you ever heard of Bradford? It's not too far from here. You'll make new friends when you start school. I have a job; I am going to teach fifth grade, and your father is going to open a new pet shop. We won't have to depend on Grandma anymore."

My father? I did not say anything. I stared out at the familiar darkness, watching the birds dive in and out from under the grape arbor. Yellow, blue, and green lightning bugs began flashing above the dark grass. I wondered what it would be like to be sitting on the swing between my mother and my father. I wondered what it would be like to see him again, but I said nothing.

Grandma came down from the garden swatting the air. "Oh!" she moaned, "the punkies are eating me alive!" We shifted on the swing to make room for her. Grandma dug in the garden with her hands and her fingers smelled of the earth.

"Sometimes in life," Mom said, "we have to do things we don't want to do. We have no choice." She paused and looked up at the early stars. She spoke as though she had forgotten the freedom we sang about in the spirituals. I started singing "Steal Away" to remind her, and she and Grandma joined in on harmony. After we sang two or three other songs, Mom said we were lucky to have stayed at Grandma's as long as we had. She also said that we were lucky she had a job and that Dad would have a chance to do better with his pet shop. She talked about our lives as though Grandma was not there. After awhile Grandma got up and went into the house to take a bath and rub olive oil on herself from head to toe.

"I don't feel lucky," I told her, and she laughed. She said I was one of the luckiest people on God's earth, only I did not know it yet. She asked me to close my eyes and sit still, making me pretend that I could not feel the swing lift as she got off or that I could not hear the creak of the screen door as she went inside.

"Did you keep your eyes closed?" she asked when she came back. "Well, then," she said, "keep them closed. Now. Open your hand."

It was a dime, but I found it hard to say thank you. What good was a dime? I thought. It was like a cookie if I had a stomachache, or it was like tickling me when I wanted to cry. I didn't want to leave Grandma's, and I wasn't sure what it would be like to have Dad back in the house. I missed him, but I wasn't sure.

The next day I walked into town, aware that I was breathing the dusty heat and the smell of the alley's warm tar for the last time. I looked in the window of Weidner's News and Hobby Shop at the balsa wood gliders, the dime moist in my hand. Mr. Weidner had pasted white paper clouds on blue poster paper for sky. With their wings tipped in flight, the gliders nose-dived toward the street like a flock of birds in V-formation. U.S. fighter planes, each glider had a five-pointed blue star inside a red circle on both wings and numbers on the fuselage. I did not want to move away to a different town.

I went down the alley behind the store and sat in the middle of the gravel, staring at small pieces of glass and sand between my shoes. Absently I picked up an old Popsicle stick and gouged out a valley. Just beneath the dirt, I spotted something shining. I dug deeper; it was another dime. As fast as I could, I ran to Billy's house with a dime in each fist: one for Billy and one for me. Billy and I raced back to the hobby shop together, steaming up the counter with our fists as we dropped the dimes on the glass. Painstakingly, his tongue at the corner of his mouth, Mr. Weidner put a lead weight in each nose, slipped the narrow wing through the slot under the pilot's window, then peered at the body for warps and stuck on both pieces of the tail.

We did not run back to Billy's house because the delicate balsa might split in the wind. We did not fly the planes either, because we were afraid their bellies would get scraped on the blacktop. We walked fast with stiff legs, shielding our planes like candles before us, laughing excitedly.

I liked to throw the plane as high as I could, cheering as it soared and dipped in Billy's backyard. I was lucky. My pilot knew how to drop gradually, leveling off before coming in for the perfect landing. We screamed as the gliders skimmed over the lilac bush and clothesline, landing in a mine field of rotten crabapples and yellow-jackets. Grandma had said the juice inside the apples had turned hard and that the yellow-jackets were "foolishly drunk" and all the more dangerous. We bombed them with hard green apples and called them "Japs."

I still didn't know much about the war, but I was learning about the Japs. I had seen pictures of them outside the Garby and Orpheum. They had buck teeth and slanted eyes. When we were angry, we called anyone we didn't like a Jap. To jap: that meant to jump out of the bushes on the back of a friend, to betray, to cheat. The Japs lived in palm trees like monkeys and they killed out of the blue. They were part of the spell which made us pull the blinds and turn off the lights at night, hiding in the living room behind the sofa.

I shouted to the blue pilot inside the cockpit, cheering his bravery and promising him a Purple Heart. I cupped my hands so he could hear through his wrap-around goggles, his helmet, and the roar of his propeller. If the wind swept his plane into a tree, or if it doubled back and crashed against the house, I started up my siren and rushed to the rescue, wailing like an ambulance.

When it was time for me to go, Billy dug into the pockets of his trousers, turning his back so I could not see. He stuffed a few things back, then opened both hands together.

"Here," he said, "take anything you want. For keeps." Before me were half a roll of caps, an Indian head penny, a brass war-button, and a magic white stone Billy said he had found near the tracks. I did not have to think twice about what I wanted, but I moved my fingers slowly over each object, not letting on. I was afraid if Billy suspected I really wanted one thing more than another, he might change his mind, even though John Paul was the real Indian giver. I picked up the magic stone, casually tossing it into the air. But I could not hide my excitement. Having Billy's stone made moving easier; now, I thought, the curse of the white hooded murderers was over, and I slipped the stone into my pocket.

CHAPTER 5

The Ledger

I sat in the back seat of Grandma's old Ford staring at my father's head as we drove through the Allegheny National Forest, marveling at how big he was. I had never seen him drive before, and whenever we went over bumps in the road, the top of his head brushed up against the soft beige ceiling. Whenever he spotted people standing by the road, he blew his horn to let them know we were coming. Mom was jumpy, mentioning various roadmarks to try to calm herself. By heart, she recited the names of every village along the long and barren road: Lucinda, Leeper, Crown, Vowinckel, Marienville, and Pigeon. She knew the trip to Bradford well. "Be careful," she cautioned in a controlled voice, "the road curves up ahead." Without warning, Dad swerved into a filling station, got out by himself, and drank a bottle of pop in the shade. "He shouldn't be driving," Mom hissed under her breath. "He shouldn't be driving, and he knows it. He can't even get a license. They won't give him one because of his spells. It drives me wild!" When he came back and opened the door, he was trembling. He pointed a finger at her and narrowed his eyes. She did not say another word until we got to Bradford.

Our moving van was red. Parked in front of our new house, it blocked off half the street. The first thing I noticed about the house was the drawing beneath the mail box. Some previous tenant's child had drawn stick figures on the gray asbestos shingles: a cave drawing of two men with penises and three women with huge breasts, each lined up in descending order of height like figures in a school book. Mother gasped at the sight of it and said she would scrape "the filthy mess" off with her fingernails if she had to, but the drawing wouldn't go away.

"Charles," she said, appealing to his physical strength, "use your elbow grease on this." But my father couldn't get the drawing off the wall either, and the two movers smiled and talked in a funny voice when they stepped around him as he scrubbed. Finally, he tossed the suds out into the tiny yard, a patch of dirt trampled hard as rock. Mom was also upset that the moving van took up more than our share of the street, and when an infrequent car squeezed by, she cupped her hands and yelled after it, "Sorry!" She smiled and waved until the car had turned the corner. Carrying light boxes, my father and mother circled each other politely, trying to make the move pleasant.

I kneeled on the sofa at the living room window, watching the movers stumble up the front steps with the piano. The house sat on the corner close to the sidewalk of Amm and Davis, and even closer to the yellow house next door. When a car passed, the windows rattled: when a truck thundered by, the floor shook.

The back rooms in the house were dark, and the bathroom, Dad said, smelled like cat dirt. I had seen my father only once or twice since he had come to take away the baby chicks. He promised the remaining nine chicks would grow up in a good home, on the MacIntyre farm in Elmo. Now, standing outside the van, I tugged on his shirt and begged him for a ride. I had missed him. I hoped he would call my mother "Speedunk," because, I remembered, that was what he had called her when he was in a good mood.

At the end of the day, Mom made lemonade for the movers. She walked slowly with them to the truck as though they had been company, waving good-bye as they pulled away from the curb. Mom told people what she was thinking, and she got to know strangers quickly. "Thank you!" she cried after them. "Thank you!" But the move had been a strain on her nerves. Dejected, she climbed the porch steps with her hands on her knees, closed the front door, and fell back against it. "I don't know," she said. "I just don't know." Then she buried her face in her hands and started to cry.

I could hear my father's heavy steps in the kitchen. He skidded a box across the floor to clear a path for himself, then he stood in the middle of the living room with his arms folded across his chest, glaring. "Now what?" he asked impatiently. "What's the matter?"

She took a deep breath and sighed, "I don't know, Charles. I just don't know."

"Cut the crap!" he said sharply. "Cut the crap and tell me what you're ranting about." When she did not answer he slapped the wall beside her with the heel of his hand; little chips of plaster fell inside and rattled. Mom took her face out of her hands and turned to the place where he had dented the plaster. She touched the spot and whimpered. "Goddamn it," he shouted. "Stop it! Stop it right now or I'll knock the living daylights out of you!"

She acted as though she had not heard him, rising to her feet and straightening her back with dignity, as though he did not exist. He spun her toward him, and she sat down quickly, going limp. At first she looked defiant; then she pretended to be laughing at the rattle inside the wall, shaking her head in disbelief. I wanted to get up off the sofa and walk casually between them, but instead I froze.

"Get out of here!" he shouted at me, and I tried to slide back into the couch, pushing into the cushions. "Go on!" he threatened. "Get out of here before there's a war on and you're in it!" I pulled a cushion over my head, my hands like blinders over my eyes. I heard him kick a heavy box and listened as something inside tinkled. Mom laughed the way she did when nothing was funny. Furious, Dad skidded more boxes to the side with his heavy foot, then stomped out, slamming the front door.

The next morning the house was so calm it seemed empty. Mom said she was sorry about what had happened. Dad said it was over, and we should not talk about it because things would only get worse. Saying he was out of Pepsi, he sent me to Lemage's Red and White to get him a bottle. The store was directly behind the house, no more than fifty yards away, but I ran both ways. All the houses on Davis and the street alongside Tuna Creek were close together. The water in the creek was brown and shallow; it smelled like the water that seeped into Grandma's basement after a storm. No houses stood on the creek side of the street across from Lemage's—no alleys, no yards, no places to hide. When I got back Mom was talking on the phone. School started in two days, and I would be in the first grade. I heard her say that she was not about to leave me at home alone, and that if they expected her to teach fifth grade at Lincoln School, I had to start school when I was five.

On the first day, Mom combed a huge wave in my hair and straightened my collar, making sure I looked neat. My cardboard shoes fit so tightly that I walked on the balls of my feet. My father walked up the steep hill with me, panting, taking long loping strides, asserting himself against the steep climb as though it challenged his strength as a man.

We arrived late; the other children were already inside. My father shook Miss Byrd's hand as though he knew her and folded his arms across his chest. After I had taken my seat, he was still there, standing beside Miss Byrd and beaming at the class. He told her how much he liked children, and that he had been the director of a Scout camp in Elkhart, Indiana: the largest Boy Scout camp in America. Speaking to us in a loud voice, he told all of us to have fun no matter what; then, waving especially to me, he left the room.

In the small room on Amm Street my parents bumped into each other. The house did not have a furnace; the rooms were cold. We lit space heaters, turning them on and off as we moved from one room to another. The space heater in the dining room was missing two of its six mantles; two others were chipped and cracked. My father said it was up to the landlord to buy new ones, but Mr. Fraser said that the mantles were just like lightbulbs and that we had to buy our own. We tried to eat in the kitchen, but the smell from the bathroom was too strong. Dad had been right; it smelled like cat dirt. The urine had soaked into the fir floor, mixing permanently with the resins to create an odor so sharp I held my breath when I ran inside to pee. When winter came, we ate in the dining room, sacrificing warmth to escape the smell.

Our first Christmas in Bradford, my mother and I went downtown together to shop. We had made out our shopping list at the dining room table: a pair of slacks, a flannel shirt, underwear, and earmuffs. It got cold in Bradford, Mom said, "bitter cold."

On the corner of Main and Kennedy Santa Claus stood ringing a bell and rocking back and forth from side to side to keep warm. Saint Nick, I had been taught, was sacrilegious, causing people to forget the real meaning of Christmas. He was standing with some people in blue uniforms who were playing the trumpet and trombone. Mom wished them a Merry Christmas and dropped a coin in the red kettle. Santa rang the bell toward us but Mom smiled politely, backing away.

"Did you see the pillow under his suit and his fake beard?" she muttered as we crossed the street.

"The whiskers," I said, "not the pillow."

We were going to a store that would have everything we needed, Mom said, and she read me the sign painted on the window:

MAYER BRAUSER

New and Used Furniture
Gent's Furnishings
Shoes   Luggage
Carpets   Rugs   Linoleum
Stoves   Tools   Etc.

"Etcetera," she explained as the overhead bell rang, meant everything. After the glare of the snow on the street, the store was dark, and I could see nothing. The floor was so badly warped and buckled that I ran my hand along the edge of the display tables to keep my balance. Mom introduced herself as a newcomer to town from Clarion, and a small, friendly man with bumps on his face squeezed out from behind a pile of green workpants to shake hands.

"So," he said, "you're a Downhomer. Good. Clarion? Punxsy? Knox? Everybody down there ends up in Bradford. Downhomers," he laughed. "We call them Downhomers because you're always thinking of home!" The man's name was Mayer Brauser, the name on the window of the store. After he had put our packages in a sack, he asked if we had the tree up yet. I shook my head and stared at the narrow floorboards.

"But you have to have a tree at Christmas," Mr. Brauser persisted. "Have you seen the nice ones we have leaning right outside the door?"

"The tree will have to wait until next year," Mom answered easily. "New shoes. New clothes. You know, the expense of moving." She laughed and measured an invisible stack of bills that came up to her chin. She wished him "Season's Greetings" as we went out the door, stopping to look at the trees with no intent of buying. "I like Scotch pine best," she said, her attention elsewhere. "Grandpa Crawford liked it best, too. Come on now."

The next night, Christmas Eve, our doorbell rang and Mr. Brauser stood on the porch in the snow. He was smiling and holding a tree with his arm around its waist as though they were friends. A foot taller than he was, it was a Scotch pine. He wished us "Merry Christmas" and tipped the tree forward like a soldier presenting his rifle at parade rest. "Here!" Mr. Brauser exclaimed. "Merry Christmas and a Happy New Year!" Mom covered her face with her hands. "My goodness!" she sighed. "How will we ever repay you?" Mr. Brauser waved away the question and smiled. "You don't have to." he said. "It's for you. Welcome to Bradford. A gift!"

After we brought the tree inside, Mom sat on the couch and cried.

"Why are you crying?" I asked.

"Because," she answered, choking. "Because I am so happy."

Years after, when she told and retold the story, she always ended it the same way: "It was our first Christmas in Bradford and Christ's message of love came to us through a Jew." But she did not say what had happened after Mayer Brauser stomped his feet on the porch, turned, and disappeared into the snow.

"He knows what he's doing," my father had said bitterly. "It's Christmas Eve, and he couldn't sell it. You'll be back."

Mom looked away. "Oh, Charles. He didn't mean it that way. He didn't have to give us a beautiful Scotch pine."

"I didn't say he did. All I said was that he knows what he's doing. He's a Jew, isn't he?"

"I am not going to have you ruin our first Christmas in Bradford," she said, and she sent me upstairs to bed.

I had never met a Jew before, and I liked Mr. Brauser. I did not understand the intense dislike the Jews produced in my father, but I felt relieved when he picked fights with strangers rather than my mother or me.

On Christmas morning we gathered in the living room and shivered around the tree. Dad read the second chapter of Luke, what he called the real Christmas. He lowered his voice until he found the proper key, deep and sonorous. "And it came to pass in those days, that there went out a decree from Caesar Augustus, that all the world should be taxed . . ." and on and on through the part about the angel in the sky and the shepherds being sore afraid.

My birthday came three days after Christmas. I was never aware of going without, but my mother said I always got the short end of the stick because I was born so close to Christmas. Sometimes she gave me birthday presents which had been intended for Christmas. After our first Christmas in Bradford, she gave me a book called *One God and the Ways We Worship Him.* Dad gave me a special envelope from the bank with a crisp George Washington smiling through an oval window of red berries and holly.

The next day, the new bill buttoned safely inside my shirt pocket, I ran downtown to Woolworth's to the stationery section, ogling the rulers and the compasses, the pencils and the gum erasers. After trying to decide what I wanted most, I bought a pen nib and a wooden holder, a bottle of blue-black Parker's ink, a blotter, and a book called a "Ledger." The book had a black and white marbled cover and swirls of purple endpapers. Each page was tinted celery green with a thin red line down the margin and a wide blue line down the center.

Sitting at the dining room table I drew a picture of the Christmas tree. I also entered the names of each article I had purchased and the price, blotting the drops of ink that had leaked from the tip of the scratchy pen.

"Why on earth did you go and buy a ledger?" Mom asked. "Do you want to be a businessman?"

I did not know the answer. I was not sure. I thought of my father and Mayer Brauser. After we had left Mayer Brauser's store on the day before Christmas, Mom explained that she had wished him "Season's Greetings" and not "Merry Christmas" because he was a Jew.

"Well," she asked again, "why did you buy a ledger? Do you want to become a businessman?" She looked at me and she asked me to look at her. I could feel tears in my eyes, but I did not answer. I knew only that I wanted to write down things I had seen during the day so I would always have them, the way I saved leaves and horse chestnuts, special stones and rusty railroad spikes. I wanted to keep track of the changes in my life, whatever came into it and whatever went out, but I did not know that was what I wanted to do. I did not want to show her anything I had drawn or written down, so I hid the ledger in my desk. Keeping a ledger was a little like talking to God. It was secret.

"Look at me," she said again, and when I looked up at her and our eyes met, we both broke out laughing.

CHAPTER 6

The Fishbowl

I wish in first grade I had been warned about the dangers of climbing down as well as climbing up, of moving too fast from one zone to another, of plunging in over my head, maybe drowning. But I did not know anything about caisson disease and the deep-sea diver's need to decompress slowly while coming up for air. My father kept a deep-sea diver on the bottom of his fish tank, a metallic man in a helmet hooked to a small black hose, the bubbles floating up like private thoughts from characters in the comics. The diver and I were not what anyone would call "close friends," but whenever I tried to peer behind his gridlike mask I thought I saw his lips move as though he were trying to speak. I took my early friendships wherever I could find them. New to town, I didn't get to walk home with friends for lunch at noon and, besides, both of my parents worked. Bradford's Fourth Ward School sat on Petrolia Hill overlooking town, and when the bell rang at twelve o'clock, I ran downhill to have lunch with my father. Meanwhile, the other kids who lived within easy walking distance of the school went home for lunch. Scrambling too fast, I got to the bottom of the hill and crossed Tuna Creek, feeling as though I had the bends: bubbles of gas in the blood, cramps, a tightening in the chest. But the pressure was not the result of coming up for air too soon. I had descended too quickly, leaving healthy air on the hill behind for the smoke and haze trapped in the valley below. I caught my breath in front of the Pet Shop for a moment, staring at red and black spots, my ears ringing.

Dad sat behind glass on his chrome chair doing what he did best, working crossword puzzles. Beside him, painted turtles floated in a basin of tepid water or basked on the Hanley half-brick I had seen him dig up from the sidewalk in front of the house. The turtles lived and swam inside a white porcelain pan propped up by a rubber dog bone on one end. Painted red and green and blue, some of them had decals of Pluto and Mickey Mouse glued to their shells, a kind of turtle's tattoo that made them look silly, undignified. I liked the natural green ones best. Dad fed the turtles lettuce scraps we had gathered from behind the Nu-Way Market and flies he had swatted in the store.

"The proper way to hit a fly to feed a turtle," he said, "takes time to learn. All you do, though, is stun it, never hit it so hard it dies. Let the turtle do that. Let the turtle have some fun too." By his chair in the window he kept a flyswatter so he could reach it without stirring the air. Then, like a graceful badminton player, he'd swat gently, sometimes catching the fly in mid-air. Half-buzzing, it made small circles on the water; then, in one chomp, it was gone.

I stood with my hand extended, ready to open the door at the exact instant he looked up from his chair and saw me. A smile flickered across his mouth and he said "Hi" through the plate glass, exaggerating the shape of his lips so as to express and seal a special feeling between us, but I was never certain as to what that feeling meant. If he was in a good mood, he would joke and offer me a stick of gum; but if he was in a bad mood, I was in trouble. The bell tingled as I entered the shop and crossed the tile floor to the largest fish tank. The big tank had its own light that made the water green and yellow except for the shaft of bubbles that rose up from the deep-sea diver's helmet.

"Don't get fingerprints on the tank," Dad warned. A drowsy guppy darted one way and then the other for no apparent reason, froze, then darted back again. There were Ribbon Fish, Angelfish, Gobies, Pencil Fish, Black Mollies, and Gourami. The Black Mollies were dappled with iridescent blue and green dots, and their bluish flanks had rows of orange-red dots. The Gourami came from India. They had metallic blue-green stripes and thick orange lips. On extra cold days, despite having a tank heater, my father worried about the Gourami because they were expensive; he said they would die if the temperature in their tank dropped even two degrees overnight. Those were my father's favorites: the Black Mollies and the Gourami. My favorites were the Angelfish; they were flat and thin and, when I snapped my fingernail against the glass, they didn't swim away. I felt sorry for the Gobies; they looked naked among the other brightly colored fish and had milky eyes. Actually they were about the same color as spit when I had a cold and let one fly off the curb.

I liked the fish more than the birds because the canaries and the lovebirds made a mess. They spilled their water and kicked seed on the floor in tantrums. The tank was clean and mysterious, and sometimes after school I sat for hours watching the fish cruise silently through space and through the open windows of the yellow china castle on the bottom. They bumped their noses against the glass the way a friendly dog nuzzles your hand, especially the Angelfish. Even though my father owned a pet shop, we were not allowed to have a dog or a cat at home because the landlord would not let us. That was why I liked the nuzzling Angels. But we couldn't keep tropical fish at home either: the house got too cold, and we couldn't afford to have a tank heater at home just for the pleasure of having fish. Even the white mice in the living room couldn't survive more than a few weeks during the winter, and winter in the Allegheny Mountains lasted half a year.

Best of all I liked the snails that stuck to the glass. Two of them had eyeballs that rested on the ends of their stalks, alert and bug-eyed, though I liked the ordinary everyday snails just as well. Snails did not move, or at least they didn't seem to move. I would watch one that had crawled halfway up the side of the tank, then I would turn my eyes away for a minute and find that it had snuck off somewhere else without getting caught. That was an art: one minute to be eternally stuck in one spot and the next to be off in another direction an inch away without anyone noticing. The snail moved so slowly it moved fast, crawling with such speed I never saw it crawl at all. I wanted to know the trick, so I watched and watched. My father said snails helped clean the insides of the tank, eating away bits of slime and film. After an eye-straining period of several weeks, I thought I had discovered their pattern—first they climbed up the side and then they climbed down, always a little bit to the left or the right, in rows, the way a farmer plows his field, or so I said to myself in order to understand. When my father wasn't looking, I took the eraser end of a pencil and knocked one off the side so I could watch it tumble and spill in slow motion through green space to the white sand on the bottom.

I even thought about snails in school. When our teacher passed out new pebbly sheets of white construction paper and told us to draw whatever we wanted, I drew a huge swirl from a single point in the center of the page. She said my first drawing was not a snail at all because I did not draw the antennae, and she got angry when I told her the truth, that the snail had crawled back inside its shell to sleep.

The smell of incense in the shop mingled with the scent of perfumed sand, cigarette smoke, and the faint odor of bird mess that hung in the air, clinging to the cotton of my father's shirts even after they were washed. He said that he was afraid to leave the door of the shop open for fresh air because if the birds got chilled, they would die. He said that each bird cost sixty cents, and that was why he burned incense and mopped the tile floor with disinfectant; but Mom said he had burned incense when he started smoking in college to keep his father from knowing about it. Back when my father went to college, in the early 1920s, smoking was a sin.

"Don't you want to take a leak and comb your hair before lunch?" he shouted from the back room. Without turning away from the snails in the fish tank, I knew he was standing in front of the broken mirror with his legs spread and his knees wobbly, parting his wet black hair. He ran the greasy comb back and forth under the faucet, then tapped it twice before balancing it on the front lip of the sink. The sink was chipped and rusted nearly red under the faucet. "Damn Jews," he said. "They won't even heat the place." That was why he left the water running: "so the pipes won't freeze and flood us out." It never occurred to me to ask if the pipes would freeze in the summer as well, for he kept the water running all year long. I did not ask about the Jews either. My mother told me that when things went wrong, he picked on the Jews to make himself feel better.

"Don't drown," he yelled as I dawdled in the bathroom, but I wasn't dawdling, even if he said so. I was standing perfectly still listening to him walk over to his desk. I closed my eyes and saw him writing a note to hang on the door. I liked to imagine what people were doing when I could not see them. His desk, an old oak rolltop, was cluttered with pastel note pads, cigarettes, catalogs, and black and white marbled notebooks where he kept his daily records. On shopping days just before Christmas he filled two pages, but most often he wrote only three or four entries per page. The words were almost indecipherable, but the numbers were printed neatly in pale blue ink, printed under "Income":

Fish food	15¢
Guppy	15¢
Dog collar (med)	65¢
Birdseed	38¢
Total	$1.33

The shop was narrow and long like a barbershop without its row of chairs. Dad blocked the rear of the store with empty tins and cardboard boxes, so his customers would not "snoop around back there." Left alone in the shop, I felt better if I focused on the tile floor or sat watching the snails. I think the feeling of emptiness in the place got to my father as well. Once he said he needed more canaries to make a go of it. He complained that it had rained on Sunday when he was a preacher, and now that he ran a pet shop, it rained on Saturdays. "Not many people in life have been through what I've been through," he said bitterly.

Episodes from his life, invented and real, came to me over the years in bits and scraps. He told me he had been a prizefighter, a basketball coach, a race-car driver, and a semi-professional basketball player on a franchise team for the Boston Celtics. He had taken care of a cow and chickens in Elmo once, too, but he never talked about that. The only sign I ever saw around the house that he had played basketball was a moth-eaten boat-neck in the bottom of his dresser: a bulky grape-colored sweater with a huge gold *W* in front—a varsity letter from the College of Wooster in Ohio. I found it hard to figure out what had actually happened and what had not. Both my parents had stories which held their lives together and to which they returned for understanding, sad and elaborate tales but stories which made sense nonetheless. Once, when business was slow on a rainy Saturday, Dad put his hand over his heart to explain why sometimes he knocked over birdcages and fishtanks. He said the doctors who sewed him up after his crash were to blame; they had put a tube near his heart that clotted, and that was why he had spells. The same story served to explain why he had become a minister. "Heart block," he called it. He told me he had flipped his car in a big race in Akron and was lying on his deathbed, his life as good as over. That was when he prayed to God and promised that if God would only spare him he would become a preacher. He would have preached forever, had it not been for the lousy doctors who spliced a major artery with a faulty tube, and so the heart block explained why he had to give up preaching as well. Now he sat in the shop, and when he wasn't doing crosswords, he ministered to the birds and small animals. "God speaks to us through the earth and the water, through the birds of the air, and through the little living creatures upon the earth," he said.

When I came out of the bathroom, he was standing over his desk making a sign, bending from the waist, stiffly, like a man who does not want to wrinkle his trousers. He tore out a yellow sheet of paper from one of the pastel pads, scribbling the words and carefully printing the numbers.

> At Lunch—Back
> At 12:45
> Rev. Chas. V. McKain

He scotch-taped the sign to the middle of the plate glass and yanked hard on the swollen door, rattling the thick glass in its frame. When it would not close, he pushed his foot against the bottom and heaved up on the handle at the same time, turning the key in the lock. I did not understand the complex system of suffering and reward which formed his view of the world, but getting the door to close was somehow part of it. If the door closed the way he hoped, he would smile triumphantly, but if it bound and scraped against the threshold he would blame the landlord, muttering bitterly about "the Christ-killers and the dirty Jews." I hoped each time the door stuck we would be able to muddle through in triumph. I looked for the flicker of his smile, reassurance of his strength to rise above his miserable fate: the door closed, the shop locked, our lives secure.

My father was big, half a foot taller than most men, and he weighed nearly two hundred pounds. With his hat on he looked a whole foot taller and marched, he liked to say, as straight and tall as a Prussian soldier. He wore a gold cardigan sweater and a plum-colored tie as rich as any banker's—his socks maroon, his trousers gray, his cloth shoes brown with crepe soles. He looked jaunty among the somber tones of the businessmen and the matching khaki and gray of the men in Dickie Workclothes. But his shirt pocket, the two pockets in his sweater, and the four pockets in his trousers bulged as though he suffered from random growths. His pockets were stuffed with keys, cigarettes, pens, gum, Hershey's Kisses, handkerchiefs, a fat wallet, and two fistfuls of coin he called his silver. There was no cash register in the shop, not even a cigar box, but he enjoyed it that way, I think. When he had to make change, he smiled and plunged his hand deep into one of his trouser pockets, scooping out a fistful. He spread the pile out across his open hand as though his palm were a countertop, sliding coins here and there with the tip of his index finger, the nickels, dimes, quarters, and halves all new and shining. He exchanged the old coins at the bank early in the morning each day because, he said, new coins pleased his customers. In the middle of his silver and keys he carried an over-sized coin of special value: an American silver dollar with a giant eagle on one side and the profile of Liberty on the other, along with the date, 1901, the year he was born. He used the silver dollar to flip for heads or tails and to tell children, if they asked, about his mother and father, who had given him the coin when he turned twenty-one. "My Dad could buy out this town and not even feel it," he said. "My Dad is a millionaire."

When he found an opening in the crowd he goose-stepped through it, his silver and keys jingling as he bounced. I had to stretch my legs to keep pace, my head and shoulders forward. Now and then he bowed slightly and tipped his hat to a woman from the bank or to a customer who came into the shop regularly for fish food or birdseed. But even as he smiled and bowed, he did not slow down. That too was an art: to relax the upper half of the body and tip your hat without breaking stride, without seeming to be in a hurry. At the corner of Mechanic and Main three children spotted him and ran toward us with their hands out. They jumped up and down when they saw him.

"What will it be?" he asked triumphantly—"gum or candy?"

Smiling, he dug into his sweater pocket and thumbed a stick of Black Jack forward from the pack. I hung back and looked in the window of the Bradford Building Savings and Loan: no one else's father carried gum and candy to give out to children on Main Street. The town had its share of children with a withered hand or a missing eye, a club foot or a metal back brace. They called him "The Candy Man." I watched in the reflection of the window as the children laughed.

My father's smile made me feel uncomfortable. Though endearing, it was bent and slightly hangdog, as though he carried the burden of the world on his broad shoulders. It reminded me of the pained and quizzical expression of Christ on the Sunday school calendar, suffering forth all manner of little children. I did not know what he felt, but I suspect now he re-experienced something of the satisfaction which must have been part of his notion of Christian ministry, of having little and giving much. Whenever I saw him giving away gum and candy, though, I remembered my mother's complaint that he could not even afford to pay the rent without Grandpa McKain's help.

After the children walked away, he turned to look for me. The look of contentment on his face was terrifying. At the lunch counter in Widman and Teah's he spoke to people out of an aura, a deep and holy calm which should not have been seen in public. I could not, as yet, distinguish between the unsettling look of calm and the look of holy fear which crossed his face just before he was about to fall, and this was the source of my anxiety. In the living room at home he might slide off his reading chair onto the floor, leaving scuff marks on the linoleum where he worked his feet, his shoes jumping back and forth like the paws of a dog dreaming in its sleep. But sometimes it would happen at the store, and he would smash a tank and the fish would flop on the tile next to him, or he would knock over a bird cage and a canary would escape and fly madly around the shop until it crashed into the plate glass and broke its neck.

My mother wondered why he always seemed to fall against a cage or a tank and not into empty space. But there was no warning, not for him or for anyone else. Sometimes I thought I could detect a faint quiver at the corner of his mouth before his eyes swam back and he crashed backward off the stool at the lunch counter, but I was never quite sure. Once, near home on Amm Street, he dropped straight back without even sticking out his arm to break the fall.

I felt relieved when we got up from the lunch counter to pay our check. Dad tossed a dime under his coffee cup, so that everyone could hear and see it was a generous tip. At the cash register, he asked Miss Faye to break open a roll of quarters so he could have four new ones in exchange for a soiled dollar bill. He spread the change from his pocket out in the center of his palm, skidding coins here and there, according to value. A nickel fell, and I scampered after it, catching up to it before it went dead, like playing flies and grounders. When I gave it to him, he handed it back and told me to buy myself a box of Cracker Jacks. I don't remember the prize at the bottom of the box, whether it was a small lead monkey or a soldier with a machine gun, but I left the store feeling happy. I thanked him for the candy and ran, jumping up to swat the awning of Fanny Farmer's, spilling caramel-coated popcorn on the sidewalk.

Perhaps I landed funny on my foot, or I heard the muffled thud of coins inside his pocket, but when I glanced back over my shoulder, I saw him lying between two parked cars, his head on the curb, his face the color of a possum. Already his eyes had rolled back and his tongue was working to get back inside his mouth. With the heel of his hand he was rubbing himself just below the truss he wore, his fingers arched backward, groping to take hold of something with the top of his hand. I ran to get his hat, not thinking about the double line of cars moving up Main Street. The hat had wobbled to a dead stop a few feet into traffic. I grabbed it and held it in both hands over my stomach, the way I had seen my father hold his hat at Mrs. Peterson's funeral, his arms extended, his head bowed.

A woman put her hand to her mouth and stooped in front of me; she looked me in the eyes as though I was the one who had fallen. I handed her the hat and took out my handkerchief and tried to put it in my father's wandering hand, so he would wake up and stop rubbing himself.

"Dad!" I cried, but he didn't wake up and his tongue was bleeding. A crowd had formed above him tisking softly; one woman mumbled, "It's a shame." A policeman came through the wall of knees and squatted down, touching his shoulder.

"You okay, Reverend?" he asked. The policeman spoke calmly and hunkered down as though he might pick up a stick and draw a circle in the dirt. "Well," he said, "you don't want to sleep out here all day, do you?" He lifted my father up under the arms and gently dragged him out of the gutter and propped him up against the marble facade of the Savings and Loan, the same spot where the man without legs sat on Veteran's Day, brand new yellow pencils in his hat. In a minute or so he opened his eyes. A faint flicker of a smile crossed his lips as he looked from one face to another in confusion.

"What happened?" he asked in a thick voice: the question without an answer. When his eyes met mine his smile broadened. I went over and stood beside him, leaning against the building and looking up at the faces in the crowd.

Lieutenant Dennis and Mr. Deloe from the church helped him stand up. A taxi had parallel-parked with its rear door open. Brushing the sidewalk dust from his trousers with one hand, he held a handkerchief to the gash over his ear with the other. He smiled at me again, made his way to the waiting car, and crawled into the back seat alone.

As soon as the taxi pulled around the corner, the crowd disappeared. A thin film of dust settled on the tidy pool of blood at the edge of the curb. His hat was balanced on the head of a parking meter. Pretending not to see it, I started off down Main, but Mr. Deloe called after me. He was dusting off the hat and reshaping it. "You had better take this home, Dave," he said in a friendly voice.

I carried the hat carefully in front of me as though I was carrying the king's crown on a pillow, but once Mr. Deloe was out of sight, I raced up Pine Street, swinging it at my side, pumping my arms for speed. I got as far as the Free Methodist Church and stopped. I wanted to go back to school even though I knew I would get in trouble for being late, but I couldn't walk into class carrying my father's hat because then everyone would know what had happened. I crossed the street and watched a trickle of green scum in the creek flutter downstream from a rock. The creek stank the way it always did at the end of summer, an acid and sulphur smell mixed with the odor of human waste. I held the hat over the railing and looked at it carefully, but I could not let it drop.

CHAPTER 7

The Second Smartest Man in America

My father and I ate lunch together downtown every day. When he was in a hurry we wolfed down a grilled cheese at Widman and Teah, but when he had enough time we ate at the Home Dairy Cafeteria. I preferred the pace of the drugstore, because the rhythms of the cafeteria moved like a church service. The room was as big as the railroad depot, the walls the color of egg batter, splattered with tiny islands of gravy and grease. Each ring of splatter was like a flat dry rock in the creek when the Tuna got low enough to wade across. I jumped up the wall from rock to rock until the islands ran into a strip of wood with coathooks. The old men who ate there sat with their coats on at square wooden tables. The tables nearest the windows threw short shadows across the floor, and the tables farthest away threw long shadows. The shadows grew longer in the silence of the place, each voice floating upward into the hollow space above the blades of the slowly turning fans. As one old man pushed back his chair, a shriek rose up into the air like the sound of a nail ripped from green wood. The other grizzled old men sitting nearby slowly turned and lifted their heads, like turtles on a log. My father liked to eat there because he liked the cherry pie.

"It's nice to be friendly," he said under his breath, "even if it's just to say hello." He greeted the men standing in line, the women ladling out the soft and runny food, and the peach-colored woman at the cash register who gave him her shiniest coins. I carried my tray behind him toward the middle of the room and watched as he tried to take off his hat. I had watched him grimace as he put on his hat in the morning, and I knew the cut under his bandage hurt. He had stood spread-legged facing the mirror in the hall as he always did. Stooping spread-legged made him look bigger than he was, and he buckled his knees whether he had to or not. But when he was hurt he seemed smaller, and I wasn't as afraid of him. He looked more like Grandma Crawford putting on her blue straw hat for church: fussy, careful not to mess up her permanent. But the bandage inside the sweatband stuck, and he yanked hard once, reopening the cut and staining the gauze with wet spots the color of pennies. He shook his head and smiled as he hung his hat on the hook just where the islands hit the shore. His pale blue eyes filled with water.

I liked to watch my father and that morning I had watched him shave. After he dried, he patted his cheeks with Cashmere Bouquet, screwing up one side of his mouth and then the other as he made his cheek long and smooth, slapping on the powder in tiny puffs of dust. By lunchtime the powder had caked and dried, exaggerating the bruise under his eye and the curious blue lump on his chin. His lips were also blue, as purple as grape, as though he had been swimming in cold water. I did not like to be reminded of the time we swam in cold water, but I often thought about it despite myself.

We had gone to Chautauqua to see Grandma and Grandpa McKain, and as always when we went to Chautauqua I had to be on my best behavior. My mother made me shine my shoes and wear a clip-on bowtie. "Look nice," she insisted. "Get into the habit now of doing things for others." The "others" at Chautauqua were as old as the men who ate in the Home Dairy Cafeteria, but more respectable, their rules strict. No one was allowed to walk on the grounds in a bathing suit, not even heading down the long stretch of lawn to the lake. One Sunday morning we listened to Reverend Norman Vincent Peale in the Amphitheater, but he was so far away it was like listening to his voice on the radio. The old people fanned themselves with church bulletins, their free hands cupped to their ears. In the afternoon we returned to the Amphitheater to listen to a girl in red glasses play the French horn. We sat in back again even though there were seats down front. My mother bent over and whispered, "If there's ever a fire . . ." her voice trailing off into the obvious. The rambling old building was made entirely of wood, whitewashed like the walls inside the milking room in the MacIntyres' barn.

Grandma McKain called Chautauqua her second home because they had been going there for forty summers. When my mother and father and I stayed overnight, they rented us a room in one of the Victorian cottages across from the Carey Hotel. The three of us slept in one room. Dad sprawled out on his bed in his underwear, and Mom sprawled out on her bed in a slip, breathing heavily. They had joined two wicker chairs for me in the corner and, from there, I watched them.

"It's suffocating," Mom said, opening and closing her mouth.

"It's hot all right. I like the cold. I'll take the cold any day. What do you say, Pal? Tomorrow we'll go swimming."

"You don't have a bathing suit," my mother said wearily.

"Don't be so negative, Ida," Dad said in a voice that proved he was strong enough to rise above the heat.

"Dave doesn't have a bathing suit. That's all I said."

"That doesn't matter. He's only six years old."

"Yes, it does. He needs a suit. And what about you? You need a suit, for Pete's sake."

Dad narrowed his eyes the way he did before he got angry.

"I don't care if we go swimming, Dad."

"Listen! Don't you think I can get us bathing suits? I've been swimming in this lake for thirty years. My folks know everyone." He half-sat up in bed and looked around the room as though he had just awakened. Then he collapsed back down on his pillow.

"You don't have to raise your voice, Charles. The walls are thin enough. You don't have to shout."

"I'm not shouting. We're talking about swimming. It's idiotic to worry about a bathing suit. I could get you a suit, too, if I wanted to. Do you want me to get you a suit?"

"That will be the day," she answered coolly, turning over on her side and pulling the sheet up over her shoulder as if, in the midst of the heat, there had been a sudden draft. The porch light shone in through the lace curtains, throwing the shadow of her hips and shoulders like a range of mountains on the wall. "Please, Charles. Pull down the blinds," as if she could feel my eyes on her shadow.

The next day we ate lunch at the St. Elmo Hotel. We sat at a table with ice water in beaded glasses, with linen and silver and a basket of sticky buns. Whenever we went out to dinner with my grandparents, we ate at fancy restaurants, and I got a stomachache because I was nervous. Grandpa said I could eat the whole basket of buns by myself if I wanted to, but Grandma said he was being mean. She wrapped a sticky bun in a linen napkin and put it in her purse. "This will be for you later. When you get back from swimming with your father."

"What about the napkin?" Grandpa asked.

"I'll bring it back, dear. You know I'll bring it back. Why do you ask me that in front of David? David knows I'll bring it back."

I glanced at my mother, and she smiled. Outside of St. Elmo's my father took my hand, and we set off across the great sweeping lawn in his long sweeping stride. "We can't go in right away, Pal. After we digest a bit . . ."

We walked across the plaza beyond the Amphitheater toward the wooden stick houses with plumbing on the outside walls. "No one lives here in the winter," Dad said, pointing to the pipes. "Too cold. I wouldn't care, though. I like the cold. I love winter." Beyond the houses stood an open-air pavilion, a brown roof on white pillars. Dad said it was the Hall of Philosophy and that Thomas Edison and half a dozen presidents of the United States had spoken there. He took my hand and led me to another building with tall columns. "What do you notice first?" he asked.

The building looked closed. "There are no windows," I said, "and it's got a big front door."

"Right!" he said, smiling. "This is the Hall of Christ. The Hall of Faith. Of Belief. We live in darkness, but if you give your life to Christ, you live in Eternal Light. Christ is Light. We don't need windows. We need light. Christ said: 'Stand at the door and knock. I am the door!'"

He stood in the sun and talked about Christ as though Christ were his friend. He lit a Camel, took a couple of puffs, then snuffed the cigarette out between his finger and thumb, sliding it back into the pack. Smoking was not allowed at Chautauqua, least of all in public. "Come on," he said. "Let's go down to Palestine."

We walked back past the Amphitheater toward the Park of Palestine and the lake; old people fanned themselves and chatted on the Promenade. I did not understand why, but they made me feel uneasy. Not only were they old, but they smiled expectantly. The Park of Palestine was modeled after the Holy Land, and my grandfather had taken me there the day before to explain the scale. "When you put one foot in front of the other," he said, "you travel over a mile of Holy Land."

"Do you know what that is?" Dad asked, pointing to a hollow in the sand. It looked like a puddle without water. "That's Jericho: the city defeated in battle by Joshua. And over there, beyond Jericho, that's Samaria. Do you see the Holy City of Jerusalem? And over there, in the middle of the park, what's that?" He pointed to the shallow, warm puddle Grandpa had called the Dead Sea.

"I don't know," I answered.

"That's the Dead Sea. And what about there?" He spread his arms toward the lake. "What is that?"

I knew it was the Mediterranean Sea, but I did not answer.

"That," Dad said eagerly, "that is the Great Sea. The Mediterranean. And where we are standing? What is this place?"

"The Holy Land," I answered, caught up in his enthusiasm.

"That's right!" he said, taking my hand. "We are in the Holy Land!"

He stood on Mt. Lebanon above the Holy Land with his arms extended, the muddy water of the lake lapping the shore behind him. Heavy and sad, his voice dropped and rose when he spoke, pausing in the middle of the word "Christ," dividing it into two syllables. I had never seen him preach before. His eyes clouded over, and he trembled with emotion as he mentioned "the man from Nazareth," pointing to a tiny village between Mt. Carmel and Mt. Tabor.

I followed a few feet behind him as he strode toward the bathhouse. A young man and a young woman were handing out numbered wire baskets and brass keys attached to a garter. Dad introduced himself as the son of Walter McKain, Walter C. McKain from Youngstown, Ohio. The boy pivoted on his bare feet, turned down the radio, and asked him what he could do for him, as though he had not heard. I clicked an empty basket on the metal counter so the young woman wouldn't hear my father asking for bathing suits, but I knew she would hear him anyway.

"Isn't that right, Pal? We're going swimming."

I nodded without looking up. There was a large wooden box on wheels behind the counter, and the young man reached in and grabbed two suits off the top. He and the young woman exchanged glances without expression.

Inside the locker room my father handed me the yellow suit and said it was a cheerful color. Dark purple with a rusty gold buckle, Dad's suit had moth holes. His skin was white through the tiny holes. When I told him I did not want to go swimming, he laughed and tousled my hair. He had taken off his truss and folded it carefully in the bottom of the basket. He wore a truss every day and gritted his teeth when he mentioned it, touching a spot below his belly button. The truss left indentations on his stomach, flattening the black hairs against his belly-white skin. He rolled his shirt and trousers into a ball and jammed our things into one basket.

The big yellow bathing suit made me feel even skinnier than usual. A wind blew in across the bay from the direction of Palestine. The sun hid behind the cloud-covered sky. Dad dipped his arms in up to his elbows, turning his wrists and lifting his hands in the air like a doctor washing his hands at a sink. "Don't be an extremist like your mother," he said. "Get used to it gradually." I thrashed my arms in the water and hid behind the spray until he pushed off and swam away, slicing through the water with his fingers pointed. The water was cold. I waited until he had kicked beyond the floating dock into the deep part, then I moved in toward the shore and kneeled down in the water to pee.

He was still swimming out beyond the ropes when a lifeguard blew his whistle. The lifeguard stood on a tall chair and waved his arms and yelled through a megaphone. All the people on the beach turned and looked out at the gray water. My father stopped swimming, waved back, and then stiffly started swimming in, each stroke perfect, as though he were giving a demonstration. On shore, he staggered slightly, pushing his hair back with both hands, tightening his arm muscles in the same exaggerated fashion he used when he stooped in front of the mirror.

"They didn't used to have ropes," my father said. He gasped, caught his breath, and spit. "I've been swimming here before you were born. I've swum across this lake a dozen times. Back and forth." He was frowning slightly now, frowning and smiling at the same time, smiling as though some inner peace meant more than the presence of the life-

guard or even the lake. I was afraid he might start a fight or
that he would tell the lifeguard he was a good friend of
Johnny Weismuller's, the man who swung on a rope and
played Tarzan in the movies. He had told me that once, and
when I told my friends they had laughed. But he just stood
there and smiled, running his fingers through his thick black
hair the way Tarzan did in the picture show.

I was squatting in the water with my face forward, pretending to blow bubbles. At first he hadn't paid any attention to
me; then he came over and put his hand on my shoulder.
"Don't be a sissy," he said. "You don't have a stomachache, do
you?"

I looked up at him through tears, nodding that I did.

"Well, come on then. Next time don't eat so many sticky
buns." He smiled pleasantly as we passed the lifeguard, as
though he had forgiven the young man in the presence of
God. A breeze picked up across the lake and we shivered. His
lips turned blue, purple . . . nearly grape.

In the cafeteria, his hand shook as he lifted the heavy tan
mug. He stared over my shoulder at the wall, his eyes vacant.
A bite of cherry pie had missed his mouth and had dribbled
down his chin. He wiped his lips with his sleeve and pulled
out a pack of Spuds, loosening a single cigarette from the
pack with a flick of his wrist. After he lit up, the cigarette
stuck to his lip, leaving a tiny piece of paper and a single
bead of blood. Abruptly, as if to push back the pain, he
pushed back his chair so that it shrieked, and all of the old
men turned to watch as he stood in the middle of the aisle,
smiling and frowning, waiting for me to gulp my milk. At
first I thought he was going to carry his hat. Then, cautiously he lowered it on top of his head with both hands. As
we left the cafeteria, he blinked in the bright winter sun and
tipped his hat to a woman who worked in Fanny Farmer's,
flinching as he did so and laughing at himself for forgetting
how much his head hurt.

The hat was grimy where his thumb and forefinger tugged at the front of the brim when he said hello to women. A tiny wash of salt rose from the band, a faint shoreline of frost, thin and jagged. He never boasted about the size of his hat, and that was unusual. He did boast about the length of his trousers and the size of his shirt, his height and even his weight, but not his hat. One day Mom picked it up off the floor of the hall closet and put it on my head. "Go on, go look in the mirror!" she teased. "Take a look at yourself!"

The hat came down over my eyes, and I tipped my head back to look up under the rim. The inside of the hat smelled of dirty hair, dried blood, Jeris, incense, and the faint odor of hat cleaner.

"He has a big head," she laughed, taking my hand and leading me toward the sofa. "But it isn't his fault. He can't help it. No matter what, you must remember that. He is your father, and you must love him." She reached over and took the hat off my head and fingered the little white bow and the black leather tab with the size inside. She said she loved me and that everything would be all right.

What was it about the size of one's hat and one's head? I went downtown to Evan's Men Store the next day to find out. The hat department was in back where hats were hanging mid-air. There stood a plaster statue of a man with two hats: a hat in his hand and a hat on his head. On block heads and special metal stands along the shelves sat brown hats and tan hats, and there were hats in the half-open drawers along the wall. I fished hats out of the drawers and took them off the hatracks to check the size. The largest size I found was 7-¾, although there were several 7-½'s. But there was nothing in his size: 7-⅞. Grandma McKain had been right, I thought, and Mom was right, too. Grandma told me they had sent him to the Mayo Clinic for tests to find out why he fell and hit his head. The doctors said he had the second highest IQ ever recorded at the clinic, and everyone decided that was the problem. I thought that meant he was the second smartest man in America. Mom laughed when I told her that, then quickly frowned. She said she did not know how bright he was, but that he had a photographic mind. That meant he could read a book or look at a page and it would always come back to him, the way he sometimes showed off and spelled long words backwards and forwards. No one really understood what was wrong, but Grandma said he was too smart for his own good. My mother said the same thing: he was too smart for his own good, and there was nothing he could do.

CHAPTER 8

Things of the Earth

The men who stayed home from the War wore oily
brown baseball caps with ear flaps or red and black
checkered caps with a hunting license pinned over
the visor, but most anyone who could walk fought
overseas. Many of the houses had Gold Stars in the front
window. One house around the corner on Kennedy Street
had five Gold Stars hanging in the window: a star for each
son lost. Born in 1901, my father was too old to fight in the
War, although he often spoke passionately about joining the
Canadian Mounties. "How about it, Dave?" he would ask.
"Let's you and I go up to Ottawa where we can do some
good." He showed me a magazine picture he kept folded in
his wallet of a tall, handsome man in a red uniform riding a
white horse. Tall fir trees and a mountain stream with
white-capped mountains stood in the background.

But I was beginning to feel at home in Bradford and did not
want to go anywhere. I had found two friends who lived in
the same block and on the same side of the street as we did.
Vincent Bailer wore glasses and seemed to be as smart as
John Paul Chamberlin, and David Albright would go anywhere and do anything, like Billy Schneider. David would
even cross that great neighborhood divide which protected
us from getting beaten up—Davis Street. But we had to be in
the right mood to dare each other to cross Davis.

Everyone knew that if you were not Italian and walked on
the other side of Davis Street, you were asking for a sock in

the stomach or a punch in the mouth. Sometimes, feeling daring, David and I explored the cinder paths down where the Italians lived anyway: families named Cherilli, Camilla, Colestro, Patuto, Vigilottis, and Lama; large families that lived between coal sheds and warehouses in narrow unpainted houses. Vincent's father said they built their houses out of scrap lumber that washed up with the spring floods and from whatever materials they could find lying around Reichenbach's Junk Yard. One family I knew lived in a tarpaper shack and had a bathtub stuck vertically in the ground to shelter the Virgin Mary. The houses smelled musty and damp, like the smell of powdery dirt and air that gets trapped under a porch. Mr. Bailer said some of the Italians lived on berries, wild greens, woodchucks, and squirrel, but all of them ate beans and macaroni, a dish they called "pastafasule."

David and I picked our way down the dirt roads like combat soldiers, ducking and running, then stopping and signaling each other from behind a shed when the coast was clear. Our mission was Reichenbach's Junk Yard. There, scrap iron lay heaped in piles just for the taking—springs, boiler plates, railroad car wheels, rods, radiators, pieces of old oil derricks, and twisted hunks of railroad track. Milkweed bloomed, and every pod of silk we gathered we took to school for what our teachers called "the War effort." Milkweed meant warm leather jackets for American fliers, and I imagined them parachuting out of the skies hanging onto a million white seeds.

The tracks of the Erie and the B & O followed the winding course of the creek. Hoboes slept in the boxcars. David pointed to the turntable at the end of the line and drew an imaginary hara-kari knife across his stomach. "There's where Frankie Lama got cut in half," he said, tossing a clinker underhanded to the exact spot. "Two pieces! Right across the middle!" He dared me to jump on the platform and I did, jumping back quickly at the tick of my heels on steel.

David and I stoned the DANGER signs to watch them wobble, to hear them twang. On his way home from school one day Honey Myers got electrocuted climbing the transformer. The big letters on the front page of the *Bradford Era* read: BOY EIGHT ELECTROCUTED. One day Honey was in school and the next day he was not. Miss Pike did not mention it in class and the kids who lived up on Jackson Avenue did not seem to know anything about it. In second grade, since we sat two to a desk, Miss Pike asked Susan Lake to slide over a space to make room for Lee McKinley, but she did not mention Honey. Susan Lake wore torn and dirty dresses without a belt, and sometimes she did not wear underpants. She did not blow her nose and snot slid down her upper lip. We teased her for being poor and dirty. Once she even had lice in her hair and the teacher sent her home for a week.

Bradford, Mom argued, was a tough town to grow up in, and to prove it she pointed to *Historical Bradford*, an illustrated volume of mansions published to celebrate those who had struck it rich. With pride, the town's only history boasted that "during periods of oil excitement Bradford was one of the toughest towns on earth. For picturesque wickedness the city was equaled by few, and excelled by none." There existed dancehalls, whorehouses, and saloons, and the founders of the town added to the excitement by staging bull-and-bear fights in which the animals hooked and hugged each other inside a ring until one or the other died. According to the history, Bradford men were "rough, brawny, and hard-fisted . . . gamblers, adventurers, speculators, pimps, roustabouts, roughnecks and hustlers." That was only fifty years ago, Mom observed significantly. Their sons and grandsons were still around, or they had joined the Army.

Vincent Bailer's father wore thick glasses and wasn't allowed to join the Army, but we looked up to him anyway because he was the produce manager at the Market Basket. He wore a businessman's hat, a tie, and a sweater with buttons. At the end of the day when he came home from work, he often carried a full bag of groceries in each arm. Mr. Bailer would not let Vincent play across Davis Street because of the Italians; he said they stole food from the Market Basket.

David's father was too old for the Army, too, but he did not wear a businessman's hat like Mr. Bailer and my father. Even in second grade, my two friends and I discussed how we felt about our fathers not being in the Army, although David accepted it easily. If anyone had suggested that his father was a coward, David would have made him eat his words. Of the three fathers on the north side of Amm, Mr. Albright fit into our neighborhood best. He wore a red and black checkered wool cap with a license, and he went deer hunting every season. Whenever he shot a deer, he hung it upside down from a tree in his backyard where the blood dripped and froze on the snow. During hunting season people hung deer up on their front porches and, downtown, from the roof over the pump in front of City Motors and Woodley's Filling Station. Before hanging them anywhere, the hunters drove around town with their deer lashed across the front fender of their cars. Mr. Albright said my father must be rich because he did not hunt or fish. Mom snickered when I told her. "Oh, sure! We're rich all right! In a pig's eye!" Mrs. Albright took in laundry, and Mr. Albright worked morning to dark. As foster-parents, their children were called, Mom said, "wards of the state." A little boy named Patty lived with them who wore braces and stayed in his crib. Patty had been named the national poster baby for cerebral palsy, and the Albrights were proud of him. David also had a sister named Alice, and the five of them lived in a one-floor cottage with four tight rooms. A davenport in the living room blocked the front door so that everyone had to use the back door into the kitchen. I did not like to go into the kitchen because I couldn't breathe. Mrs. Albright heated her irons on the stove, and a thick cloud of Patty's baby powder choked the air.

The streetlights were on when Mr. Albright left for work

in the morning and the streetlights were on when he came home at night. At the end of the day, he collapsed into his chair, leaving a puddle of melted ice on the linoleum. A roustabout in the oil fields, he wore two heavy wool shirts, double-ply longjohns, and thick gray wool slacks that fit into his calf-high outer socks. He undid his long leather laces, dropped his heavy boots to the floor with a thud, then wiggled his toes inside his steaming socks. Stripped down to his longjohns, he stooped and picked up his clothes with the tips of his fingers, draping socks, shirt, sweater, and trousers on chairs and doorknobs all over the living room. He held each piece of clothing at arm's length as though the smell would kill him, waving a steaming sock back and forth in front of my face like a snake. In a loud and boisterous voice he said, "Well, goddamn it, that's pretty good, isn't it? There's Patty. Yes, sir. Right there. National poster baby."

Mrs. Albright had thumbtacked the poster of Patty to the living room wall next to the poster of Clyde Beatty fending off a tiger with a bullwhip and a kitchen chair. "What do you say, Ray," Mr. Albright said with his arm around an imaginary friend. "Let's have a beer?" "Well," he said back to himself, moving into the empty spot where his imaginary friend had stood. "Don't mind if I do."

Mr. Albright was the first man who swore around me without apologizing, and the first man I had ever seen drink anything stronger than Grandma Crawford's grape juice. I was never quite sure what he would do next, but I liked the gruff man enormously. He flipped his boots under the kerosene space heater and hissed as he tossed his gloves on top, matching to perfection the sizzling of the ice as he sprayed the air, shaking his fist at the stove and making himself red in the face.

About hunting and fishing, ice and fire, earth and oil, my father knew nothing. He came home after I did and called me into the living room to look at a lamp which had not been lit for weeks. "Here," he said with an air of mastery, "let me show you how to fix it." He rattled the dead gray bulb close to his ear, then held up the new bulb like a magician, turning it slowly between his thumb and finger. When he pulled the brass chain and the bulb lighted, he smiled and put his arm around my shoulder. "We can do it together," he said proudly, but he would not replace the broken mantles on the space heaters.

"We won't be able to do anything together if we don't get some heat. I can't stay here after supper in this cold." Mom had just gotten back from school, and she blew out her breath in little white clouds so my father could see it. Dad had only been home for a short while, and in his excitement to change the lightbulb he had forgotten to turn on the gas space heater.

"Mrs. Duke came into the shop at five-thirty. Mrs. *Duke*. She told me to call her Pauline. She said, 'Charles, money is no object. I want the best Schnauzer you can find.' You just don't walk away from a sale like that."

"Did she buy the dog?"

"What do you think?" Dad shot back. White, he glowered at her for an instant, his lower lip trembling. Then he took long strides and left the room.

Mom said it was a good night to go to church. Sometimes she said it was cold or sometimes she said she needed to pray, but we went to church after supper two or three times a week. My father sat under a cloud of blue tobacco smoke, sunk in his overstuffed chair, his head poked in the paper.

I sat on the floor buckling my galoshes so I could look at my father reading with his flesh-colored eyeglasses. He looked at peace as he read, a faint smile on his lips. Everything about him fascinated me, even his chair covered in a chintz patterned in wine-colored swirls of giant hollyhocks. The few pieces of furniture made the living room feel large. My father's chair sat in one corner on the edge of a huge expanse of linoleum, the color of desert sand. An upright Sunday school piano sat in the opposite corner of the room, and a fat maroon sofa sat under the front window. Kitty-corner, away from the cloud of smoke and my father, stood a fish tank of sawdust with two white mice, their feet pink, their eyes red, the only pets I was allowed to have.

"Take off your galoshes and put on your leggins," Mom said through closed teeth; she was anxious to leave. Dad ducked behind the *Buffalo Evening News* so she would not see him smiling; sometimes he smiled when she lost her patience. Two straight-back chairs flanked him on either side, serving as tables. On one chair lay a box of Fanny Farmer pecan-turtles, chocolates, peanut-brittle, and a pack of Spuds; on the other chair a book of crossword puzzles, the stub of a pencil, gumdrops, a bottle of Pepsi, and a mystery novel by Erle Stanley Gardner. He cradled a dish of rocky road ice cream in his lap.

As soon as I started buckling up my boots a second time, Mom walked toward the shadows of the front door. "Good night, Charles," she said into the pleated curtain. "We're going to church."

The night air was black and the snow was white. Three blocks upstream along the Tuna, yellow oblongs of light fell in uneven rectangles in the snow outside the First Free Methodist Church. After several months of evening prayer meeting, I dreaded all the talk of Brother and Sister at the door. Inside, pale people in worn gabardine and faded wool sat with their coats on, the men holding their orange and red hunting caps on their knees, the women folding their four-cornered scarves in their laps.

It was colder by far in church than it had been at home. Cushionless, the backs of the pews fell at right angles to the floor. With no carpeting and no stained glass, little indicated that this was the House of the Lord other than the pews on either side of the center aisle. The only hint of decoration appeared in an ordinary double-casement window, tinted green, over the altar. The windows on the sides of the sanctuary were pebbly and frosted like the windows in a public restroom. None of the women wore makeup or jewelry.

Reverend Woods stood up and praised the Lord with his ten fingers over his head stiffly pointed toward heaven. He said he wished to welcome us warmly because the church was so cold; then he corrected himself and said, no, the church was not cold, it was only the building. The Church of God was always warm. After we sang, Reverend Woods asked people to stand up and offer testimony in behalf of God's love.

A man in the second pew rose slowly, clutching the back of the seat in front of him, wavering for a moment, trying to remember, his voice deep and coarse. He told how he had lost his job four years ago and, with it, his faith and hope. He began to cry when he said he turned away from the Holy Spirit to the Evil Spirit, drinking in order to forget and escape. He forgot, he said, his wife, his daughter, his home. He said he even forgot who he was and, worse, he had forgotten God. One day, he said, he fell over and did not wake up for two weeks. His family thought he was dead and, he said, he really had been dead: dead in spirit, dead to Christ.

After he stopped talking he stood there shaking until the woman beside him helped him sit down. Reverend Woods bounded up four steps to the edge of the platform, gathered his toes together, and pointed his hands over his head, ready to dive. He closed his eyes but I could tell he was squinting, peeking out at the congregation. Still poised like a diver, he held his hands straight up over his head, waiting for the right moment; then, in a high-pitched voice, he prayed:

Dear Lord. This is Reverend Ed Woods in Bradford, Pennsylvania. Sometimes lost, Lord. In the mountains. Can you hear me, Lord? The roads are ice here to Kane. Here to Kinzua. Here to Salamanca. Here to Shinglehouse. O Lord, everywhere. The roads are ice.

Yet this man has cometh into our mist. Cometh into our mist to pray for your forgiveness. To repent. To pray for his sins.

After four years of dark, he has come to ask for your Light.

After four years of emptiness, come to pray to you to fill his heart with love.

Four years! Four years!

We are all sinners, Lord. All fallen as this man has fallen.

O Jesus we are lost. Sheep. We are lost sheep and you are . . . you are our Shepherd. Do we all know that hymn? "Savior, Like a Shepherd Lead Us."

Come on now. "Savior. O Savior! Like a Shepherd Lead Us."

Reverend Woods led the singing. We all stood up and pushed the words out as loudly as we could so that the walls rang and everyone smiled that we had lifted the spirit of cold and pushed it out of the room. The man who had forgotten who he was stood up and took off his glasses and waved to us, his arms outstretched like a soldier home from the War riding through town in an open car.

Then Reverend Woods lowered his arms and everyone sat down in silence. I squirmed a little and my mother touched my knee. After a short while she stood up herself. She said nothing at first, her fingers curled over the top of the pew in front. People lifted their shoulders and sighed, and a shudder rippled through the congregation.

"God bless Brother Patterson," she said slowly. "God bless him and bless his family. Bless all our families here tonight. Families broken by drink. Families broken by pain."

Again she paused, stating every word carefully, saying too much. I was ashamed that she told these people so much. Wouldn't they know about my father and our problems at home? Her eyes were shut when she spoke, but my eyes were open. We were not really brothers and sisters, and our family, my real family, my father was at home.

"Bless Brother Petterson's family," Mom continued. "Give

them the strength to pray for him too. Give them the strength to ask for God's help and forgiveness. Bless all children. My own David here . . ."

I pulled the collar of my Navy pea jacket up over my ears and held it there with both hands, arranging the collar so I could peek out through the buttonhole. I could see my mother holding onto the pew as Mr. Patterson had done, but her voice did not crack. A lay minister herself, she spoke slowly, in control. She spoke about all of us needing God's help, but she did not seem to need that help herself. People were weeping all around us. I was glad when everyone stood up, and we sang the final hymn with passion.

The next time Mom wanted to go the First Free Methodist Church I bent over to buckle my galoshes and stayed bent over until she noticed. When she asked me why I was taking so long, I held my stomach. I did not say anything until she asked me if I would rather stay at home and go to bed, and then I shook my head pitifully, "yes."

After she was gone, Dad suggested I play with the white mice, but I preferred to sit on the sofa and watch him reading. I had come to love and fear him with the same mix of emotions that I felt in the presence of all God's mysteries. The Bible presented a world in which the bizarre and the miraculous seemed commonplace, a world so strange and yet believable that whatever happened in this one seemed perfectly tame and ordinary. The room was so quiet I could hear the mice scattering the shavings Dad called excelsior. I could also hear my father breathe, and I liked to watch and guess how long it would take him to wet the tip of his finger before turning the page of his mystery. I liked him best when he was reading because he was sitting down and could not fall.

CHAPTER 9

Strangers

Strangers roamed town. One day an old man snuck over from the railroad yard, poking cautiously out of a narrow alley between two houses and crossing Davis Street like a fugitive coming out of the woods. He wore a dirty tan overcoat, white socks, and black shoes without tongues. Leaning back against the telephone pole as though it were a tree, he looked up both sides of Amm Street, inspecting the houses. I kneeled backward on the couch and watched him out the front window, confident he would choose our house. I shouted "company" as he climbed the front steps.

"Who is it?" Mom yelled back from the kitchen, but I had already answered the door, eager to see the man close up. The stranger reminded me of the old man who sat on the iron pipe fence feeding pigeons in front of town hall. Both men wore baggy gabardine coats and had streaks of rust through their long white hair. The man at the door made no attempt to smile.

"Mom or dad home?" he asked in a hollow voice. I could not see his eyes; his dark figure filled the doorframe, the sun behind him. I could hear Mom's footsteps behind me.

"I'm Ida McKain," she said in a puzzled voice, drying her hands on her apron. I was surprised she did not shake his hand.

"I need somethin' to eat," the man said.

"Are you hungry?" she asked. "You've come to the right house. We're just about to have supper. Wash up in the bathroom. Dave, you show him where."

Most strangers knocked at the back door with offers to mow the lawn, even though we did not have a lawn, but Mom would hand a plate of hot food out through the screen door anyway. "And there's no wood to chop either," she would laugh as she hooked the screen shut. But strangers who knocked at our door did not have to work in order to get something to eat. " 'Ye know neither the day nor the hour wherein the Son of Man cometh.' " Mom said to me after we were far enough away from the door to talk. "But when he does come, He will say, 'I was a stranger, and ye took me in.' "

As I led the old man through the living room, Dad snapped his paper, looked up over the top, then ducked behind it again. He did not say hello; he did not say a word until we were seated at the table, and then he said, "Let's bow our heads in prayer." Except for Sunday blessing, he used the same prayer at every meal: "Bless this food to our use and our lives to Thy service. In Christ's name. Amen." With the stranger present, he changed the grace. In woeful tones he said, "Thank you, Jesus, for bestowing your bounty upon us. And thank you for sending this stranger to our house. It is better to give than to receive." Then he added the usual blessing, invoking the name of Christ with a sharp, crisp sound close to swearing.

I had heard him say it was better to give than to receive before, but I wished he had not said it in front of the stranger. The stranger hung his head. What could he give? We had no lawn to mow or wood to chop.

"I wish we could offer you something else," Mom said, apologizing for macaroni and cheese, but the stranger remained silent. He ate steadily without gulping and Mom passed him the casserole for seconds. He had long, thin fingers and thin, red wrists. After he was finished, he got up from the table, thanked us simply, and left.

My parents talked about food and rations every day. Dad picked up the groceries for supper on his way home from work at night. Meat, butter, sugar, and other staples were rationed, but, even when they were not, we rarely could afford them. If we did not eat macaroni, he brought home canned sweet potatoes, canned beans, or canned Spanish rice. When we ate meat, I was taught to save a "chew" as Grandpa Crawford had done. After his first mouthful, Grandpa cut off the best bite and saved it at the top of his plate for the end of the meal. Then, smiling, he held it up on the tip of his fork for everyone to see. At least that was what Mom had said. Grandpa had gone without, and his chew reminded the family of how much we had to be thankful for.

Once a year, at Christmas, my mother put out a wooden bowl of unshelled nuts, oranges, tangarines, and dates. "Feast or famine," she said cheerfully. The dates were sticky with a dark creosote-colored sugar that oozed out of the package. On the brown and gold medallion, four camels lumbered across the desert toward an oasis of feathery palms. When she was out of the room I ate half the dates and licked the wrapper.

The next day I blotched out all over, and my mother put me with a fever in their bedroom. The faded rose wallpaper had scorch marks through it like iron-marks on an old and yellowing Sunday shirt. Dad kept the window open at night almost all year long, even most of the winter, and when he had to spit he let it fly from the bed in the dark toward the cold draft; the cold air, he said, was good for your health. But sometimes when he spit he missed, and when he was too tired to walk to the bathroom, he pissed out onto the rooftop. Stains grew beneath the window frame, a little pile of snow remained on the floor. Mom shut the window with a bang, shaking her head in disgust and wiping her hands.

I propped myself up and looked at pictures in a book she had brought me from school. The cover of the book showed a boy in bed who was also reading, and for the longest time I thought that people only read when they were sick in bed. Inside the book, a boy was walking down a dirt road shouldering a stick with a red bandanna tied to the end. Mom said the cloth sack contained all the boy's earthly belongings and that the boy was leaving home to seek his fortune among strangers. She said he was like the men who came to the door looking for something to eat—out of work, his stomach grumbling. The road he traveled narrowed to a line, ran downhill past a castle, then dropped off the edge of the world.

"Why do you think the road drops out of sight?" she asked. Asking questions was her way of keeping me company; I never felt I had to answer unless I wanted to. "Because there's a risk in everything," she said. "Especially when you set out on your own." She pointed to the clouds over the boy's head and called them cream puffs. "And the cream puffs? What do you think they mean?" she asked. "That's an easy one. They mean the boy is happy. For now at least."

A large black bird circled the castle, its wings throwing a shadow over the entire road. "What do you think will happen when the boy walks down the road?" she asked. I did not answer, nor did she; sometimes she asked questions without answers. "See the boy's bandanna? See his dark skin? The boy's a gypsy," she said with a smile. "I bet he never gorged himself on dates as you did. Come on now, get some sleep."

Come summer a procession of real gypsies passed through town. I was riding my bike out Congress Street when I saw them. The women wore red bandannas around their dark faces while the men wore them wrapped around their dark necks. They moved by slowly—a band of wagons and trailers hitched to old horses, pick-up trucks, and beat-up cars.

Something terrible was going to happen, I thought. At each end of the line a policeman rode a black and silver motorcycle. The policemen tried to look blank the way they do in parades, but both of them looked impatient, frowning in the glare of their own machines. The gypsies stayed close to the side of the road, going just fast enough so that the motorcycles would not tip over and so the old and tired horses could keep pace.

I pedaled alongside in the middle of the pack and across the road, far away from the policemen. The gypsy women smiled at me, the children stared, while the men did not seem to notice me at all. The clippety-clop of the horses echoed off the road up under the wagons, a rhythm of freedom and gloom. The policemen wore guns and carried nightsticks.

We had started on the outskirts of town, and after a mile or so my heart pounded as I breathed in the smell of the horses and looked at the wagons silhouetted against the hills. For a moment I forgot we were heading into town; I forgot where we were entirely. I wanted to sit up on one of the wagons behind the horses. It would be easy to be a gypsy, I thought: just wandering through the world seeking my fortune. A third policeman waved his arms at the intersection of Main and Congress, holding up traffic so we could pass through but stopping me when I tried to stay with the wagons. "Go on home, kid, where you belong."

"Interesting," Mom said when I told her the story. "A caravan of gypsies was escorted by the police? Now why do you suppose the police were there?" She untied her apron, sat down at the kitchen table, and folded the apron on her lap.

"I'll tell you," she said. "The town thinks it's too good for them. Afraid the gypsies are going to steal something. But gypsies are no worse than anyone else. They're dark, that's all. That's why the police were there. The gypsies to them are colored."

She stopped, nodded to herself, and told me a story about the gypsies and Jesus, back when the gypsies were slaves. Jesus was going to be crucified on the cross, and the Romans needed nails, four of them. They needed three nails for His hands and feet, and a fourth nail for His heart. But the gypsy blacksmith and slave didn't want to see Jesus killed, so he swallowed the nails instead. And that's when God gave the gypsies their freedom. All over the world, gypsies were set free: free to wander, free to beg, even free to steal.

"What do you think of that?" she asked.

I did not know what to think. My mother often talked about freedom in ways that were beyond me. "It must of hurt to swallow a nail," I said. "Did the gypsy die?"

One day I found a book hidden in the bureau. I knew Mom had hidden it because it was wrapped up in a tablecloth. The book, *Jim Crow*, was full of pictures of people with black faces and black hands. She had other books on Negroes, but this was the first hidden book that I had ever found. Most of the men in the pictures in *Jim Crow* were farmers, but some of them wore white suits, white hats, and fancy shoes. I had never seen a real black person, even though the gypsies were dark. One picture showed a black man dangling from a rope. Men dressed like ghosts stood in an orderly circle around the tree, eye-holes cut in the sheets.

When Mom got home from school she grabbed the book out of my hands. She said I was too young to see such pictures and that I would grow up with "a warped view of the world." Soon after that we began getting *Ebony* in the mail, the first and only magazine subscription in the house. She left it in the living room for me to read, then stacked the old copies in the hovel. After the stack grew high enough, she bundled them up with twine and the two of us marched off with them to Mrs. Oley Cosby's house. Mrs. Cosby lived over the Army and Navy Store on West Washington Street.

The venetian blind inside the plate glass of the front door was broken, and the narrow hall leading upstairs smelled of urine.

"She can't do anything about it," Mom explained. "On Saturday night the bums step inside the door and spray all over like cats."

"Can't she lock it?" I asked in disbelief.

"No," she said firmly, "now come on." As we stepped into the hall she put her hand on the small of my back, coaxing me up the stairs.

Mrs. Cosby was a tiny woman the color of a new can of brown shoe polish. She must have been close to ninety; her hair was white and she could hardly see through her glasses. Whereas most old people fussed over me and spoke to my mother about me as though I wasn't there, Mrs. Cosby shook my hand and ignored me. I liked her for that. She was polite but formal, and she did not ask us to sit down. After Mrs. Cosby finished with the magazines, she passed them out among the congregation of the Copeland African Methodist Episcopal Church—the AME for short. Pretty soon Mom got to know the Allens, the Collinses, the Cosbys, the Grays, the Jacksons, the Russells, the Saddlers, and the Walkers. We would be walking down Main Street and she would stop every colored person we saw. If she did not know the person, she would walk up and introduce herself. "I'm sorry," she said, "but I don't believe we have met. My name is Ida McKain, and I am good friends with Mrs. Cosby."

Mom said there were only thirty-three Negroes in town and it should not be hard to get to know each and every one of them. "That is," she said, "if you can trust the census. I don't. The census is crazy. They call the Negroes 'non-whites,' as if you are either white or nonexistent. Why don't they just call them colored people and be done with it? There are no other 'non-whites' around except the Indians, but according to this foolish census they don't count either.

According to the census people, the Senecas have their own nation."

She shook her head. "At school they want to know your age, sex, race, and Lord knows what all. They give us these forms. Do you know what I put down for race? I leave it blank. Yes I do. Or sometimes I'll put down a question mark. Mr. Heineman loves that! But I told him, 'I'm sorry, I really don't know. We all go back to Adam and Eve as far as I'm concerned.' And what color were they, pray tell? Nobody knows. We're all mixed." She paused and laughed. "Both ways. We're all mixed and we're all mixed up."

My mother told stories like that often, stories that were like parables from the Bible. She seemed angry and determined when she spoke, but also uncertain, like a little girl who was afraid of telling the truth. I did not share her indignation. Mrs. Cosby and all the other colored people I met seemed fine to me.

The nature of suffering was beyond me, but I was learning. One day in third grade I met a strange boy named Yankel. He could not go to the picture show on Saturday, and I could not go on Sunday. Going to the picture show meant a great deal to kids my age growing up in Bradford, and I felt sorry for Yankel that he had to go alone on Sunday. Sometimes my mother gave me eleven cents to go to the New Bradford Theater for the Saturday matinee. The excitement began as I raced to the end of a line which stretched half a block up the street to Abe Yasgur's furniture store. Bigger kids in line were asking smaller kids to count their money, knocking their coins to the ground and pretending to help them find them, pocketing whatever they picked up. I spotted somebody's mother and stood in line next to her, clutching two buffalo heads and a penny.

I liked to sit in peanut heaven. The theater was always packed, and as soon as the lights went off over one hundred fifty kids shouted. We cheered when Woody Woodpecker came on, the previews, Hopalong Cassidy, the "Adventures of Brick Bradford," "Superman and the Mole Men," and even the weekly horrors of the cattle cars and barbed wire—the zebra-shirted men with sunken eyes, the gas chambers, and the human skeletons stacked for burning outside the ovens. When they showed newsreels, the announcer lowered his voice, the violins playing in a discordant minor key. The first time I heard the rooster's crow announcing the newsreels, I thought the concentration camps were part of the show. My mother corrected me sharply, appalled that I did not yet know the difference between the horrors on the "Pathfinder News" and the "Adventures of Brick Bradford."

But the War was distant and unbelievable. Any understanding of it came in scraps, in bits and pieces, like my experience with Yankel. Yankel spoke very little English, maybe a dozen words. He had gentle eyes and, in his dark and heavy clothes, he looked as out of place as I often felt. My mother said he was a Displaced Person, but everyone called him a DP. After a week or so we became friends. One day after school I invited him home to play.

"Yankel," I said, "give me your hat and coat." I gestured and he gave me his coat, but he would not give me his hat, a tiny little circle on his head, without ear muffs or a peak. I pointed to his beanie again, but he shook his head. Finally I lunged for it, but he ducked, and soon we were wrestling on the floor. I was surprised by how hard he fought and by the wild look of fear in his eyes.

Mom ran into the hall and broke up the fight; she called his hat a skullcap and reminded me of the picture of the boy in the book I had gotten for my birthday, *One God and the Ways We Worship Him*. She explained that Jews wore their skullcaps wherever they went, even inside. I did not understand. She had always made me hang up my hat and coat, and whenever we had guests she told me to hang up their clothes, too. Yankel stayed for a game of Chinese checkers in the living room, but he remained distant, abruptly excusing himself and bowing stiffly to my mother as he left. Later we found out that he had lost both of his parents in the War. My mother told me I might have seen either his father or his mother behind barbed wire in one of the newsreels on Saturday afternoon. Our friendship changed after he came to the house and we fought. He stayed in town for only a couple of months, then moved to Cleveland to live with a family who escaped before the War, but I felt I had deserted him.

If it had not been for "circumstances," as my parents put it, my mother would have been a preacher. I did not know this until we had moved to Bradford, and then she showed me the announcement in the *Clarion Democrat:* "Word has just come to hand stating that Mrs. Ida Crawford McKain, of Parkers Landing, had been licensed to preach, at the recent session of District Conference of Grove City District. Our information is to the effect that Mrs. McKain passed a most creditable preliminary examination and was given a unanimous approval. The people of Clarion to whom Mrs. McKain is well known as Miss Ida Crawford, are sure that she will prove equal to all responsibilities given her, and hope she may be able to accomplish a great work for the Master's kingdom."

"Oh, well," she had said easily. "I don't have to stand in the pulpit to spread the Word." Actually, she had always wanted to be a missionary, and sometimes she and her friends met in the living room to discuss missionary work in Africa and China. My mother had first traveled to Bradford as general secretary of the Loyal Temperance Legion for the Woman's Christian Temperance Union. She told me that she had been called to this outpost as Albert Schweitzer had been called to French Equatorial Africa, and as Pearl Buck's parents had been called to Chinkiang, China—to save souls and to spread the word of Jesus. The temperance workers set up counseling centers, prayer meetings, and the Reading Room Association, a body of schoolteachers and housewives to whom my mother had spoken on her first visit. The WCTU in Bradford also opened up a temperance restaurant and a station house to serve the moral and spiritual needs of newsboys; on Thanksgiving they sponsored a dinner for newsboys and bootblacks alike. But the War put an end to all of that. Nonetheless, my mother was recognized for her work throughout the Alleghenies, and she showed me her picture one page after Grandma Crawford's in the *History of the Pennsylvania Woman's Christian Temperance Union.*

She also helped start a local chapter of the National Association for the Advancement of Colored People. Although not terribly supportive, Dad agreed with her WCTU work, but he had views of his own when it came to colored people. One day when he came home tired from work, he hurled *Ebony* against the wall.

"Get that nigger-lover magazine out of here!"

Dad did not own a hood or a robe, and he did not ride in the night, but he blamed the Jews, the Negroes, and the Catholics, in that order, for everything. He was an armchair Klansman, attracted by the well-aimed platitude and the well-chosen cliché. He liked the rhetoric of violence, but after dark he never left home. The Klan met in the dance hall over McCory's 5 & 10 on Main and Chambers, right next to the Methodist church. Some of the members were welders who squirreled away short sticks of pipe, welded them into crosses, then wrapped them in kerosene rags to set them ablaze in the hills. That way the crosses could be used over and over.

Dad rolled up his sleeves and tightened his fists when he spoke of Roosevelt. "The country is going to the dogs for one simple reason. A Christ killer is in the White House." He pronounced the president's name so that the first syllable rhymed with Jew, dragging it out slowly. "Roosevelt!"

He kept a KKK pamphlet in the top dresser drawer under his Boy Scout badges and handkerchiefs. A card inside the pamplet said the KKK was dedicated to the principles of

Jesus Christ, and that all of its members were "of good character and sound mind."

One evening after Mom left the house to go to prayer
meeting, Dad jumped up from his chair and ran to the window to watch her disappear, making sure. It was hot and my
bare legs stuck to the prickly sofa.

"I'll tell you what," he said. "Let's listen to the fight! Billy
Conn and Joe Louis. The greatest fight of all time. The
heavyweight championship of the world!"

I had never heard of Joe Louis or Billy Conn, but I knew
that whoever they were, they made my father happy, especially Billy Conn. He said his name as though they were
friends, rounding it out with affection and admiration:
"Billy Conn!"

Dad pulled down the blinds and picked up around the living room, clearing ashtrays, stacking newspapers, and fluff-
ing pillows. He tossed a pillow on the floor beside his chair
facing the radio. "For you, Pal. It's cooler down there. Gets
hot at ringside."

The radio was a Philco console which took up nearly the
entire wall. A loose wire crawled out the back, snaked up
over the doorway, and then ran out through a BB hole in the
window. The radio looked like a kerosene stove and took up
almost the same amount of space. Dad listened to the evening news every night, and on Wednesdays he listened to
"Town Hall." On Sunday night he listened to his favorite
program, "Amos and Andy," and that was when Mom left
the room because she wouldn't laugh at people making fun
of the colored. He cocked his ear and listened to the dials
with the tips of his fingers, like a man cracking a safe. No
one else could touch it.

"Billy Conn will lick him," he said when he got KDKA.
"Wait and see. Louis is no boxer. He's all brawn. Conn's got
the brains. Conn's from Pittsburgh. I don't care if Louis does
outweigh him by twenty-five pounds. Conn's the boxer!" He
stood up tall and assumed a fighting position, curling his

fists, leading with his left, his right arm cocked in readiness. He used the word "lick" when he talked about his days as a prizefighter, rolling up his sleeves and posing. "I could lick half the men in this town right now, and that includes the strangers that pass through. One arm tied behind my back."

As the evening grew darker, the yellow light of the radio spread out into the corners of the room. Dad's face was bathed in a kind of chlorine glow, a sickly green. I liked the songs about razor blades and the sound of the bell, but I did not understand the fight. While the radio crackled, the announcer's voice faded in and out in waves. When Dad jiggled the antenna wire, sometimes it crackled louder. He frowned; "I hope Conn kills him."

Between rounds we drank Pepsi. Dad clenched his fists, jabbing, punching into the dark. As the fight wore on he became bitter, and when Conn sagged to one knee, he stared straight ahead without leaning forward to adjust the dial. Conn weakened in the seventh and, in the eighth, Louis finished him. The fight was over.

Sweating and exhausted, Dad sat in his chair a minute before getting up, as though he had been the one who had been knocked to the canvas. "The fight was fixed," he said bitterly. I looked at him closely from the safety of the shadows, his face bleached by the radio light. Strangest of strangers, he got up stiffly, moving awkwardly as though in pain. "I could have told you that from the second round," he said. "Conn never had a chance. The fight was fixed."

CHAPTER 10

The Great Flood

T he only time I ever saw my mother set foot inside the Pet Shop was on the day of the flood: May 27, 1946. My father had come home early that day, his soaked shirt clinging to his back. School had let out at noon, and ever since she got home, my mother had paced back and forth in front of the window, drawing the curtain and shaking her head. The curbs had vanished, and Dad said the creek was up to the footbridge on Pine Street. The rain streaked the talcum on his cheeks and slanted his hair forward. He had a funny little bang that made him look like Hitler.

"You mean the shop is going to get flooded?" Mom asked.

"Get your raincoats on," Dad yelled, and he ran out the door still dripping wet. I skipped through the water as the three of us waded downtown, the street a vast puddle from one side to the other. The wind drove the rain in spirals and whipped the edges of the puddle into a froth. I felt I could do whatever I pleased, as though the rules had been suspended. By the time we got to the shop the water licked at the front step.

Inside, yellow seeds of hemp and millet floated on an inch of water. Mother and I picked up the cartons while Dad stacked them on the sink and toilet in the bathroom, as high as he could reach. Then he covered the canaries under dark blue hoods to calm them, warbling softly, cooing from the back of his throat like a pigeon in Veteran's Square. He chortled to the finches and, pursing his lips, kissed the air to please the lovebirds. He reminded me again that if the birds caught pneumonia they would die.

Water lapped at the throw rugs sandbagged at the door, and Dad swung his mop back and forth in huge arcs across the tile, but the water kept on coming. He was frowning.

"It's no use, Charles. You've filled three buckets and it's getting worse."

He straightened his back for an instant, stared at her once, and kept on mopping, proving he could stay calm in a crisis.

"Won't the fish be okay?" I asked. I knew they were tropical fish and would not be okay, but I wanted to say something encouraging.

"You've done all you can do, Charles," Mom persisted. "Now it's time to think of your family."

It was still pouring outside and the water continued to push in under the door. Mom said the water would be higher on Amm Street because we lived downstream from the shop. Dad only smiled and continued to mop. "Don't add insult to injury," he said. I was afraid he would get angry and fall, or that he might push her down to keep her quiet.

"The fish look good," I said. "They're swimming in all directions."

At last he put on his hat and searched impatiently through his key ring for the right one. Mom asked him to take her arm so she would not lose her balance. Sometimes she asked him for help just before he was ready to explode, but he never seemed to catch on. By the time we reached Kennedy Street the swirling water was over my knees. It raced down the street from the direction of the creek, making holes around the base of the stop sign and around the trunks of the trees, roaring like a river. The light green shingles on David's house had turned dark, like moss.

"You'd better swim," Dad said. "You can swim, can't you?"

I looked at him to see if he was teasing. He had forgotten

the wind off Chautauqua Lake, my yellow bathing suit, his blue lips. I plunged into the water, kicking my feet and dog-paddling, trying to keep my nose up. The current pulled me toward Main Street before my mother grabbed my foot and stood me up straight. The last block home I dangled my feet between them. Dad held me up under one arm, Mom under the other. They dipped me up and down in the water as we walked, for the flood had made us giddy.

"The rich live in the hills, the poor live down here," Mom said. We were watching the water lap over the fire hydrant and inch its way up the pole of the street sign. "It's going to bury both Amm and Davis," she said, staring at the sign.

People in orange and black rain gear waved from boats while we waved back from the porch. Half a dozen rowboats with outboards went by before someone cut the engine and drifted toward us. The man cupped his hands and shouted that we had better take the next boat. The creek was rising fast. The railroad tracks were already torn up by Hanley Park; the bricks ripped up out of the road. Mom laughed when I wrestled my small desk upstairs, but my desk and the ledger inside were the only belongings I cared about.

"What about David Albright?" I asked after another boat went by.

"That's just it. We can always go upstairs if it gets much higher. The Albrights don't have an upstairs." She looked at me and added, "But they'll be okay. Nothing will happen to your friends."

Since our house was higher off the ground than most, Mom kept waving the rescue boats on down the street, down toward the Bailers and the Albrights. The power went out. Dad looked at his watch and shook his head. Dark at five-thirty, we had to light candles. I sat on the stairs in the front hall clutching the banister. The front door was open and dark brown water covered the porch, pushing into the hall as high as the second step. Every once in a while the faint light of a boat floated up the street. Finally Dad said he had had enough, and he stepped into the doorway swinging his flashlight back and forth like a lantern.

"Here comes one!" he said with relief, and we watched the prow creep closer across the black water. When the boat pulled up over the porch, the captain held onto one of the posts until we boarded; the three of us were unsteady. Mom could not swim and Dad's weight tipped the boat dangerously to one side. Mom waved good-bye to no one on the porch and bit her lip.

After the boat swung around, we headed through the dark up Davis Street toward the bridge and higher ground. The water bubbled and churned in all directions. No other boats appeared on the water. A barrel and a tree were pinned against the bridge railing. Up in the distance where the hill began we could see four or five sets of headlights shining over the floodwaters, lighting our path. A small cheer rose up as we scraped bottom. A soldier said we were the last ones to be rescued and that was why they were cheering. Mom looked toward the crowd and waved. The headlights of the Army trucks grew brighter as they raced their engines.

"Goodness," Mom said. "There's Mr. and Mrs. Leary!"

The next day I discovered that Linda Leary had been in my mother's fifth grade class at Lincoln School. Mr. Leary was in the oil business and he owned the Frosty Lunch and Dairy, the best store in town. They made homemade ice cream and homemade candy and popped their own popcorn right in the front window.

Mrs. Leary threw a blanket over my shoulder and gave me a slice of fudge. Mr. Leary carried our rope-tied suitcases around to his car trunk, one in each hand. "Hurry! Hurry!" he shouted. "We're gonna get drowned!" We drove for a long time in the rain before he turned into a long steep driveway to a red-brick house lit by spotlights on the lawn. He parked the blue car next to a white one and, together, the two cars glowed under long fluorescent bulbs like new cars in a showroom. Toys and tools jumped out in bright detail. Red and blue bikes leaned up against the wall along with a row of long-handled shovels, brand new hoes, gleaming rakes, and a lawnmower. I had never been in a new house before, and when we entered the kitchen hallway from the garage the click of the door behind us blocked out the whipping noise of the wind and the hammering of the rain. From inside the storm's shout became a murmur. We were inside the house of a rich man who lived on the hill. My senses were muffled, my instincts numb.

Mr. Leary asked me to help him build a fire. I followed him into the living room across a thick carpet. Dad sat in a stiff-backed gray satin chair which matched the color of his face. His trousers were wet to his knees, and when he crossed his legs water squeaked inside his shoes. Mom was wearing a pair of shiny black slacks and white ankle socks.

Mrs. Leary served coffee and hot chocolate, announcing high tea. Mr. Leary said we'd have been better off sticking with the Red Cross because they had doughnuts. Mom said, "You're better than the Red Cross. You found us on the side of the road and have taken us in, like the Good Samaritan."

Dad frowned and lit a cigarette. He said there was no one on earth like his father. "Dad," he said passionately, "Dad would do anything for anyone. As rich as he is, a millionaire, he would do anything for anyone."

His eyes had gone hollow; they had that faraway look he sometimes got before he had a spell. He could topple off the satin chair and smash the lamp and the table in an instant. I shouted to him as though he were in another room, startling myself as well as the others. He blinked and turned his head slowly, smiling toward me vaguely.

"Well," Mom said, "it has been quite a day."

"They say you got it worst," Mr. Leary said. "Hilton. Forman. Lower Amm. All the flatlands." He adjusted himself in his seat and leaned forward, touching his fingers together. "You hear about people out Willis and down Sixth Ward?

The Tuna caught fire right in front of the houses down there. Just below Kendall. Leak in the gasoline line and the whole creek was up in flames. Talked to one fellow who said they're lucky the whole refinery didn't blow. If the leak had busted wide open, every home down there would have burned. The people would either been drowned or burned alive."

"That's Bradford," Mom said in mock despair. "The only place on God's earth where the Final Day will come both ways. Fire and water." Mom spoke about the flood as though we were living through a story from the Bible, as though somehow it were not really happening. Mr. Leary spoke with authority. His voice was not particularly loud or deep, but he spoke touching the tips of his fingers together, with knowledge, as though he was bringing together two sides of an argument. Like most people in Bradford, he said "crick" for "creek" and, although he did not mean to, he made me feel uneasy. I did not like being taken in by rich people, watching my parents squirm, rattling china cups and saucers on their knees.

"They say you can strike a match down there any day of the week and the creek will burn," Mr. Leary continued. "It's all that phenol and chloride from the refinery. Oil brine and ammonia. You can scoop the damned stuff right off the top of the water and heat your house with it. I know people down there who say the gas fumes get so strong they burn your throat and eyes just breathing." He paused and looked at each of us. "That's a fact," he said, as though no one in the room believed him.

But it was not that we did not believe him; we just did not know what he was talking about. Mom did not even know the location of Willis Avenue, let alone anything about the oil business. I knew more about the layout of the town than she did because I walked from one end to the other and kept a map inside my head. My mother's knowledge came from God's plan as set down in the Old and New Testaments: a knowledge that lifted her above the floodwaters and the burning creek, above the names of the streets, pain and suffering.

Dad smiled quickly out of embarrassment; he had not been paying attention. Mr. Leary leaned forward in his chair, the light from the fire catching the bald spot in the middle of his thin gray hair. "Al Jenkins come across a boat that capsized. Five people hanging onto the sides. The father tossed the baby up into a tree. Tosses it right up into the crotch of a tree and crawls up after it! Just like that!"

Nobody spoke. Mr. Leary looked up at each of us, measuring his impact. After a long period of silence he rubbed his hands together and stood up. "I don't know about anybody else," he said, "but it's time for me to catch some shuteye."

In the morning the sun was shining. "Where's the dove?" Mom joked as we were driving back to town. "Where's the olive branch in the beak of the dove?"

A man with a red flag slowed us down as we bumped across the planks and the railroad tracks by Hanley Park. The water was below the bridge but the planks on the bridge were weak. "Praise the Lord," Mom said as we crossed to the other side. A Chevy coupe and a Ford sedan on Amm Street had watermarks up to the rooftop.

Mr. Leary got out and opened the trunk. He had been silent all morning, sitting near the window so he could blow out his cigar smoke. He had given Dad a cigar, too.

"My goodness," Mom said, leaning into the car, "there's no way we can ever thank you for being such Good Samaritans."

"Thanks for the lift," Dad said, looking away. "And the cigar."

Brown silt and muck greeted us in the hall. A few boards in the living room had lifted and the glossy surface of the linoleum had broken into chips so that patches of it looked like tar paper.

Mom and I scooped up the muck and mud with the snow

shovel, carefully scraping it over the side of the porch. Afterward we went downtown for a new roll of linoleum. Other people had been hit harder than we, people who lived in one-floor cottages. Upturned beds and tables, sofas and chairs, stoves and refrigerators littered the sidewalk. We had to walk out into the street to get by two little girls sitting on a bright blue sofa. As we passed, Mom said hello cheerfully, then she whispered under her breath that I should always remember them sitting out on the street like that. "Always count your blessings."

Downtown was devastated: a slick brown film stuck to everything. Some of the merchants had put their shoes and clothes into wooden bins and wheeled them out onto the sidewalk for a rummage sale, but most of the shops were boarded up. I was surprised that the door to Mayer Brauser's store was wide open, his high tin ceiling crisscrossed with clotheslines of socks, overalls, and workshirts. He shook his head when Mom told him it looked as if he were hanging out the wash.

"What'll it be?" he asked wearily.

With effort, Mom and I steered the long hollow tube of linoleum out the front door, Mr. Brauser shuffling and shouting instructions every foot of the way.

"Once we start we can't stop," she shouted back through the tube. Along the muddy street we walked past the bright blue sofa where the little girls had played. "Another block!" she hollered, her words hollow, as though we were still under water.

"Oh my," she sighed as we collapsed on the living room floor. "Our yoke may be easy, but our burden isn't light. Not today." The linoleum was tan so that it would not show the dirt.

Dad came home from the Pet Shop and read us the news from the *Evening Star.* "Listen to this," he said. "Water carrying dark brown silt swept through the first floor of homes on lower Amm, Forman, Hilton, Davis, River, Clarion, and Edgett streets. Nearly one hundred people were evacuated."

"Well, Dave," Mom said, "we're one of a hundred. Save that one for posterity. We're part of history. One out of a hundred. One of the Chosen Few."

For a month after the flood the house smelled musty, even with the windows open, while the street and the creek behind the house smelled of sewage. A powdery sand settled on the furniture when the trucks rumbled up Davis Street. Disgusted, Mom said we had more centipedes and silverfish than we had had in Punxsutawney. The new linoleum did not lie flat on the living room floor, and she was forever catching the heel of her shoe on it. A watery bathtub ring stretched around the entire room an inch above the baseboard. Middle C and some of the black keys stuck whenever she played the piano.

Outside, city sanitation workers spread white bleaching powder around the foundation of all the houses on Amm and Davis. Chloride of lime, the chemical used in war gas, stuck to our shoes when we played in the backyards and ducked under the rickety porches to hide. "Don't breathe that stuff in," Mrs. Albright warned. "It's poison." I got some in my eye one morning, and Mom washed it out with boric acid. "Let's just hope it's slack lime," she teased. "At least that won't leave a hole."

Patches of white powder stayed all summer. "You never get rid of winter around here," Mom said half in jest and half in anger. She pointed to the lime on the weeds. "There's snow on the ground all year."

"That's not snow," I quickly corrected. Mom had been complaining about one thing or another all summer, and I was learning that was a tactic she used to get her own way.

"I'm not going to go through another flood again," she said pensively. "It pretty nearly wrecked everything."

"There were only a couple of inches in the living room," I countered, repeating what I had heard my father say. The day after the flood they had argued about the damage. Dad had insisted that he had been hit much harder at the Pet Shop than we had been hit at home. "Please stop being such a calamity howler," he said evenly. "You strain at gnats and swallow camels."

CHAPTER II

~~~~~~~~~~~~~~~~~~~~~~~~~~~~~

Exposure

A week before I was supposed to start the fourth grade we moved again. The new house was only five minutes away, but it was a block farther from the creek than the old house and that was what mattered. A mustard-colored double-decker, the house had two doors on the front porch: a door to our apartment and a door for the landlord, who lived upstairs. On the day we moved, the FOR RENT sign was still thumbtacked above the mailbox. My father ripped it down and was about to shred it, but my mother held out her open hand. "Give me that please," she said evenly, exactly the way a schoolteacher talks to a boy caught defacing school property. My father looked at her harshly but handed the sign over.

The move was simpler this time than last. All the furniture was set up in a couple of hours. Our new apartment was small enough so that we did not have to close off two rooms for lack of furniture. "It's a lot less barren than the house on Amm," Mom said as she shivered. "It's warmer, too."

"Well, I liked Amm," Dad said. "And I don't like those two Colosimos up there wrangling all day in Italian."

"Oh, Charles. What's the difference? I would agree if we knew what they were saying. But we don't understand a word."

"That's not the point. They're noisy and inconsiderate. They won't even fix the toilet. They charge a king's ransom for rent and won't even fix the toilet. That's not my idea of how people should treat one another." The running toilet was right off the kitchen. Sometimes jiggling the handle helped, but most often it did not.

The older Mr. Colosimo was deaf and spoke no English; Louie, his younger brother, had to shout to be heard. On warm days late into Indian summer, the two of them marched arm in arm twenty paces back and forth in front of the house in a kind of wedding shuffle, but much slower. Each man wore a matching brown fedora and purple corduroy slippers. Every once in a while they would stop while Louie put his mouth close to his brother's ear and shouted. Mom liked the two old men because they were tiny and smiled warmly.

"They certainly can't help the fact they were born in another country," she said, reminding us that her father had been born overseas.

"I never claimed they could. You're twisting my words. I didn't say I objected to them because they're foreigners. They're inconsiderate and noisy, that's all. They have no respect for others. They shout when I am trying to sleep, and the damn toilet keeps running. I can't eat with that thing running. It's like Niagara Falls."

"Oh, Charles," Mom said slowly. "Lord have mercy."

The apartment on North Center Street was small. My mother and father and I lived too close: boxed in. Mom went out almost every night, more than she had gone out on Amm Street when the cold drove her to testify in church. She had friends from school and at several churches around town, but I had never seen my father with a friend. One night after she had gone to choir practice he told me she treated other people better than she treated members of her own family, and that was why she was always gone; she never had any time for us. He did not usually complain about her to me, and he was bitter when he spoke.

The next morning when I opened my bedroom door Mom

was sitting in a heap on the floor, her nightgown ripped at the shoulder. She held the torn flaps together when she saw me standing in the doorway. A red welt stood out on her cheekbone and she was sobbing. I had taught myself to remain cool during such moments, and in a measured voice I said good morning. Mom tried to drag herself off, moaning softly.

Just then their bedroom door flew open, and Dad stood there yelling, his eyes narrowed. Unaware that she sat at his feet, he looked toward the living room, shouting "Ida!" When he saw her slumped against the wall in front of him, he kicked her outstretched legs, flapping his arms to maintain his balance. He kept kicking her legs even as she reached down to cover them with her arms. He braced himself against the wall to jump down on her, as though he was trying to put out a fire. When he had had enough, the feeling gone out of his face, he tripped slightly as he tried to walk over her, turning in annoyance as though he had stumbled over clutter on the steps.

She lay there crumpled, her fingers rubbing her knees, her lower lip quivering. When she sat up, she rolled the back of her head from side to side against the wall as though the gentle rocking soothed her. I was afraid of what he would do to both of us if I got in the way. She wiped her sleeve across her nose, roughly, deliberately hurting herself, tearing at her face with the crook of her arm.

"Mom?" I asked. But she did not answer. She looked at me, her eyes welling up again as she heaved three or four sighs and groaned. Then she smiled slightly and shook her head, saying she was sorry, that I was not to blame. Her words made no sense to me. I did not feel as though I were to blame.

"Ida!" he yelled from the kitchen. "Get out here this minute or I'll be late for work." The danger was nearly gone from his voice. Now it was my mother's turn; unaccountably she would do something to provoke him, to bring back the rage.

When he shouted, she sprang to her feet and ran back inside the bedroom, slamming the door, both to annoy him and to hide.

"Dave!" he hollered impatiently. "Hurry up or you'll be late for school."

I took my place at the table. The space heater had not been turned on, and faintly I could see my breath. I made X's on the cold oilcloth with my thumbnail, shallow little indentations which lifted and faded away. He was running water into the coffee pot, over and over, filling it up and pouring it out.

I did not hear her come into the kitchen, but when I looked up there she was, standing naked in the middle of the doorway wearing only an apron. "Don't be a horse's ass!" Dad shouted. "Take that goddamn apron off! Get dressed!"

"No!" she said in a voice too perfectly calm. "If this is the only dress I have . . . ," she caught her voice, ". . . then I'm going to wear it. . . . I'm going to wear it to school."

"Get dressed!" he shouted. "Get dressed!" I had never seen him so outraged, as though her nakedness was a sin which spilled over onto both of them, as though he had been stripped naked beside her. He screamed and shoved her down, then kicked her across the room like an object he was trying to push out of sight.

A breast stuck out of her apron and she tucked it back the way Grandma McKain stuffed her handkerchief into her dress. Sobbing, she staggered through the living room into the front hall and pressed her forehead against the curtain and the frosted glass.

"Don't" I shouted, running at her as she wrinkled the curtains in her fist. She had always insisted that the curtains be kept ironed and neat, but now she was balling them up as though nothing mattered. "Don't!" I shouted a second time. "You're ruining the curtains!"

But she did not hear me, or if she did she did not listen. She turned the knob of the door and started to walk out onto the front porch. The wind was bitter and blew snow into the house. Dad grabbed her arm from behind and pulled her back inside, flinging her back down onto the floor. He hit her only once this time, a deep dull thud between the shoulder blades. Her arms shot out and she gasped, trying to catch her breath. Her eyes were frightened in a new way, as though she was drowning; then it was over. Her apron had come undone. She did not clutch at the bow or act embarrassed, but, slowly, stood up and walked toward the bedroom, the battle over.

In a few minutes she came out powdered and dressed, ready for school. I watched as she put on her red scarf in the mirror, and then she turned to me and smiled. "Boy!" she said, "I'm a wreck." Gingerly she touched the welt under her eye and patted rouge to her cheeks. Her lower lip was swollen, her eyes raw.

She moved toward me for a hug but stopped at the sound of Mr. Waller blowing his horn. I followed her to the door, pressing my forehead against the wrinkled curtain, breathing in the stale, wet smell of cold glass, watching her walk briskly down the front steps. Then she waved to the car full of teachers: the lighthearted one smiling, holding up one gloved hand to gather snowflakes, making light of the season's first storm.

Dad loved the cold. From October to May we were sealed in for winter. During our first year on Center Street we got so much snow people called the winter "closed." But there were few blizzards severe enough to close school, only a steady white spit that froze mid-air and melted in my eyes. Snow was not just snow for my father; it was a mark of his character, a source of his pride. Every morning he listened to the weather report at breakfast, and when it was reported that the temperature had dropped below zero, making Bradford the coldest spot in the nation, he would rub his hands together in glee, blowing air out through his lips and exclaiming, "Brrr!"

Mom waited for summer. She was always cold, and they would argue about whether or not she could turn up the heat. "Put a sweater on," he would chide. "It's no wonder you're cold."

When summer finally did come around, doors clicked open and slammed shut after supper as kids up and down the street raced outside to play. With no full-crowned maples and elms on Center Street as there had been on Amm, by mid-July the sun was relentless. Bricks were missing in the sidewalk; the street was dusty and dry, over-exposed. On one of those rare evenings when Mom did not have choir practice or a meeting, the two of us went for a walk after supper. Although we had lived there for nearly a year, she called it "getting to know the neighborhood." We crossed West Washington Street and walked past the Bradford City Garage and a row of city buses. At Barbour Street we stopped on the bridge.

"There," she said, gazing over the railing. "There's our little friend. It doesn't seem so dangeous, does it?"

I looked at the green slime wriggling downstream between the flat, dry rocks; the creek smelled raw and sulphurous. I glanced at my mother as she peered at the pathetic trickle, her eyes sparkling. The sun threw our shadows together on the rocks and trickle.

"Look!" she said with obvious pleasure. "That would make a perfect picture, wouldn't it." The two of us stood huddled over the iron railing, our shadows touching in silhouette. I felt embarrassed. I knew when she cropped a picture for our scrapbook, she carefully scissored out the entire background so that we seemed to exist in space alone: just arms, legs, and a head, or whatever stage prop she wished to feature—a flower, a book, or two lumps of coal for the snowman's eyes. In pictures where I had posed in front of the house on Amm Street, she had cut out the house completely, as though we lived without background, without struggle, without a town. On North Center Street she made sure there was no house to cut out. She took my picture standing beside the bush in front of the house next door.

"I like the shadow of the latticework on the water," she said, already picking out an acceptable prop for her picture.

"I like the old tires and broken bottles," I added.

"What?" she asked in surprise.

"If you took a picture, you'd cut out everything but the two of us," I said in a troubled voice.

"Well, you wouldn't want trash in it, would you?"

"I like it the way it is," I said, raising my voice. "The trash and everything."

I did not fully understand my anger, but I vaguely sensed that every time she trimmed down a picture to the two of us I felt weaker, less secure, as though I was losing a creek, a house, the sky.

CHAPTER 12

Boys

The town became my main escape. Phil Chicketti led a gang of kids in our neighborhood, and for a while I was one of them. He was the shortest boy in the fourth grade but the toughest kid in the school. Everybody called the Third Ward the "Bloody Third" because kids fought all the time. The "Bloody Third" was tougher than Davis Street, and I joined Phil's gang for self-protection. He fought with his fists and aimed at your teeth. Sometimes he started fights for no apparent reason, punching kids just to see them cry. He called his friends "Kikes and Dagoes": Richie Fishman, Guy Besutti, Mark Rosen, Harry Goldman.

"Hey," he shouted, touching all ten fingers to his chest dramatically, "Fishman's my friend. If I wanna call Fish 'Kike' I call him Kike. It don't bother nobody. Right? He calls me 'Dago,' 'Guinea,' 'Wop.' Every other fuckin' thing. Tell 'em, Fish, am I right? The rest of you guys fuck off. A Kike's a Kike."

"What are you?" he said to me one day, his hand twisting my collar. "You ain't no Jew or Guinea. What are you, a mackerel snapper? Yeah," he laughed, "you're a fuckin' mackerel snapper. Am I right?"

I nodded that he was right. If he wanted me to be a Catholic I would be a Catholic, but I stayed away from the neighborhood as much as I could. When school got out I escaped downtown, wandering up and down Main Street by the hour, taking inventory, counting stores, looking in windows. I felt important on Main Street because it was the center of town. I looked ahead at the people walking toward me; I looked forward to smiling and saying hello. I smiled and spoke to everyone. Both Mom and Dad encouraged me in this: to talk to strangers, to make them feel welcome and at home. Someday, I imagined, I would know everybody in town. I even waved to people as they drove by in their cars.

But my father was not pleased when I dropped in unexpectedly on him at the shop. He said if people looked in the window and saw me they would not come in.

"It's not good for business," he reasoned. "People will think I'm busy. We don't want to scare away the customers, do we?" When someone stopped outside the window to look at the turtles, he pretended he was reading a magazine. Then, under his breath, he would say, "Quick! Into the bathroom!" If the person came in, he jumped from his chair, tossing his magazine behind him on the seat as though he had been surprised. He smiled and sang hello in a rising and falling voice, making the word long and liquid. "We couldn't ask for a better day, could we?" he would say, or, "We could use a little sunshine for a change. What can I do for you?"

After Christmas, business was slow. Dad said he would close up until spring if it were not for his regulars, the little old women who came in for powders and seed. He had not even put a sprig of holly in his window for Christmas, while almost all the other stores downtown had fancy displays: magic worlds of gnomes in leather aprons dancing in a circle, jumping out of doors in trees to clap, some opening and closing their arms around accordions, others playing the violin and ringing bells. My favorite display was in the window of the Emery Hardware: a woods scene of stuffed squirrels, stuffed grouse and pheasant, even a stuffed deer. Although its fur was mangy and its ears torn, the deer had lived in the hills and something of its magical power remained, as though at any time it could turn and leap through the glass.

A black bear had recently roamed up and down Main Street, so anything seemed possible. Dad said the bear was looking for garbage cans and that, if it did not find food, it would simply disappear into the woods. Most people in Bradford seemed to expect bears to wander up and down the street. Wild stretches of unbroken woodland surrounded the town.

The display of Emery's reflected the spirit of the place, of who we were in Bradford. The outline of my face lined up with the deer's head; antlers grew out of my earmuffs and our eyes met in a single gaze. Dabs of cotton were pasted to the inside of the window, while a carpet of cotton lay on the floor. It was snowing outside, too, and the snowbank at the curb reflected in the glass. I did not necessarily want to be a hunter, but I wanted to own the .30-30 which was part of the display. I wanted to polish the walnut stock and oil the blue metal barrel. Someday I wanted to hang a gun over the sofa in my living room, whether I became a hunter or not.

As I stared into the deer's glass eyes, a boy wearing a red hunting cap looked into the window beside me. I pretended not to see him at first, but he moved closer, as though we were friends.

"You like to hunt?" he asked.

"Sometimes," I said, surprised that he had spoken.

"You want to see my guns?" he asked.

"You have guns?"

"Yeah. I have three rifles. A shotgun. A pistol. And a .22 for rattlers and copperheads." He counted slowly, as though he had so many guns it was hard for him to remember.

"Gosh!"

"Come on, I'll show you."

The boy took a key out of his pocket and opened the door to the right of the window in front of us. He looked up and down the street before we went in. The wind was gusting and the people on foot covered their faces against the snow.

I followed him up the darkened stairway where he un-locked another door, reached inside around the corner, and turned on a dim light. Once inside, he clicked the dead-bolt behind us. The room did not look like an ordinary room in a house, but I did not know what else it could be.

"I don't have any brothers and sisters," he said.

"Me neither."

"You aren't supposed to say you were up here," he said. "Okay?"

"How come?" I asked. We did not know each other well enough to share secrets.

"Because."

I had never seen a stainless steel sink before. Beside it stood a matching cooking stove. A picture of a horse jumping over a rail fence hung on the wall. The picture was lit by a brass light.

"That picture is worth money," he said. "I could sell it and buy a dozen guns if I wanted to. Hey, you still want to see my guns?"

"Yes," I said. "But I have to get home pretty soon."

"Okay, I'll show you the guns in a minute." The boy sat down in a black leather chair, looking sad. "Wait," he said thickly. "First . . . first you have to take down your pants."

I looked away as though I had not heard him; maybe he was in junior high school.

"Come on," he said, "take down your pants. It's no big deal."

I backed up toward the sink, looking for a water glass.

"Okay," he said, "I'll take mine down first." He undid his buckle and the buttons on his fly, then he sat back down on the edge of the leather chair.

"I don't want to," I said as calmly as I could.

"If you don't I won't show you my guns."

"I don't care," I said. "I don't want to." I moved toward the door, and he stood up quickly. He had something in his hand and he was smiling.

He pressed down his thumb and a blade sprung out. "A pig-sticker," he said, opening it and closing it. "I could kill

you easy with this. Take down your pants and you won't get
hurt." Awkwardly, he pulled down his own trousers and underpants without letting go of the knife. "Come on!" he
shouted, "hurry up!" He waved the knife in a small circle
between us.

My face got hot. I looked at the white horse jumping and
the rider in red britches half-standing in the stirrups. For the
first time I noticed a fox at the edge of the woods. The boy
with the knife seemed more frightened than I was. I faced
the older boy without knowing what he would do, unbuttoning my trousers and slipping them down to my knees.

"Your underpants, too," he said. He was touching himself,
making his penis stand up.

I looked at the knife. The boy's face was angry. I slid down
my underpants to my knees.

"Come here," he said in a funny thick voice. "Sit in my
lap."

"Where are the guns?" I asked without moving.

"In the room behind that door."

"You promise to show me then?"

"Promise. Just come sit on my lap. I won't hurt you."

I covered myself with my hands and limped over to the
leather chair. I sat down on his knees and my skin tickled; I
jumped back up. "I want a glass of water first," I said. "I'm
thirsty."

Pulling up my underpants and trousers, I walked toward
the sink as though it was perfectly understandable for me to
want a glass of water. "I don't know where the glasses are," I
said, trying to sound casual.

The boy impatiently rose from the leather chair and wad-
dled toward the sink. As he turned his back to reach over his
head for a glass, I grabbed my jacket, slid back the bolt, and
flew down the stairs three steps at a time to the street.

"I'll kill you!" he screamed. He was standing at the top of
the landing with his pants around his ankles, brandishing
his knife.

The cold wind burned my face as I ran home. I took off my
shirt in the bathroom and covered my shoulders with a
towel. I filled the sink and dunked my head up and down,
drinking the water slowly as though from a mountain
stream. After I quenched my thirst I combed my hair, making sure the part was straight. It had grown dark in the empty house. I did not care what Dad said about the electricity. I
turned on all the lights in the living room and the kitchen.

My mother called it moping. "What are you doing in the
house on a day like this?" she asked after church one day,
throwing open the windows. I was rolling a ping-pong ball in
the corner of my room, watching it ricochet and hoping it
would wobble to a stop inside a magic circle. The deaf Mr.
Colosimo had caught a cold in July and died. It was much
quieter upstairs. We had been living on North Center for
over a year. I had stopped going downtown or playing on
Howard Street. "Well," she said, "I called Mrs. Hale. She said
you can play with her son tomorrow after school." Mom
turned in the middle of the living room and asked me to
unzip the back of her dress. Dad was sitting in his hollyhock
chair reading the Sunday paper; he did not look up.
   "Who is her son?" I asked.
   "Richard. Richard Hale. He's a nice boy but he has no one
to play with. I told Mrs. Hale you would wait for him after
school tomorrow." I did not unzip the back of her dress, and
she reached around to do it herself. "Come on, Dave!" she
said with exasperation. "That's the least you can do. He has
no one to play with. You know how hard that can be."
   Richard was in the fourth grade and no one would play
with him because he was different. His shirt hung out and he
buttoned it tight at the neck. He wore Coke-bottle glasses
and spoke with a lisp.
   I walked around in figure-eights in front of the school the
next day waiting for him. As the final bell rang, out he came,
curling his thick soft lips in a grin. White and flabby, he

looked like a large bird that could no longer fly. Some kids called him Dodo. "Hi," he said in a low and gurgly voice. At the curb he reached down and took my hand as we crossed the street. When we reached the other side he held on, skipping and laughing. His hand was smooth and moist, softer than any hand I had ever touched. He sputtered when he laughed, coughing and drooling as though he had choked on a bone. At one moment his face was white and flat, and at the next tongue-red. He sprayed me with laughter.

Mom said he acted the way he did because his parents were nearly seventy. Mrs. Hale made apple pies for the Free Methodist picnic; his father wore a stained gray hat and leaned on a blueberry cane, his face in shadow. Mom said they were good people who feared God, and that was all that mattered. She said they were doing their best to make Richard happy and that in God's eyes Richard was a favorite; from God's point of view Richard was the ideal friend.

Despite the fact that he was odd, I liked Richard, too. He did not tease me for carrying a violin to school, and when I smiled, he smiled back. After school we often went back to his house to play King of the Mountain. In fifth grade I weighed less than seventy pounds; Richard weighed at least twice that and stood over six feet tall. I said he could be king, but I made him kneel on the ground before I touched each shoulder and crowned him gently with a picket that had fallen from their fence. To play the game properly, I had to crawl up the hill on my hands and knees; then Richard started kicking, whizzing his high-topped boot by my ear. He laughed when I told him kicking was against the rules. I tried to stand up and grab his legs, but he pushed me harder, spilling me head over heels to the bottom.

I crawled as close to the top as I could without standing, taunting him until he leaned forward to shove me down again; then I grabbed his hand and pulled with all my might. It worked; the biggest part of Richard, his head, listed forward, and he came toppling with it, sprawling headfirst to the bottom. Face down in the leaves, he did not move.

"Come on, Richard," I said, "let's play some more. You can still be king."

"Wichard! Wichard!" he lisped, jumping to his feet. "Wichard! King of the Mounting!"

Richard was the only boy at the YMCA who had hair over his penis. In swimming class, only the lifeguard wore a suit. I did not like taking Richard to the Y because he held onto the side of the pool and kicked, splashing chlorine in my eyes. We were on the buddy system, but when the whistle blew I did not have to look far; I stayed close to him because I was afraid he might drown. After swimming, he took forever to get dressed. He had recently learned to tie his shoes, methodically placing one lace over the other, grunting each step of the way, his purple tongue touching the tip of his nose as he bent over. Then, after one shoe was tied, he checked the bow and loose ends to see that they were exactly the same length, and if they were not, he untied them and started all over again.

We took a shortcut to the Y through the Tuna Lumberyard, a wetland along Tuna Creek that had been filled with slag and gravel. We took our time, lobbing stones over the shed rooftops into the creek, skipping stones, and firing at the reflectors on the telephone poles. One day we found a black and white puppy lapping from a puddle. Although the dog had mange, Richard picked it up and stroked its quivering back. Even after it peed on his sleeve, he laughed and cuddled it. "Come on," I said. "I'm going to the Y."

Richard would not put the dog down, so I ran ahead and hid behind a stack of lumber. I waited for the sound of his footsteps in the gravel, ready to whistle a stone inches in front of his nose. Instead, I missed, and the stone sailed through the half-inch of space between his glasses and cheekbone, smashing the thick lens to bits. His nose started to bleed and he pressed his knuckles into the sockets of his eyes, his shoulders shaking.

I strolled out from behind the lumber with my hands in my pockets. "What happened, Richard? You all right?" I picked up his broken glasses and jabbered about a Jap, a sniper's stray bullet. Without his glasses on, the hollows of his eyes were damp and pink; standing awkwardly in the sunlight, he looked naked. I held his soft hand on the way home while he sobbed hysterically, his breath hot. "Boy, Richard!" I said soothingly, "you're really lucky. You could have lost an eye."

Mrs. Hale did not believe that we had been attacked by an unknown enemy lurking in the lumberyard, but I stuck to my story. His glasses had a life of their own, and no one could bring the dead back to life. Richard's glasses grew out of his face like a nose or a chin; without them, he looked mutilated, maimed.

Mrs. Hale sat down at the kitchen table and folded her arms, staring straight ahead and sighing. I lumbered around the table imitating Richard's heavy gait, grabbing my eye the way he had done, gaping open-mouthed, screaming, and falling to my knees. Richard was wearing a second pair of glasses patched together with adhesive tape. He laughed as I staggered about, blubbering and drooling, his voice hollow, an octave too low, ecstatic. Mr. Hale stood in the shadows laughing too, and then Mrs. Hale laughed. At the end of my little performance I bowed foolishly, slid out the door, and waved good-bye.

Part Two

CHAPTER 13

Some Moves

On Good Friday before school I stood in front of the mirror, clipped on my salt and pepper bowtie, and sang "Were You There When They Crucified My Lord?" Whenever I sang spirituals, my eyes watered, and I had to fight against the sadness by channeling its power into my voice. My favorite songs started deep inside me so that I swayed, lifting my voice higher until the music broke free, soaring all by itself while I fought back the sadness. But that was in church; in church the music blinded me to the congregation. It was easy to sing a solo. I just stepped forward from the rest of the choir and closed my eyes. At home, in front of the bedroom mirror, I let my eyes fill with tears, watching in fascination through the blur. I took myself so seriously in the mirror, a look of puckered pain twisted my face; I looked so ugly I finally laughed.

School let out at twelve so that everyone could go to church in the afternoon. Other kids also dressed up for Good Friday, wearing their Sunday best and sitting at their desks with wet hair. It was pouring outside and dark. Mrs. Starkweather had to turn on the lights. By ten o'clock the wind rattled the panes in their sashes. Mrs. Starkweather told us stories and let us draw pictures on the blackboard. Finally she even let us stand at the windows and look outside: at first the glass was so dark we saw only our own faces. Beyond our reflections, white water bubbled up out of the storm drains and foamed angrily in the gutters. When it thundered, the girls put their hands over their ears while the boys laughed, pretending they were not afraid.

I sloshed my way to the Methodist church, stopping on the iron bridge at the foot of the hill to listen to the roar of the creek. Branches and bottles raced by under the bridge. Just two stores beyond the creek, Dad sat smoking in the window of his Pet Shop, staring up at the ceiling calmly, searching for a puzzle word.

At church, I poured water from my shoe while Reverend Zinger read Matthew 27, the story of the Crucifixion. Thunder cracked outside the stained glass windows and "there was darkness over all the land," just as it was written in the Bible. During the pause when the children's choir gathered itself to sing, the church lights flickered. Miss Dunn smiled up at us bravely from the piano and winked so we would not lose heart.

By the end of the service, water had risen ankle-deep on Chestnut Street. My mother and father were already at home, grabbing shoes and boxes off the floor and wrestling with chairs and tables to get everything up on the beds. Nothing else could be done. The hills were piled high with snow; the rain was warm.

The Tuna waited until the next morning to overflow its banks, but by eleven o'clock, North Center Street was under water. We listened through the crackle on the radio for flood reports.

The announcer said we were tuned to WESB: "The Friendly voice of WESB—the High-Grade Oil Metropolis of the World—Where Every Sponsor Belongs." He said that eight feet of water stood at the corner of Main Street and Davis Street and warned people to stay upstairs and wait for the rescue boats. The water was still rising. It was the first day of the station's broadcast, and we listened attentively.

"We don't have an upstairs," Mom said.

"I'd rather drown than ask that SOB for a single red American cent," Dad said.

"Oh, Charles. The poor old man doesn't even have a brother anymore. I wish there was something we could do."

"Like what?" he asked, but Mom did not answer. Then the radio died, and they both laughed. "That's it," Dad said, snuffing out his Camel. "So much for the voice of the High-Grade Oil Metropolis of the World. What'd it last? Half an hour?" He smiled faintly and shook his head.

Dad said he wasn't going to wait for the last boat to China as we had done on Amm Street. So we lined up behind him to push open the storm door against the wind and rain. The three of us shuffled arm in arm, looking down as though we expected to step in a hole. The water felt colder than the first flood. I sucked in my stomach as I stepped in over my waist. We were moving with the current on the street, so we had to plant our heels and drag our feet to avoid being swept away. High ground was beyond State Street, a block and a half from the house, and we grabbed onto bushes to get there.

My legs felt heavy as we struggled up the hill to the Third Ward, which, we had heard on the radio, was being used as a temporary shelter. Major Appleby's son David issued me a pair of dry socks and trousers. The Major said the Salvation Army had given out over nine hundred loaves of bread and five hundred coffee rolls. He thanked my mother for her help. I did not know what she had done, but people often stopped us on the street to thank her for something. Sometimes to say thanks people brought us cuts of venison, homemade bread, and sassafras root.

By Easter Sunday the water in the street was gone, as though someone had pulled the plug in a giant drain. A ring of brown foam clung halfway up the windows of every house on the street.

"Oh, no!" my mother said as we walked back down the hill from the shelter. "We've lost everything!"

"Don't be an extremist," my father warned. "Most people count their chickens before they're hatched, but you smash the eggs."

We tossed out an old chair and scrubbed the mud off the sofa and Dad's hollyhock chair, but otherwise our losses were few. The linoleum buckled, and when we pressed down on the ridges it cracked and fell apart. Water sat on the bottom shelf of the refrigerator, but it was an old GE with the motor on top, and when Dad plugged it in it whirred right up. We had stuck the Philco Console Radio on the bed, and there were no other electrical appliances to worry about.

Dad turned on the radio the first thing. Mom let out a little cheer. WESB crackled and sputtered, back on the air. The announcer said that this had been the worst flood in the town's history, even worse than the last one. This time there had been twelve feet of water on Main Street; during the last flood there had been only eight. Mom stared off into space, drumming her fingers on the tin-top table. A spokesman from Penelec asked housewives to skip the Monday wash and Tuesday ironing until later in the week. Mayor Ryan promised one thousand bags of chloride of lime from Harrisburg. "Just what we need," Mom said. "More poison."

"Listen!" Dad hissed, and there was a special warning to boil all water before drinking it.

"I guess the first flood didn't wash our sins away after all," Mom said. "We had to have a second one."

The next day my mother and I slogged downtown to Mayer Brauser's for a roll of linoleum, the same desert-tan we had bought the last time, a pattern that didn't show the dirt.

After the second flood, City Hall pronounced our neighborhood "blighted." The Health Department nailed up a "DO NOT ENTER" sign on the house across the street. The empty lot out back smelled as though something had crawled inside the wall and died.

A group of men with small white flowers in their lapels walked up and down the street, picking their way through the mud in their shiny black shoes. Mom said they had come to "gawk," and she did not like it. An Army jeep pulled up, and a man in uniform got out to take pictures of the abandoned houses and broken porches. Mom pulled down the blinds.

People all over town began to talk about flood control. Mrs. Starkweather said that living in Bradford was like living at the bottom of the ocean, for that was what the Alleghenies had once been—the bottom of the ocean. Every spring the snow melted and raced down into the narrow valley off the steep and rugged hills. I felt proud when she said the lowest spot in town was the junction of the east and west branches of the Tuna Creek. David Albright and I had stood on the Davis Street bridge and watched the bottles pick up speed when they got close to the spot where the branches joined. I raised my hand. "We used to live there," I blurted out. Mrs. Starkweather said that was very nice.

Colonel W. E. Lorence of the U.S. Army Corps of Engineers said that in three years money from the Rivers Appropriation Bill would allow the town to reforest the hills, cement the banks of the creek, and put up a dike downstream from where David and I had bombed the floating bottles. "Three years!" Mom exclaimed. "I don't care what the Colonel says. We're not waiting."

Before flood season hit a third time, we packed our things and called Wingard's Trucking. Wingard's van was yellow and red with black handpainted letters and a phone number scratched on the door. I would have preferred a Sneath Carting truck with gold letters neatly embossed on dark green, and not just for aesthetic reasons. Wingard's rusty truck was like a billboard on wheels advertising all over town: "The People We Move Are Poor." The pale skinny driver had long black sideburns of steel wool; he wore a soiled leather cap that was too small for his head. Mom and I had to get on his end of the sofa to help him load it into the truck. When he slammed the truck door twice to make it close, Mrs. Aiello ran out on the porch in her apron with her hands on her hips as though there had been a crash. The truck sputtered and coughed as smoke filled the air, the fenders flapping.

This time we moved to the other side of Tuna Creek to the high side of South Avenue and upstairs over a garage. Just beyond our alley at the foot of Cliff Street, rickety wooden steps teetered up the side of Quintuple Mountain to a plank sidewalk. We could also see a brand new oil well out the back window, and I thought our neighbors were rich. But, I soon discovered, the mineral rights belonged to somebody who lived up one of the hills or just outside of town. In Bradford, the owner with mineral rights could come in, dig up your lawn, bang up a shed, stick in a rusty five hundred–gallon tank, and drill for oil right outside your front door.

But from our kitchen window we could also look out eye-level to the roof of the Emery Hotel, one of the tallest buildings in town. "If we aren't safe here," Mom observed, "Judgment Day is at hand."

Shortly after we moved in, Mom started sleeping with me. She had slept with me before when Dad had the grippe, but this time the arrangement seemed permanent. One morning I woke and there she was, shivering on top of the covers in her housecoat, clinging to the edge of the bed.

"He won't share," she said. "He won't budge an inch, and that's all there is to it." Then, after a few weeks, she cried. She showed me the black and blue marks on her arms and legs.

She went to bed much later than I did, and she got up earlier. She kept on her side and I kept on mine, each of us aware of the unspoken insult to the other. I was glad she had decided not to talk about it; not talking helped preserve the pretense, and I was getting used to that. Under the rules of silence, my room was still mine. My pennants hung on the wall, my hairbrush and my comb collected dust on the dresser, and Mom kept her perfume, jewelry, and clothes in her room. But sometimes the anger rose up on its own, and I climbed up the rickety wooden steps on South Avenue to bomb the passing cars below with huge balls of snow. At other times I broke out crying and could not stop. I never knew when I would cry; it just happened. I could be sitting at supper or taking a bath when all of a sudden my eyes welled up. That was the first sign; then I waited for the deep howl to rise, and it happened fast, like the flooding of Tuna Creek. I howled five minutes, then shuddered, trying to catch my breath.

"Why can't you sleep on the sofa and leave me alone?" I once demanded, but I had forgotten the black and blue marks and the cold. Dad turned down the heat at night to fifty-five and, as he had done on Amm Street, he opened the window, rain or snow.

Every morning exhaust fumes rose up through the heating registers from the garage. Mrs. Ringo started her Buick inside the garage to warm it up. The sting burned our eyes. Once at breakfast Mom fanned the air in front of her face and laughed. She said we might be choked and cramped but in other ways we were lucky. She said we would never be flooded out again, and the rent was only thirty dollars a month, one week's pay.

By fifth grade I had become unruly. I walked to school in the near dark; the morning reflected the color of unpainted houses and smoke, of metal warehouses and the thick lead sky of winter. Sometimes the sky was so dark that only the snow on the street and the rooftops brightened the day. But the usual shade of gray matched the color of the hornet's nest that Mrs. Starkweather had hung over the pencil sharpener, the gray of dirty snow and dishwater. When the teacher turned her back to write "poinsettia" on the board, or stooped to pick up a fallen piece of chalk, I bellowed "Waw-Waw!" as loudly as I could. During the winter months of school I shouted "Waw-Waw!" every day.

Mrs. Starkweather phoned my mother, who promised, in a

troubled voice, "to sit Dave down for a talk." That meant we sat at the kitchen table and she asked me how I felt, and I said "good."

"Ah, Dave," she pleaded gently, "try to do better." And that was the end of it; she did not try to make me account for myself, perhaps because she knew I couldn't. Whatever her reasons, she wasn't clear how she felt about my poor performance in school, and I knew it. Sometimes she expressed a kind of spiritual disdain for achievement of any kind, despite letting me know that she had been salutatorian of her high school class. But she also felt that whatever my troubles, all of them could be traced back to one single cause: I had started first grade too early, and that was the nub of it. Any other problems she turned over to God, acknowledging that they were too great for us to face alone.

I shared her suspicion that our lives were out of control. After sitting in school at my rock-maple desk for a couple of hours, silence seeped under the door like a yellow gas, growing more oppressive until I hollered "Waw-Waw!" as loudly as I could, throwing open the window. When I heard nervous giggles from the back of the room, I relaxed and breathed more freely. But sometimes I needed even more response, and I "Waw-Wawed!" until Mrs. Starkweather turned pale. By shouting "Waw-Waw!" I cast a spell of my own over the room, rearranging the silence and making it mine. I had to be careful, though, or the teacher would slap me across the face in front of everyone. That risk became everything. With a single shout I turned myself into a daredevil. Gradually I got the reputation of being crazy: a kid who would do anything.

I did not resist the pressure to act crazy; I enjoyed it. I never felt happier than when I did something others considered dangerous, inside school or out. I did not seek wild adventures; they just came naturally. Once on a slow and quiet Sunday afternoon, Michael Robertson and I headed out East

Main, just beyond the railroad station and depot. At the foot of Mount Raub, the street rose thirty feet above the creek and the tracks. A railing to keep pedestrians from falling ran alongside the inside of the sidewalk for eighty feet between the bowling alley and Clara's Kitchen.

On impulse I jumped up on the wobbly two-inch railing and steadied myself as I had done at the Y on the tip of the diving board, squirming my toes until I felt secure. Arms spread, I inched my way across the top without looking down at the rocks and broken glass below. Michael shouted and tried to pull me off, but I hissed him away. I warned him that if he touched me again I would fall. But I knew I would make it; I saw only the two-inch rusted iron railing, more than wide enough for my narrow sneakers. Slowly I inched my way across, flapping my arms now and then to heighten the drama. Michael called me a fool and threatened to tell my mother, but the angrier he became, the happier I felt.

The power did not last. School came the next day, and Mrs. Starkweather usually found ways to control me. Before devotions she came over to my desk and whispered in my ear as though we shared some nasty secret. "David," she said, "I'd like to see you out in the hall." George Wheeler joined us and the three of us walked down the corridor in silence to the stockroom. Two desk chairs had been set with a spoon and a paper towel neatly folded like a napkin. Mrs. Starkweather told us to sit down and wait while she opened a can of stewed tomatoes and heated them up on a hot-plate. As the pot steamed, she broke a slice of Butter-Krust bread into each of our bowls, then poured the tomatoes on top.

"Don't worry, boys," she said. "There's nothing wrong with not getting enough to eat at home. You should not feel ashamed. But you do need to start the day with something."

George and I did not look at each other. We hunched over our bowls and blew on our spoons when she opened the door to leave. After she was gone we laughed angrily, looking around the room. The stockroom, filled with rows and rows of erasers, pads, pencils, and chalk, had always been off-limits. I took down a gallon jar of white paste.

"It's better than tomatoes," I said. George agreed. We scooped out a couple of mouthfuls with our fingers, then hid the opened jar behind the new ones.

The Good Friday flood had hit the Pet Shop hard. Water covered the seat of my father's chrome chair, leaving a little puddle on the red plastic cushion. The eyes of the canaries clouded over like turtle eyes, damp and gooey. The parakeets sneezed for a time, then slumped to the bottom of their cage, quivering. He lost over half the birds and fish, some leather collars, and almost all the seed. When I walked by the shop on my way to school, I crossed the street so he would not see me.

One night at supper he said, "When we get some warm weather we'll see. Right now I'm afraid I'm going to catch the same pneumonia that killed the birds."

After school ended in June, he asked me to help him move the shop to Olean, a town up the Allegheny River just over the Pennsylvania line. "I've got to make some money somehow," he said. "Bradford's dead and so are half my birds."

Bob McNutt drove for Greyhound and said we could move the stuff from the shop on his bus for nothing. While Dad and I carried the surviving birds to the bus terminal, the ticket man watched over our boxes. The birds blinked their eyes in the sun and cocked their heads in all directions, flapping their wings when a car drove by. On our last trip we carried a quart-size potato salad container of tropical fish in each hand. The wire handle pinched my skin, but I didn't mind. The pain made me feel grown up.

Bob McNutt said we could sprawl out in the last four rows on the bus and "make ourselves to home"; he didn't care. Unlike Wendell Wilkie, Bishop Wilbur Hamaker, Mayor Ryan, or Johnny Weismuller, Bob McNutt really was my father's friend—the first and last I ever knew him to have. Although he did not visit the house, Mr. McNutt looked right in my father's eyes when they talked and called him "Reverend" in a friendly voice. The parakeets sprayed seed out into the aisle and some of the water from the fish trickled up and down the narrow furrows of the black rubber floor mat in a network of rivers, carrying the tiny seed downstream. Dad sat behind the driver's seat and I sat in the back of the bus guarding the birds. After we crossed the river and pulled into Seneca Junction, we had to change from one bus to another. Mr. McNutt waited and asked the other driver to let us off wherever we wanted to go, then he waved and his air-brakes whooshed as he spun the oversized steering wheel toward Salamanca and Buffalo.

Dad took the Greyhound to Olean every morning. When he got home for supper it was dark, even during the summer. "This is killing me," he said one morning at breakfast. "God didn't intend a dog to live like this." He started coming home on Saturday night and returning Monday morning.

"That's the way he wants it," Mom said as she shrugged her shoulders.

But after a couple of months Mr. McNutt quit working for Greyhound, and the new driver did not wait for the Salamanca-Olean connection. Dad had to stand outside at Seneca Junction, the wind hard off the river on his back. Within a few days he had a heavy cold which became, he said, bronchitis mixed with pneumonia. Bedridden for a week, he hacked and held his chest; the Monday after Thanksgiving, he moved to Olean for good.

The move, he said, was "the only sensible option." Every once in a while he would say something like that, or he would spell "incompatibility" backwards. I knew he wanted to impress me when he spelled difficult words backwards, but I was really only impressed when he tossed off a phrase like "the only sensible option." Then he seemed important, a man who could talk on the radio. Whenever I found a chance to be proud of him I was proud, and sometimes I wondered if he really weren't good friends with Wendell Wilkie and the mayor.

Mom told me he was seeing a medicine man who lived on the reservation just beyond Seneca Junction. From the bus I had seen the sign with an Indian chief in headfeathers outside the medicine man's house. Dad saw him for the pains in his chest: the pains he called pneumonia and the pains he blamed on the heart block. The Indian sold Salamanca Cream, a poultice and salve made from a petroleum base, ground beth root, and secret ingredients. Dad did not trust local doctors. Regular doctors, Mom said, reminded him of his spells. Since I was becoming more self-conscious, I was glad the medicine man did not live in Bradford.

After his move to Olean, we did not see my father for a month; then, on Christmas Day, the bell rang. I knew it was he. I jumped down the nineteen steps, five at a time, to open the door. He stood in the snow smiling and ashen, a turban-style bandage on his head. We shook hands; then he handed me a large paper sack from the drug store, shaped like a basketball. He said he had slipped on a patch of ice.

Mom did not look at him until his back was to us; then she shook her head and touched her cheekbone with the tips of her fingers. She offered him a seat and wished him "Merry Christmas" as though he had never been to the house before. He sat in his hollyhock chair and smoked while I spun the basketball on my knees to show him how much I liked it. Mom stared at him in alternating waves of pity and horror as though he wouldn't notice. I resented her for making me see him through her eyes. She even asked him if he was going to stay for Christmas dinner, as though there might be reason for doubt. Inside I screamed, "Of course he is staying for dinner!"

He narrowed his eyes and smiled ironically.

"I wouldn't eat here if my life depended on it," he said evenly. "With my son Dave, yes. But not you! Not even on Christmas! Not you! Never! Never again!"

The narrowing of his eyes became a glowering. "You've ruined my life!" he shouted. "It will take more than food to pay me back for the years of pain!"

He was up on his feet now, standing over her as she cowered on the edge of her chair. He leaned his legs against hers and pushed at her with his knees. She turned her face.

"Listen to me!" he shouted.

She looked up once, in time to duck, and then she tried to run, but he grabbed her. Off-balance, she spun as he held her arm; she stumbled, crashing full-tilt into the tree, knocking it down. The lights went out, and for a moment no one moved. Moaning, she lay on the tree, icicles in her hair. She stayed still for a long time, making sure her suffering was not lost on us. In icy silence she looked at the broken balls and the crushed manger at her feet. A king had lost his crown, two lambs their legs; a shepherd had lost his arm, and Mary had a hole in her side. The roof of the manger had caved in, and Jesus, in Japanese porcelain, had tipped out of his crèche and lay face down in the hay.

It was odd wondering how long she would wait before getting up, how long Dad would wait before helping her; but when it was time, he reached forward with one hand and pulled her up clumsily. He did not take the cigarette out of his mouth, the smoke burning his eyes. He tipped back his head and squinted, his eyes red and watery.

Mom wobbled on her feet and looked back at the broken ornaments. Tiny pieces of silver and colored glass stuck in her arms, sparkling in the light like sequins on a dancer. The two of them stood in the small space of the shattered corner, breathing heavily.

"This has nothing to do with you, Dave," Dad said, panting. "Your mother is a horse's tail and that's all there is to it. She treats me like cat dirt even on Christ's birthday. You and I are pals, Dave. You and I will always be pals."

He put his arm around my shoulder and squeezed to show me how strong he was.

"Next time we'll put up a real basket out there. Next time I'll show you why I played with the original Boston Celtics. Here," he said, "give me the ball!"

I followed him downstairs and held his hat and coat as he shot imaginary baskets in the snow. "Like this!" he shouted, faking a pass to his right and dribbling to his left. "How's that for a move?" he shouted, bending over unsteadily to pick up the ball which had not bounced. Snow danced around his bandaged head like bees around a hive; he passed me the wet ball and smiled broadly. "Get that basket up and I'll come over and play again. Then I'll show you some moves!"

We shook hands and he wished me Merry Christmas, and that was the last Christmas I saw him.

CHAPTER 14

The Most Important Person in the World

Soon after my father walked away at Christmas, Grandma Crawford came to live with us and take his place. At supper she sat at the head of the table and sprinkled salt in her palm, tilting her head and squinting at the invisible grains. "Salt isn't as salty as it used to be," she harped. "It's lost its savor."

"Does she mean flavor?" I asked Mom.

"No. It's savor." Mom rested her knife and fork across the top of the plate according to Emily Post, then folded her hands in her lap. Even though Grandma had interrupted our meal, Mom smiled at her as though everything were all right.

"It has no savor!" Grandma said furiously, tumbling salt from the shaker until it spilled over her hand and frosted her spinach. "I said it has no savor! Nobody listens anymore! Nobody listens!"

"May I have the salt, please?" Mom asked diplomatically. "You're ruining your supper." Grandma didn't listen; she kept on pouring.

Mom tried to lean forward without being seen, bending slowly toward the table to snatch the shaker out of her hand mid-air, but it didn't work. Grandma pushed back her chair and jumped up at the same time, spilling her milk.

"Now look what you've made me do!" she cried. "I will not be treated this way in my own house!" And with that she clenched her teeth and turned red.

"Oh my God," Mom whispered harshly, "she's going to have an attack!"

Grandma choked and crossed her hands under her throat, stumbling forward out of the room as though she had choked.

"Let her go," Mom warned, her jaw set like a ventriloquist, speaking from her belly, mumbling through her teeth. "She'll calm down better if she's left alone. The poor woman. She can't help it any more than the man in the moon. One of these days I'm going to end up just like her. You mark my words."

"I'm not going anywhere," I said angrily. I hated it when my mother projected her misery into the future. I sat wedged in by the table and the sink, and I had no intention of going after her. Grandma was no longer the woman I loved who had strung her kitchen with green and red peppers, who had baked delicious pies and had taught me to peel perfect apples. Now she sat around in her bathrobe all day talking to people in *Life* magazine, scolding Esther Williams for wearing only a bathing suit in public, wagging her finger in the swimmer's face and shouting, "Who do you think you are parading naked through my house? The idea! Not enough on to dust a fiddle!" Sometimes she slapped Esther Williams with the back of her hand, tearing the magazine to shreds.

I ran home after school to make sure she had not set the house on fire. We hid the matches and disguised the stove with an old sheet and a couple of bottles of toilet water, a mirror, a comb, and the lamp from my mother's dresser.

"I can't find a thing in my own house," Grandma complained. Sometimes she wandered downtown to the post office with our unopened mail, or sometimes she hid it in a safe place so she would not lose it. When I got home I opened the door noiselessly so I could watch her talking to *Life*, but

I also liked to watch her stalk through the living room, swatting the air with a rolled-up newspaper.

"There's one!" she cursed. "And there's another one! A black one! Oh, my!"

"Oh, my!" I teased back in her sing-song voice. "There's another one. And there's a black one, too!" I wasn't sure why, but in her presence I became cruel; I hid and squirted water over her head so I could watch her hold out her hand for rain. "Well, the Good Lord knows we need it," she said, staring at the ceiling.

"Where did David go?" I asked, mocking her with the question she had asked me as a little boy. "David used to live here. Have you seen him? He was such a nice boy, little David."

Or I would ask more pointedly than she ever realized, "Where did Grandma go? She used to live in Clarion. Have you seen her? She was such a nice Grandma. I miss her." I teased until she chased me around the room, her jowls and upper arms quivering, her face beet-red.

Miss Hawkins also quivered, especially when she had to write up high on the blackboard. A massive woman with a parrot's beak and the chest of an admiral, whatever dress she wore draped over her like a sheet over a refrigerator. In class she marched up and down the aisles, stopping to shake her finger under an unsuspecting nose to make her point. One morning she stood beside my desk in the front row by the window, a position she had given me early in the year which she called "the seat of honor." She stood so close I could smell her perfume and feel the heat of her massive body.

"Well, David!" she shouted. "Who is it? Who?"

I looked down at the floor.

"Please," she said gently. "If you don't have the answer, at least show the courtesy to look up at me in your ignorance. Now, again. Who? Who is the most important person in the world?"

Her dark-rimmed glasses reflected the overhead lights like rows of ice-cube trays in her eyes. The room was silent, her teeth gleaming. I did not know the answer. I wanted to say my mother but I knew everyone would laugh.

"God," I whispered. I knew that was not the answer, but I knew no one would dare laugh.

"Ah!" Miss Hawkins mocked. "The most important *person* in *this* world."

God was of this world, I thought to myself, but I said nothing.

"Maybe this will help," she badgered. "To you. That makes it simple, doesn't it? The most important person in the world to you."

Bud + Audrey had been gouged into the top of my desk, and I ran my fingers into the plus sign between them.

"Oh, no!" she shouted, her smile widening as she came closer, bending over my desk. "Not the names of the idiots who have defaced school property. Not . . . let's see . . . Audrey or Bill."

"Bud," I said without thinking. "The boy's name is Bud."

The whole class laughed. Miss Hawkins laughed, too.

"Is the answer Bud, then?" she asked. Heavily she swung away from my desk toward the blackboard, her heels walloping the hardwood floor. She grabbed a piece of chalk from the trough, plowing each line into the slate, chips and powder flying. She was breathing fast now, scrawling two simple letters up and down across the entire blackboard, her arms and jowls quivering: first "M" and then "E."

"Me!" she shouted "Me! Me! Me!" She jumped up and down in little hops that shook the floor. "That is," she said, pointing at me, "you! You, David, you! You are the most important person in the world to you." She turned to the class and let her head fall to one side as though the ordeal had exhausted her.

"David," she said, addressing her remarks to the class, "listen. I am the most important person in the world to me,

and this is as it should be. This is the nature of civics. This is
what makes America the greatest country in the world.
Civics. Civ-ics. Civ-ilization. *Sibi.* That's Latin for me. It
starts with one person. Just one. If you don't have that, you
don't have anything. One little word. Me. The biggest word
in the vocabulary. The beginning of everything. Freedom.
Democracy. Capitalism. America!"

She paused and checked the eyes of her favorite girls in the
middle row for approval. They were beaming. "Do you understand?" she asked, turning toward me.

I nodded, thought for a moment, and answered, "yes."

But I did not understand, and I did not believe her. I did not
think that I was the most important person in the world, and
I did not want to think about myself at all. I had been taught
that I was important only as I worshipped God. Otherwise
God would not have sent His only begotten Son, and if God
had not sacrificed His only begotten Son, all of us would be
damned for all eternity. Alone, I was nothing.

Since Grandma had come to live with us, Mom spoke
more frequently about trusting our problems to God. She
said life was beyond our comprehension, and my own experience bore her out. Besides, hadn't we read Walt Whitman in
Mrs. Ordiway's English class, and hadn't the greatest of
American poets asked, "What is man anyhow? What am I?
What are you?" And didn't Emily Dickinson write, "I am
nobody. Who are you?"

If others exceeded me in mind or body or spirit, as they
surely did, how could I ever consider myself the most important person in God's world? When I told Mom about Miss
Hawkins' question in civics class, she looked perplexed for a
moment, then she got up from the kitchen table to fetch the
Bible.

"If a man imagines himself to be somebody when he is
nothing," she read, "he is deluding himself." She closed the
book on her thumb and smiled. "Galatians," she added.

The problem, for the moment, was solved. I felt weightless in my nothingness, free, and exalted. Transported by my own selflessness, nothing could hold me back. The world revolved around me and yet I was nothing. I could bring myself back down to earth at any time just by opening my eyes, just by smelling the skin above my wrist.

But Miss Hawkins had unsettled me. Her challenge encouraged me to think of myself with a heightened form of self-consciousness which made me blush. If she was right, I could do anything I wanted to do. I began to struggle saying my prayers at night. No word in nine years of school had unleashed so many doubts. "Me": it was the answer to a question I had never asked, and it forced me to ask other questions as well. Among my many selves, who was I to begin with? To whom did "me" actually refer? Was it Mike Robertson's friend or Ida McKain's son? Was it the small voice inside of me who had trouble with his prayers? Was it my father's son, and would I grow up to be like him? Was I the skinny boy in the plaid shirt who could not concentrate in school—foolish, something of a clown? The very meaning of the trees had changed, the meaning of the deer and wild turkey, the meaning of my face in the mirror.

The power of God's spell and His mysterious authority had been challenged. For the next six weeks I made my bed, picked up my socks, practiced my violin, and, with something in it every Sunday, took my pledge envelope to church. I also kept track of Dr. and Mrs. Piper from the Methodist church who were missionaries in darkest Africa. I tacked a large *National Geographic* map of the dark continent on my wall and with red and yellow pushpins marked their travels up and down the wild rivers. The Pipers were looking for a new place to found a mission, and Reverend Zinger reported on their progress every Sunday. Perhaps one day I would become a missionary and spread the Word of the Lord.

For a short burst of time I picked up groceries for old Mrs. Coit on the other side of town and called on the ancient Mr.

Cody. The most delicate humpbacked man I had ever seen, Mr. Cody was four-and-a-half feet tall, had white hair, and wore a three-piece suit with a heavy gold chain that dangled from his vest. Ninety years old and second cousin to Buffalo Bill Cody, he was senior deacon of the First Baptist Church and he treated me as an equal. He lived alone in a big dark house with green window shades, lace curtains, and tassles hanging from the floorlamps. Lace doilies covered the arms and backs of the chairs and the tops of the tables. The two of us sat across from each other in the living room for five minutes of excruciating silence; sometimes Mr. Cody seemed to pray. But I did not remember a word he said until he raised himself stiffly from his seat and it was time to go. Then he shuffled over to a big table by the window, leafed through a folder, and shuffled back.

"Here," he said. "I have found two more." He handed me two clippings from a magazine: pictures of a church, any church—it didn't matter so long as there was a steeple.

"Why do I have to go see Mr. Cody?" I asked Mom one day after I began to tire of my good deeds.

"Because he enjoys your company and it is good for you."

It was becoming harder to visit him whether it made him happy or not, and Mom compounded the problem by telling him his pictures were among my favorites, as though I had a vast and significant collection. She did not know I had thrown them away. The next time I went back I could hardly look him in the eye. As usual we sat in silence for five minutes until he got up and shuffled over to his folder of pictures.

"Someday," he said in his ancient wrinkled voice, "you'll have a bigger collection than mine."

After that I could not go back at all. I still thought about helping others, but I was becoming more and more confused about church. I had never walked down front when the minister called us forward to give our lives to Jesus, not even at the special salvation meetings for children. The shaking and ringing of the preacher's voice repulsed me as much as it moved me, and I stayed in my pew. Still, my mother took me to services all over town. We went to the Assembly of God, to the Christian Missionary Alliance, to the AME, to the United Brethren, and to the First Church of Spiritualists, led by Dr. and Mrs. S. Van Duyzers, co-pastors. Dr. Van Duyzer held my hand at the door in both of his. I thought he would never let go.

But the harder I tried to live up to what I perceived to be the church's standard of submission, the darker my thoughts became. One day, when I must have been feeling particularly hopeless, my mother suggested I join the Boy Scouts.

"Come on," she urged, "it will do you good. And it will mean a great deal to your father, too. He was an Eagle Scout."

"No, he wasn't," I said bitterly. "That's just another one of his stories. Go see for yourself. Look under his handkerchief and his KKK manual. He left all of his badges in there."

"Oh, Dave," she said, as though I was responsible for what my father left behind in his dresser drawer, but had she looked she would have found the silver eagle pin with the red, white, and blue bunting right on top. I wasn't mad at my father, I was mad at her, and I tried to punish her by blaming her for my father's lies—even those he did not tell.

In a few months I stood rigidly with the tips of my shoes touching the red line on the basement floor of the Methodist church. Twenty of us stood at attention as Mr. Lyle presided. Most of us wore an olive drab Boy Scout shirt, but only one or two scouts had matching trousers. Mr. Lyle was the only one in the troop in full uniform. He wore green socks and a canvas Boy Scout belt from which he hung a compass and a water canteen, even when we were not hiking. He also wore a nickle-plated whistle around his neck and an olive sash with cloth badges and metal pins across his chest. Mr. Lyle's head was shaped like a torpedo, and he was fat.

"Gentlemen," he said, rocking on his heels, "today is a very special day in the annals of Scouting. Today is Awards Day. It is that day you have been working toward and waiting for—some of you to join the ranks of Scouting with your first degree, some to climb even higher, to Life and Star. It is my special honor and privilege to bestow these badges upon you. When I call your name I want you to step forward proudly, give the Scout salute, and repeat the oath."

The ceremony lasted so long I felt lightheaded. Mothers and fathers scraped forward to shake Mr. Lyle's hand and pin a medal over their son's heart. Mom had to be at choir practice on Wednesday evenings and Dad lived in Olean. I tried not to think about it, but I couldn't help wonder who would come forward and decorate me with the Tenderfoot badge. Mr. Lyle read each boy's name from a yellow sheet of paper, adding, "You have successfully climbed the ladder of success," just as though there were an actual ladder. When he turned to the card table for another badge, I pumped my knees in the air and reached one hand over the other, climbing the ladder to the top. Each time Larry Gildersleeve and I laughed, and, finally, Mr. Lyle caught us. Sputtering, he claimed we had embarrassed the entire troop, and he asked us to stand outside in the hall until the ceremony ended. Later that evening he called my mother and told her I had not conducted myself in a manner suitable for a Scout and that I would not receive my Tenderfoot badge until I conducted myself with the proper deportment.

At the next regular meeting I raised my hand when Mr. Lyle asked for a show of Scouts who wanted to work on their Woodsmanship merit badge by hiking up Quintuple Mountain, the mountain in front of our house. I had been looking around at the colorful sleeves with merit patches, and I could feel the weight of many medals on my chest. I had hiked up the mountain a hundred times. On Quintuple I could show everybody the abandoned grave of Daniel Kingsbury, the man who had built the old mill and pond at the

foot of what had become Main Street. I knew where chestnuts grew, acorns, and wild pig nuts. I knew where the wild
turkeys slept, where they scratched at the spring seeps, and
where deer bedded down, crushing the tall grass. If the
Scouts sat under a tree and listened, they could hear the wild
turkeys yelp and cluck; they could hear their kee-kee calls,
the putts, kutts, and box calls. On top of the hill I could
show everybody the flame that burned all day and all night;
where, in winter, grass and flowers grew inside a brain of
yellow ice. I could even show people where we could get
rich: where amber oil seeped up through the leaves and
snow, lying in pools on the ground, there for the scooping.

We met at the church after school and marched in single
file for three blocks to the foot of Cliff Street, thirty yards
from our front door. Cliff Street was steep. Nothing but a
Power Wagon or a Jeep could climb it, and only three houses
clung to the shale and yellow clay. Mr. Lyle paused at the foot
of the hill, his bullet-shaped head topped by a broad-brimmed
bugler's hat, his canteen bulging at his waist. After he caught
his breath, he blew his whistle and off we marched, a gaggle of
olive drab geese with spots of red. As we passed Mrs. Mabelle
Matthews's house, I whispered to Larry that a Negro woman
lived there. Mrs. Matthews was a friend of my mother's and
the caretaker of the Citizen's National Bank where she
worked nights. "Really?" Larry asked, impressed. I wanted to
tell others too, but Mr. Lucas was standing on his porch with
his arms folded, gazing down at us sternly. No one but the
mailman and members of his own family ever walked that far
up Cliff Street. Mr. Lucas considered the street his private
road.

"Hi, Mr. Lucas!" I shouted.

Mr. Lyle turned around and blew his silver whistle. In a
loud voice he said that if I acted up again we would have to
break rank.

"This is a hike, gentlemen, not a tea party."

The rutted dirt road gave way to a lease road and humped

grass; then it petered out into a deer path along Quintuple ridge, the side of the mountain hooking south and paralleling the west branch of Tuna Creek, six hundred feet above the valley. Mr. Lyle continued to lead us in a thin, broken line. We walked for an hour in silence, our eyes on the trail. When I saw a gray patch of road down in the valley through the leaves, I fell back to the middle of the pack. I grabbed my stomach, then told the rear guard I had cramps, squatting down behind a tree. The troop marched on down the hill and I waited until I saw them cross Route 346, dropping over the bank and out of sight. I decided to walk back to town alone.

A mud-spattered Jeep pulled up beside me. The driver, who wore aviator sunglasses, reached over and pulled back the sliding window. "If you're goin' to town," he said, "hop in back. Be dark in twenty minutes."

He watched me carefully as I climbed into the tightly packed rear of his tiny Jeep, stepping between bushels of freshly picked apples.

"Help yourself," he shouted into the noisy wind. The chill air was heady with apple bruise and ripeness, the hills red and yellow, the sun aflame in his rearview mirror. I watched a pair of groggy yellow-jackets crawl in and out of the brown holes of the windfalls lying on top. I had never been in a Jeep before and the ride was a treat.

The next day Mr. Lyle called my mother at Lincoln School to tell her I had been suspended from Troop 21 and that I could face criminal charges for stealing apples. Using one of those adult words which didn't mean much, Mom said she was growing "alarmed." Perhaps, I thought, the man had not filled his order for a store, or, when he had parked his Jeep, someone else had stolen the apples. But the charge was so outrageous I didn't care.

"You don't belong to anything anymore," Mom said unhappily. "You have stopped going to church. You no longer sing in the choir. You refused to join DeMolay. And now this."

"I wasn't asked to join DeMolay. Wimpy Zinger black-balled me."

"Winthrop! Winthrop Zinger! Winthrop!"

"Well, he did. Besides, I do belong to something. I belong to the YMCA, the Young Men's Christian Association."

I shot baskets every day after school at the Y and nobody bothered me. I was winning nickels and dimes playing Around the World. Basketball was becoming my salvation. I was also beginning to think that maybe Miss Hawkins was right—if I were not the most important person in the world, I was, at least, one of them. By the end of the year none of my friends at the Y could beat me one-on-one.

CHAPTER 15

Play

As the thin walls of the apartment shook, Grandma's handpainted fruitbowl skittered across the piano top, wobbling to a stop at the edge. I dribbled inside the house and out, rolling the ball up one arm and down the other, spreading my fingers as far as I could, trying to palm it like the great Goose Tatum. I slept with the ball next to my bed, checking first thing in the morning to be sure it was there. A basketball was expensive; no one else in the neighborhood owned one. I would have taken it to school if I could, but the teachers wouldn't let me.

My mother did not like it. The frivolity of sport, for her, was close to sin, but the thin veneer of her authority and control had vanished with my father. I had stopped practicing the violin and going to church except on Christmas and Easter Sundays. After school one day she collapsed on the couch and covered her forehead with a damp washcloth, waving an open bottle of camphor back and forth under her nose.

"I can't go on this way," she said wearily. "Please get that horrible ball out of this house!"

Ice clogged the alley from November to April, and the ball bounced at odd angles, ricocheting off the frozen ruts and hummocks. My fingers raw, my mittens frozen, I wiped my nose on my sleeve and timed my moves to each erratic dribble, keeping the ball low.

I played Twenty-One, Horse, and Around the World with

whomever I could persuade to come home with me after
school, usually Eddie Layton, Harry Goldman, or Reeder
Huff. But I also played One-on-One by myself, taking the
ball out of bounds, juking left or right, driving past All-
Americans, boxing out, and crashing the boards against
George Mikan and Easy Ed McCauley. When friends played
pepper in the spring and tap-pass in the fall, I dipped my
shoulder low, gave a little head fake, and drove to the hoop,
pulling up for a fade-away jumper, a second showing on the
clock.

Tryouts for freshman basketball began toward the end of
November. I bought a pair of white wool sweat socks, a Bike
jock strap, and a pair of white high-top Converse sneakers
with Chuck Taylor's name inside a special circle. No one
carried a gym bag, and I practiced rolling my gear into a
white towel like the guys returning from last year's team. I
smoothed the dry towel out on the bed and folded the bor-
ders lengthwise toward the middle, squeezing socks, shorts,
and jock into a tidy little roll. After a shower I kneaded the
wet towel even tighter, tucking it under my left arm, jamming my hands into my jacket, and slinging my sneakers
over my shoulder so I could practice strutting like Eric Parker and Kid Landry. Eric and Kid had the best walks in
school, a kind of rhythmic shuffle which defied the world.
They took tight, efficient steps and rolled their shoulders,
their bodies coiled. Actually they had two walks: in one they
dragged their heels as though holding back their power, in-
timidating rival teams and classmates; in the other they
pushed off from the balls of their feet with more spring,
creating a sense of boyish lightheartedness. But even this
lighter gait had its sinister appeal—they did not care what
anybody thought. "Hey," Eric grunted in greeting, flicking
his head and raising an eyebrow like a man bidding at a farm
auction. The coach called him "Sleepy."

Before tryouts I went to Rocco Rich for a brushcut, proof I
would do anything to make the team. My mother wanted

me to keep my wave in front. "Oh, Dave," she sighed, "don't go and ruin your hair, too." Mr. Rich hung a certificate with a gold seal over his cash register:

> Rocco Rich—President
> Journeymen and Master's
> Barbers Union Local

On Saturdays he charged twenty-five cents extra for brush-cuts to discourage kids from coming in; Saturdays were the day for the men who worked all week. When my father still lived in Bradford he used to have his hair cut on Wednesdays by a nonunion barber who charged a little less.

"It's not the money," he said. "It's the principle of the thing. Unions are ruining America." Unions, for him, meant immigrants and Catholics—like the Jews, enemies sapping America's strength. Sitting in Rocco's chair, I wondered if he knew my father; the possibility made my stomach ache. "Don't move your head now. Come on. Sit still." Rocco swung my chair around and jerked it to a stop, tossing my head to the side. He did not ask how I wanted it cut, he just waved his scissors and kept talking to a sour-looking man smoking a cigar and reading a magazine. The trip to Rocco's provided a lesson. I was beginning to recognize the town's code. The code, like the style of the haircut, came out of the War: men chopped off their hair or they got lice; men followed military orders or they did not come home; men faced danger in the oil fields and in the factories or they didn't eat. Spider wheels snapped and crushed bones; nitroglycerin blew up in their faces.

People lived at the edge, between extremes. Winters lasted half the year and sometimes it snowed in May. Men drilled two thousand feet below the ground, and the hills rose up two thousand feet above sea level. They either struck it rich or they lost their savings and their homes. But people had grown accustomed to losing and doing without. During the

War there had been no meat, no sugar, no gas, no butter, no steel, no money, no rubber, no leather, no clothes. Instead there had been scarlet fever, diphtheria, polio, meningitis, and the lingering poverty of the Great Depression. The men in town played it safe, denying any sign of comfort for themselves for fear it would be taken as a sign of weakness. In Bradford, a man showed his toughness not in order to impress others, but to convince himself he was strong enough to survive. I admired the slow and sullen men. I sensed the strength they hid. To me, they were heroic.

Rocco snapped my pin-striped bib and grunted "okay," signaling my haircut was finished. Every bristle of hair stood at attention, a full half-inch on end. I had bought a wooden hair brush and a jar of Yardley's Brilliantine, a green and spicy goo which, when mixed with sweat, trickled down my neck like a light-weight oil. But I never did master the sullen gait of taking small steps and rocking slightly side to side. Restraint was against my temperament. The tight towel and bonehead brushcut made me look even more nervous and wired up than I was, but after tryouts began I forgot the controlled swagger of Eric and Kid. I dove for loose balls, pushed, jumped, ballhawked, and ran from wing to wing with my arms flying; all I wanted to do was to make the team.

I made the team, and I didn't. After a week of tryouts, the coach told twelve of us to report to the nurse's office for a physical; it looked good. We lined up in our skivvies, coughed left and right, and that was, for everyone else, the end of the examination. But Dr. McCreary asked me to cough over and over, his finger probing.

"I'm sorry, Dave," he finally said. "You have a small left-sided varicocele which could get worse: a soft compressible tumor. In all honesty it represents a potential hernia. The school can't take the risk with your future. If you played and got hurt you might really hurt yourself. And we wouldn't want that, would we?" He winked at the reference to my future sex life.

"Oh, well," my mother said at supper. "Things could be worse. Basketball isn't everything."

"Oh, yes," I said in a steely voice, "it is." I could taste salt in my mouth, I could feel myself losing control. She took a long look at me, got up, and called Dr. McCreary. No, he told her, the school could not afford to let me play; it would not take the risk, nor would it absorb the additional insurance. He suggested that we take out a separate policy and sign some sort of waiver, but my mother thanked him in a way I recognized as final. We could not afford to carry unnecessary insurance.

I moped around for a day or two but that was all. I really didn't care if I played for the school just as long as I played. I needed to run, to move. I played basketball in gym class every day, and I played at the Y three days a week. I played invisible One-on-One in the alley, and I played ping-pong basketball behind my closet door. Best of all, I played in the SCAFO Class A League on Saturday afternoons. The SCAFO League had referees, a clock, and a scorekeeper who hand-delivered box-scores to the *Bradford Era* after every game. The games were real. The teams in the league were sponsored by local companies and service organizations, their names sewn in white felt letters on the front of our shirts: The Lions, The Exchange, Larson-Benjamin, Bottone Painters, The Rotary, South Penn Service Station, and two ringers, The Beavers and The Pioneers. My team, The Dukes, was named after the oil family who lived in Duke Center, the family that almost bought a schnauzer from my father.

The Dukes won the championship that year, and against Larson-Benjamin one Saturday I scored thirty-seven points with a cast on my leg. I had broken a bone in my foot playing basketball in gym class, but for a day or two after scoring so many points I walked around on a cloud. The story was on WESB, and that evening the *Pittsburgh Press* and the *Buffalo Evening News* phoned long distance for an interview.

"What's your father's name, Dave? . . . Reverend Charles

McKain. . . . Hey, he must be pretty pleased, huh? Does he pray you'll score lots of points? No, just kidding, Dave. What's his church? . . ." I was glad the interviewer did not ask any more questions about my father or, worse, ask to speak with him.

On Monday morning the headline on the sports page of the *Era* read: "Davie McKain Fails to Let Cast on Foot Stop Him in Cage Game—Hits 37 Points." The *Era* story went on to say, "Davie McKain likes to play basketball and he doesn't let much get in his way to keep him from playing. On Saturday, Davie, who is the son of the Rev. and Mrs. Charles McKain of South Ave., went down to the YMCA to play in the SCAFO Class A League WEARING A CAST ON HIS RIGHT FOOT. Davie, 14, not only played but he led his Dukes to a 71 to 32 victory over the Larson-Benjamin team. He scored 37 points."

I wished that they hadn't mentioned my father's name. Seeing Rev. Charles McKain in print made me aware that he was gone again, and I did not know where he was or how he was doing. I was afraid someone might ask.

The assistant head basketball coach collared me in the hall on Monday and teased me in that special way coaches pay compliments. He squeezed my shoulder muscle until it hurt. After the season ended I begged my mother to call Dr. McCreary again. It worked: the doctor gave me another examination and scheduled an operation for Easter vacation. He assured us that the operation would settle the insurance question and with it, I believed, all my other problems as well. A basketball in my hands, I had no time to brood or to think about myself. I did not even think about my shots. Here was the ball, there was the basket: the two went together; I was just part of the process. I got to know the angles of the floor and the bounce off the board, thinking with my fingers. In a kind of religious fervor, I lost all self-consciousness. And, for the first time in my life, being a beanpole helped. Reeder Huff said that after they castrated me at the hospital I would put on weight and be much tougher.

But the day before I was to go into the hospital, Mom's face got long at breakfast. "You don't really need it," she argued. "It's nothing but a waste of money. The doctor told me these things sometimes disappear all by themselves. Besides," she added abstractly, "you can do without basketball. Lots of others have, and you might even be better off if you didn't play. Look at you. You haven't practiced your violin in so long I'm surprised Mr. Duhart keeps you in the orchestra." She looked over my shoulder as she spoke, her mouth set.

I quit the orchestra on my own in the fall. I should have been excited about entering high school, but I wasn't. Basketball season didn't start until December, and I didn't even know if I would be able to play. Kitty-corner from the hospital, Bradford Senior High School sat low to the ground and looked like a factory that manufactured wooden novelties: perhaps birdfeeders or salad bowls, wall plaques or salt and pepper shakers. Only the plants down by the Tuna were larger: Bovaird and Seyfang, Kendall and Dresser. Built of Hanley red brick, the high school was flat with a gable roof supported by tall white columns over the entrance.

My mother advised me to sign up for College Prep, and, since I didn't know what else to do, I did. Supposedly students chose their own programs according to interest, but, after a couple of months of school, I had begun to doubt this. Students were grouped into College Preparatory, Commercial, General, Home Economics, and Shop by wealth and family position. Poor kids from the country chose Home Economics and Shop, and poor kids from the city chose General and Commercial. The rich and a handful of kids in the middle chose College Prep. Occasionally, bright and attractive students from working-class families were tracked into

College Prep, but it never worked the other way around; no matter how dull they were, the rich kids always prepared for college.

I was not a rebel, I just didn't like school, and that was what drove my teachers mad. In the first month or so Miss Russo kicked me out of the library for laughing. "Don't you ever take anything seriously?" she shouted. I had been asked to write a book report on a biography of Bernard Baruch, investor and financier, and as our class sat around a big round table reading, no one dared whisper. Miss Russo sat up front at her desk peeking over the top of a magazine pretending to read; if she caught someone "stepping out of line," as she put it, she jumped up from behind her desk and shouted "Please!" All such breakdowns of adult authority made me laugh, and Miss Russo screaming for quiet in the library sent me under the table. I bent down to tie my shoes so she would not see me, but I did not hear her circling around behind my chair. Sobbing, she grabbed my shirt and shook until the cloth tore and two black buttons popped off onto the floor.

"Get out! Get out!" she shouted. "And don't ever come back! Ever!"

Miles Fink had been kicked out of the library too. "S'not bad," he said, smirking, speaking in his drawl from the hills. "I just go down the gym and smoke." Miles Fink was in Shop, and like most of the Shop kids he dressed sloppy with a vengeance. Miles and his friends roamed the halls with their cuffs and collars rolled up, flaunting Luckies and Camels in their shirt pockets. They wore low black shoes and white work socks, clicking their taps wherever they prowled. They stood with their legs spread and their hands in their pockets inside the big front doors before the bell rang, clicking their Zippo lighters open and shut, each click sharp, like the latching of a bolt or the cocking of a trigger: a brazen sound, angry and defiant.

I envied the Shop boys. They could slouch in their seats and go hunting half of deer season, and the teachers didn't say a word. After morning devotions, they dug their taps into the tile floor and clattered down the stairs, pushing and shoving while the rest of us had to walk. Then, at the bottom of the stairs they slid and slammed through the back door to their separate quarters, a small, red brick building behind the school, the only Vocational Trade Center in McKean County. Cupping their cigarettes the way their fathers had done in the trenches during the War, they held the butt between the finger and the thumb to hide the glow. They leaned against the fence as though on a factory break, one boot up, the heel hooked in a chain-link diamond.

By the time I was in eleventh grade, I had been suspended from Spanish class, history class, and typing class and told in each class to go to the library. The first two or three times I actually knocked on the library door, but Miss Russo cracked it only an inch, blocking the narrow entrance with her body. She shook her head slowly back and forth, smiling.

"Never!" she said defiantly. "Never again, David McKain! Never!" So I never went back. Miles nodded from a dark corner of the locker room as he leaned up against the wall, puffing on a weed, a crooked smile on his face. I went to the gym.

Coach Booker was a gentle cross-eyed man with a wisp of white hair above each ear. He wore a red varsity letter sweater and an oil-stained hat. "Coach," as everybody called him, allowed us to decide our own lot. He nodded to Miles Fink smoking in the locker room and let me go to the gym whenever I wanted. When class started, he came down from his office upstairs with a basketball under his arm, raced through the roll call nonstop, and blew his whistle.

"Okay, men," he said. "Shirts and Bares. Jump Ball!" Then he cranked his stiff neck upward toward the rafters, bent his knees, and tossed the ball in a random arc between the two tallest players on the floor. And that was the last we saw of him until jump ball the following period. In a school of hard-nosed coaches and teachers, old Mr. Booker was kind. On some days he let me play basketball third period and fourth period, come back after lunch fifth period, and stay around for sixth. "Why not?" he smiled. "Keep you out of trouble."

The pretty girls in school wore gold circle pins and cashmere sweaters, dickies, Peter Pan blouses, and pleated Pendleton wool skirts with a four-inch gold-plated safety pin at the knee. They kept any loose strands of their soft, shampooed hair in place with turtle-shell barrettes. They also wore subtle shades of red lipstick and a drop of perfume, the entire outfit touched off by a gold bracelet with good-luck charms and scarabs. The College Prep boys wore baby blue V-neck sweaters, charcoal grey slacks, argyle socks, and oxblood shoes; or, if they played a sport, they dressed in khaki slacks, coarse cotton football sweatshirts, and clodhoppers.

There were General and Commercial students as well, kids studying business math and bookkeeping, but the only serious fights at school took place between the College Prep athletes and the Shop boys: the "Jocks" versus the "Pigs." During homeroom ceremonies the two groups often sat in quiet disdain: the Shop boys slouching and staring out the window, the College Prep boys going through the motions of pledging allegiance and listening to the Scripture. Now and then the two factions glanced threateningly at one another, but the war remained cold until the end-of-the-year Tug of War at the school picnic. The banks along Red House Brook were muddy and slippery in early June, the stream cold and deep from the late spring run-off. Spokesmen for the two groups met at the edge of the parking lot with their hands in their pockets, kicking pebbles, laying ground rules. In an obvious show of superior intelligence, the College Prep boys talked their way into taking the level side of the brook, leaving the Shop boys on a muddy incline sloping toward the water's edge.

The Jocks were ready. Members of the football backfield, the basketball team, and the track team grabbed the thick rope closest to the water while bulky football linemen anchored themselves in the rear, their clodhoppers dug in, their bare arms bulging. On the other side of the water stood the boys from Bolivar Run and Ormsby, Rew and Cyclone, Custer City and Degolia, cigarettes dangling from their lips, their collars turned. Twenty-five to a side, the two armies gripped the rope and snorted, awaiting the countdown: "... seven ... eight ... nine ... ten!" A lightweight, I was stationed near the front, looking across the brook straight into the eyes of Ebert Keestetter and Miles Fink, each one pulling steadily, showing no strain. They stood their ground and pulled evenly while we yanked in waves, jerking and letting up, as though rocking a car out of the mud. I could feel the heaves in the rope and hear the grunts behind me. I saw Miles slowly and methodically cross one hand in front of the other, do it slowly twice, then pull rhythmically, picking up speed until I slid across the gravel into the water and let go of the rope. The Shop boys had won.

Smirking, Miles Fink stood on dry ground shaking hands, greeting one dismayed Jock after another. Secretly, I was pleased. Whatever else might be said about them, the Shop boys hung tight as a group and had few pretensions. These were the same guys who had smuggled leeks into homeroom in seventh grade and hid them in the register so that, by noon, the room reeked so badly we were all sent home. With his mouth shut tight, Miles curled his upper lip, creating an outrageous smirk that infuriated his teachers. Easy-going and ironic, he kept school at a distance.

I kept school at a distance, too, but not because I wanted to. I liked the classes I still attended, although I usually got something from the lesson different from whatever the teacher intended. I concentrated on the tone of the class, its mood and tenor. I could have told the teacher what I thought she and everyone else in the room was feeling on a given day, but I had only a little to say on whether or not China should be allowed to join the United Nations. I liked the occasion of school, its theater and drama. I also enjoyed some of its substance, but not at the expense of everything else. As my father would have said, school was a battle, and I was in it.

Distrust and bad feelings exhausted me, and on some days, usually Thursdays, I stayed home. Still in bed at noon, I listened to a woman with polio from Clear Springs, Indiana win an Amana refrigerator, a new outfit, dinner, and a whirlwind tour of New York's hottest nightspots. All the women shrieked when Jack Bailey cried, in a sing-song cheer, "Would *you* like to be Queen for a Day?" At noon every day one poor woman after another told her sad story until one was chosen to rise, transformed to the glory of queen. School, by comparison, was mean-spirited and dull.

After Gabriel Heatter and the news, I got up, dressed, and went outside to shoot baskets until school let out. Then I walked a block and a half down the street to Tony's Pool Hall where I spent hours playing Harrigan. At the door a short man in a 1930s hat named Smokey kept watch for the cops. Five or six shooters gathered around the table and tossed two dimes on the felt: one for the winner's kitty and the other for the house. Tony was the house; he racked, passed out "pills," and barked out the winning number. Each pill was the size of a marble and had a flat side with a number on it. Tony shook the ivory pills out of a thick leather bottle and each player got two of them: one pill with a number for the break, and another pill with a number for the winning ball. Before deciding which of the two pills to throw in, I studied the location of the balls inside the rack for the odds, trying to decide whether to shoot high or low, depending on the position of the racked balls. If I had a low-numbered pill, I might be able to shoot second or third; but if the other pill matched the number of a ball buried in the middle of the rack, I might never get a clean shot at it. I also had to consider who else was shooting at the table. To shoot against Moze or Tony Arlia was a waste of time and money; they were pros. When they were in the game, I always tossed in my low pill first, just hoping to get off a shot.

But the next day, unless I had a fever, I had to go back to school. On Friday we had assembly; that was why I tried to skip on Thursday. Although a waste of time, assembly was a relief from classes. Often lawyers and businessmen came and lectured us on the need to develop a strong resumé. They told us we would be judged according to the attractiveness of our individual portfolios, and toward that end we learned eye-contact and gesturing in public speaking, wrote business letters in English, and studied the glories of conquering empires in world history. In chemistry we watched films championing the rise of Dupont and U.S. Steel and, on Field Day, we toured local industry: Zippo, Dressers, Butter-Krust Bakery, and Kendell. We were encouraged to compete for scholarships from Fisher Body and Dressers, join the Debate Club, and take on "leadership roles" in student government. The severe Miss Fox, our guidance counselor, spoke about "selling yourself in today's competitive educational marketplace," advising the more promising boys to pursue lucrative careers in engineering.

Miss Murry, my history teacher, wagged a slow finger in front of the class and said, "David. You must apply yourself now. If you don't, when others go on to college, you will find yourself on the outside looking in." She spoke slowly, slurring her words like someone who had had too much to drink. After she finished chiding me, I shielded my eyes with both hands and pretended to press my nose against the window, squinting through the frosted glass. All the teachers knew that during my five minutes of guidance with Miss Fox, she had suggested I pursue a career in the United States Army.

CHAPTER 16

~~~~~~~~~~~~~~~~~~~

Money

At home, long after the last Pepsi in the icebox had gone flat and ice crystals crazed the last half-eaten pint of chocolate ice cream, we found sweets stuck under the furniture, hidden behind books, jammed behind cushions on the sofa: gum drops, caramels, kisses, and, once or twice, a chocolate-covered turtle. My mother was not a good housekeeper. "For the life of me," she complained, "I have never in all my born days seen one man leave such a mess behind him. He's been gone over two years, and he's still around. I don't know if we'll ever be free of him."

For weeks on end I didn't think of him at all, and then I would look over at the bookcase and see one of his mysteries or, retrieving a coin dropped behind the piano, I would find a lump of moldy candy. First I would sense his presence, then I would become aware of his absence. One night I came home, opened the door, glanced across the room, and realized once again that he was not there; only this time the realization was more acute. The hollyhock chair was empty, the room dead. I sat down in the chair and rubbed the arms, pushing my face into the familiar slipcover. The stale odor of bird and tobacco lingered deep in the fabric: the smells of Jeris, talcum, and incense. I was late. Had my father been there, I might have been given what he called a "thrashing"; then again he simply might have looked at his watch and said, "If

you can't get back on time, you can't go out at all. Period." I
sat in his chair and wept.

Jim Johnson and I had been sitting in front of the Thorn
house talking about money, unaware of the hour. In Bradford, everybody talked about money. Kids guessed what it
would be like to live like one of the oil barons. The rich lived
in mansions with wrap-around porches and balconies,
Tiffany windows and awnings, curved arches and fluted
chimneys, cornices, pilasters, and Gothic gewgaws: testa-
ment to those who had drilled for oil and struck. Iron fences
and filigree surrounded the manors and the carriage houses,
the swimming pools, the circular drives, the private parks.

Grownups gossiped about the glitter and power. People
still remembered when Bradford had been one of the richest
towns in America, and the memory trickled down. As
though the town's history boosted his own image in the
world, my father often reminded me that Bradford had been
the third richest town per capita in the country. "It had," he
pronounced importantly, "one of the greatest concentra-
tions of money in the entire United States, second only to
Beverly Hills."

There were still plenty of Cadillacs in town, but most of
the money had already headed south for Texas. Oil people
took from the land, but they never put anything back.
Slowly, the town was being pumped dry. Fifty years ago
Bradford had produced eighty-five percent of all the oil used
in the United States, and the Bradford Oil Exchange had
been the largest in the world.

Jim and I often sat on the wall in front of the Thorn house
and talked after the town had become still, our words seeming to ring with truth in the dark. The Thorns lived in a
brick mansion with white shutters and rose gardens, herbs,
walks, and trellises. Both Jim and I loved the beauty of the
place.

"I wonder why the Thorns own Forest Oil and not the

Johnsons or McKains," Jim asked ironically. His parents were born in Greece, and after they came here they changed their name. Jim guarded his old name like a family secret; he felt as much an outsider as I did.

"Bradford's closed," he said, slicing the air in half with his hand. "The money in this town is all sewn up. A few families, that's it." He did not try to hide his envy.

"What are you talking about?" I challenged. Jim and I often argued. I did not accept anyone else's point of view easily, nor did he.

Jim looked at me knowingly for a moment. "Okay," he said smugly, "do you know what WESB stands for?"

"Of course," I answered confidently. The announcers on the station reminded their listeners everyday. "Where Every Sponsor Belongs."

"That's what you know! W ... E ... S ... B. Listen. It stands for Edwards, Satterwhite, and Bromley. The Big Three. They *own* the radio station. Do you know what else they own? They own half the town, that's all. The newspaper. The radio station. Lumber. Oil. You name it. Even Northeastern Box!" He was ticking off the names of businesses on his fingers by bending them back toward his wrist, one at a time.

"Northeastern Box! How do you know?"

Jim was grinning now, teasing with his silence.

"Well," I asked impatiently, "how do you know?"

"Dad told me," he said, and that ended it. Mr. Johnson owned the best restaurant on Main Street, and if anybody knew what was going on around town, Mr. Johnson did.

"So, Dave, you could have been a Thorn or an Edwards, and I could have been a Satterwhite or a Bromley."

"Could have ..." I said discouragingly. We sat in sullen silence.

"Seriously," Jim said finally. "We don't choose much, do we? Come to think of it, we don't choose anything." He laughed a little Santa Claus laugh. "What do we choose? We don't choose our parents. We don't choose where we're born." Jim bent back one finger emphatically again, his voice loud. "We don't even choose the century we're born in!"

"You'll wake everybody up," I warned, nodding over my shoulder at the Thorns's garage. The chauffeur and his family lived upstairs; their windows were open. The moonlight threw shadows at our feet. Jim elbowed me, and we started punching each other on the arm until it hurt. I hit him while he braced, and then he hit me while I braced. Neither of us wanted to stop and neither of us wanted to fight. Then my fist glanced off his shoulder and caught him under the eye. It was not a hard punch, but he grabbed his eye and bent forward, working the moment for all it was worth. I was trembling and so was he, but now he had the edge; I had gone too far. "That was pretty stupid," he said.

"I'm sorry," I said, meaning it. "Come on. I'll walk you home."

He continued to bury his face in his hands, then he pulled his fingers away as though he was ripping off a mask; he was laughing. "Naw," he said, "I'll walk you."

"Okay," I agreed, and we jumped up at the same time, surprising each other. Jim brushed his nose twice with his right thumb. I stood rigidly with my fists curled back, the way my father used to stand when we shadow-boxed and I was his shadow.

"We're really stupid," Jim said.

"Yeah," I said, "we really are."

Jim Johnson's nickname was "Dah," mine "Dummy." They called Jim "Dah" because he had a deep voice and sometimes paused before he spoke, muttering "dah" while he was thinking. My nickname had been given to me by Bull Correlli. We were on a picnic out at Thunder Rocks; he was with Cindy McQuire and I was with Linda Barry. Cindy had blond hair and long legs; Linda was short and had brown hair. Bull and Cindy were going steady, but Linda and I were only on our second date.

Bull had driven his father's car and brought everything for the picnic: corn, butter, aluminum foil, baking potatoes, steaks, beer, even a chef's apron and napkins. Bull liked to take charge. "Hey!" he bellowed. "How 'bout startin' the charcoal!" He had been wrapping the potatoes in foil, his back turned. When I did not respond, he shouted again. "Hey! You don't have ears or somethin'?" I stood there and shrugged, pretending I didn't hear. I had never started a charcoal fire. I had never even seen one before; I had never eaten a steak. On church picnics we had always brought baked beans or a covered dish, and those were the only picnics I had ever been on. Bull called this picnic a barbecue. I smiled at Linda and she smiled back. I did not want to look as foolish as I felt; I shuffled over to his powder blue station wagon to give myself time to think. There lay a bag in back marked "charcoal," but without directions. I brought the bag over quietly and leaned it against a rock. Bull turned around. "Hey!" he bellowed. "Do I get a fire or what?"

I stood with my hands in my pockets and smiled vacantly. Bull pointed his finger at my chest and broke out laughing. He shook his head and howled. "Come on, Dummy, light the fire!" I just stood there, and he said it again. "You gotta be kiddin' me! Come on, Dummy, light it!" I glanced over at Linda again. I wished I had known her better. She smiled back as though she knew how I felt.

"Gimme that thing," Bull said. "I'll start it myself!" I lugged the bag over to the grill, still smiling. As I pulled the red drawstring to open it, the string broke. Bull howled. "Get the hell out of here, Dummy! Now you've wrecked the bag!" I wondered if my eyes were watering. I put my hands back in my pockets and shrugged my shoulders. Linda was sitting on the blanket eating potato chips. Both girls were laughing and I laughed too, hoping, as I walked by, Linda would come walk with me. Short of breath, with the muscles gone from my legs, I didn't want to ask.

I slowed down a step or two so she would be able to catch up. I felt as though I were standing in the middle of the field even though I was walking. I wandered twenty or thirty yards before I could hear someone running behind me. "Hi," she said, smiling. "Do you want to go up to the rocks?" The rocks were concentrated on a mountaintop near Salamanca, the only nonreservation town in America owned by Indians. I did not know for sure, but I guessed that the Indians had named the place Thunder Rocks. Huge boulders were strewn in all directions as though they had been hurled down from the sky, splitting mid-aid and rumbling like thunder. It was cool deep down between the rocks, and the fissures were lined with moss.

Footholds appeared in the rocks, a kind of primitive ladder carved by Indians. I climbed to the top of a boulder and gazed out over the river and the farms below. Linda scrambled up after me without asking for help. She didn't seem to mind getting dirty and scraped. I was glad we didn't know each other well enough to talk; I didn't feel confident enough to tell her how much I liked the place. It was enough to sit on the rocks in silence, losing myself in the mountains and the valley. I wanted to ask Linda if she believed in God, but I didn't, deciding I didn't know the answer to that question either.

We must have been there for half an hour before Bull bellowed, "Dummy! Time to eat!" Linda smiled; she had nearly fallen asleep. She stretched slowly, arching her back and reaching her hands up into the sky. "It's beautiful," she said, pulling me up. "Thunder Rocks is my favorite place in the whole world."

The next time Jim and I talked on the wall in front of the Thorns's, I told him about my new nickname. His nickname, Dah, had come first. I understood why he didn't like it, but I wasn't sure how I felt about Dummy. Maybe being a dummy wasn't so bad. Bull had laughed about it in good humor; it also had the added virtue of being true. I often kept my mouth shut because I didn't want people to realize how little I understood. I hid that part of myself which was too shy or timid to come forward: some deep and private self that was more important than anything else people could see. This other self remained silent, and I protected it by pretending not to know which end was up. I remembered how the cops had grilled the gypsies and how the gypsies had shrugged and smiled innocently, staying mum and remaining free.

But other nicknames hurt. Kid Landry and Eric Barker called Jim and me "the Philosophers," and neither Jim nor I liked that. It wasn't really a nickname anyway; it was more of a label. To be a philosopher meant you put on airs, as though you thought you were better than other people. We didn't feel better than anyone else, but Eric and Kid called us the Philosophers because we asked questions that did not have answers. Sometimes it was hard to tell the difference between being a philosopher and being a dummy. People laughed at me as Dummy, but they resented me as a so-called philosopher. Over the cash register in half a dozen grocery stores and lunch counters hung the ever-present challenge: "If you're so smart, why aren't you rich?"

CHAPTER 17

Nights

On special shopping nights before Christmas music swelled the air, each clear bell suspended by the falling snow, echoing back and forth between the buildings on Main Street. No other music matched these chimes, not even the summer concerts of Little Civics in the park at Veteran's Square. Snow melted on my tongue and the simple joy of being surged through my veins as I jumped and swatted the air to punctuate the end of a refrain—just as God, mother claimed, had always intended. Rubber boots and tires whispered through the slush.

Strut was part of the concert, too. He stood in the middle of the street blowing his whistle and conducting traffic, holding his white-gloved hand high in the air like a figure inside a paperweight of tumbling snow. When he smiled for me to cross, he looked up at the sky toward the steeple of the Baptist church and grinned: no one else listened to the music with quite the same joy as the two of us. Not only did we listen, but we each saw my mother seated at the console pumping the pedals in her stockinged feet as she danced across the wooden slats, tapping the toe pistons and stomping the swells, rocking back and forth and booming "Joy to the World! The Lord Is Come!"

Then the lights in the store windows dimmed and the streets began to empty, my signal to meet my friends at the garage behind the Bradford Club, a building made of Hanley brick that stood next to the Bradford Bank in the middle of the biggest block on Main Street. Strut was usually still on duty and I had to be careful. If he saw me after the stores had closed, I waved and walked beyond the club to the pedestrian alley which allowed me to circle back to the garage. And there, at 9:15, first one, then two, three, four, and five faces appeared, each boy holding a finger to his lips. There was Mark Rosen, Jim Johnson, Reeder Huff, Eddie Layton, and me. Although we had stolen Mitch Herbert's father's Cadillac before, we pushed and punched each other on the arm. Mitch had the keys to the garage and to the car's ignition. The rest of us kept guard and raised the door just high enough to ease the long, smooth Caddie out into the dark, the aerial down. Then, lights off, we cruised the side streets and back alleys toward what everyone called the Back Road to Limestone. None of us knew the people who had been killed there, but all of us had heard the story about the girl's head rolling down the bank and into the creek. My mother said she lost it for some half-wit who didn't care enough about her to learn how to drive. The twisted body and stained seats of the wrecked car sat at the Quaker State filling station the next day, and all the town came to see. We all knew the danger spots along the road: the roller-coaster dip leading to the one-lane bridge.

We had started crossing the state line at fourteen, four years under the minimum age prescribed by New York law but old enough to be served in one of the five roadhouses in wide-open Limestone. We called the yellow beer "piss" and the Chianti "Dago Red," handing the wine back and forth in the car like a dare. The straw around the bottle crackled loudly.

"Keep it down!" Mark whispered, each of us afraid that the rustling might carry up through the padded upholstery and steel roof into the night, attracting attention.

"Here comes one!" Jim warned harshly, sitting on his knees at the back window. Each of us had a lookout. Every pair of headlights meant arrest, jail, disgrace. None of us was old enough to have a license, and only Mitch knew how to drive.

By the time we got back to town we were hopelessly drunk on bravado and fear. Mitch drove past all of our houses but his own, blaring the horn to scare us as much as he had been scared from the start of the evening. As we drove up South Avenue past my house, I knew that my mother and Strut would be sipping cocoa at the kitchen table, laughing and talking softly. An electric candle glowed in each of the front two windows. The tree lights were lit, and a Christmas wreath hung on the door. My mother would have her shoes off, and Strut's gun and holster would dangle over the back of my father's hollyhock chair.

I wasn't sure if my friends felt the same way I did, but I enjoyed the thrill of just riding in a Cadillac more than being a car thief. I had never been in a Cadillac before, and it took some time to recognize how the experience affected me. In a self-conscious way I felt heady and smug in the backseat of the big car, but I also felt embarrassed. The sense of well-being seemed to come too easily; shortly after we gave up stealing cars we started to break into some of the darkened mansions around town. During the winter, the rich vacationed in Florida and Bermuda. This time the thrill was obvious. We never stole anything; we just sat in the tall, over-stuffed chairs in the dark, sipped Coke, and pissed in the toilet as though we owned the place.

We didn't always steal cars and break into houses on Saturday night; sometimes we just went to the picture show. There were three moviehouses in town: the McKean, the Shea, and the New Bradford. The McKean got grade-B movies, the Shea got first-run sophisticated films, and the New Bradford got the cowboy and adventure pictures. Most of the time we went to the New Bradford, but wherever we went, afterward we headed for the Congress Street Diner, looking for action. The diner was modelled on a railroad dining car, and on weekends it was packed. Standing inside the door waiting for a table, we had to be quiet or we would get Mr. Bachakis angry. Mr. Bachakis owned the place, ran the cash register, and worked the grill: he wouldn't take any fooling. A sign on the door said, "Please—Ladies Welcome!" I liked to wait inside because the tassel of my watchcap brushed the ceiling, making me feel tall; but if Mr. Bachakis saw me he frowned and tore at the air over his head until I took it off.

"Here she comes," Mark whispered tensely.

"Holy shit! Look at those jugs!" Reeder exclaimed.

All of us became silent as Betty Basketballs walked by, her huge bosom heaving. Then, just as anyone could reach out and touch her, Eddie pushed Mark into her to get a feel. Betty winked.

"What d'ya want?" she asked after we sat down in a booth. She plopped the heavy brass-cornered menus down onto the middle of the table, blowing the napkins onto our laps. We tried to keep her standing there so we could glance at her large breasts, each of us chipping in a nickel to play six songs for a quarter on the jukebox. Mark reached over and turned the ivory-knob scroll-selector, choosing from the hits— songs by Eddie Fisher, Tennessee Ernie Ford, Johnnie Ray, Tony Bennett, Roy Hamilton, and the Inkspots.

"I want you, Betty," Eddie finally said.

"Oh, come on," she answered, touching the tip of her pencil to her lips.

"How about tonight then?" Reeder asked boldly.

Betty looked both ways. "Yeah," she snarled crudely. "All right. But come on, you guys. I gotta work."

After she took our order, Eddie whispered, "Hey, you guys. She's gonna go down!"

"Shh!"

"She's a pig," Jim said, frowning.

"What's the matter, Dah. You got something on the side?"

"I heard she does," Reeder said, a wrinkle starting across his forehead as he lifted his eyes. "She gang-banged a whole bunch of guys!"

Eddie held up eight fingers. "They all lined up."

"How the hell do you know?" Mark asked in annoyance. "Were you there?"

Eddie smiled and lifted his arm, rapping his knuckles in mid-air three times. "You know that rubber cement stuff in school?" he asked lewdly. "It was like somebody poured a bottle on her crotch."

"Try to be a little bit more disgusting," Jim said, drawing back.

Reeder caught my eye and winked. I knew that they were joking, trying to shock Jim and Mark. They called it "spocking." But even if I hadn't known they were teasing, I would have felt pretty removed from it all. I had been seeing more and more of Linda, and I was thinking of her. Deliberately, I held her in my mind as a kind of shield, a way of keeping myself distant and pure.

Mr. Bachakis came around from behind the counter and stood beside the cash register, his hands on his hips, a spatula in his fist.

"Ba-Jack-Ass is coming," Reeder said through his teeth, smiling.

"Shut up, Reeder!" Mark whispered harshly. "He's standing there!"

We were quiet until Mr. Bachakis went back to the grill; then everybody started laughing. Eddie and Reeder were acting crazy. "Stop staring!" Mark shouted as Betty bent over to wipe a table. Her legs joined her feet without ankles, something I would not have noticed if she had not worn a gold ankle bracelet that threatened to cut off her circulation. Mr. Bachakis rang the bell on top of the cash register, pointing an accusing finger. Jim looked across the table at me and lifted his eyebrows. "Ready?" he asked. "I've had enough." I nodded and we left.

"That's why I sat on the end of the booth in there," Jim said when we got outside. "Those guys are sick."

"Maybe," I said abstractly, but I couldn't tell Jim his friends had been spocking him. Jim put his collar up, and I walked him up and down Main Street until he cooled off. Again, the thought of Linda kept me insulated from what was going on, and I wondered why I had not called her that night.

Linda cheered for the Bradford High Owls. She wore a gold circle pin and a scarab bracelet, but her father didn't make much money so she had to make her own clothes. Her father sold animal scents to trappers and hunters, and every month he signed his paycheck over to Miller Lumber Company to pay for their new Lustron Home. My mother finally signed some waiver with the school, and in the eleventh grade I could play basketball. Before each game, Linda bounced out onto the center of the court and chanted:

> McKain . . . McKain . . . He's our man.
> If he can't do it
> Gildersleeve can . . .

She chicken-walked like an Indian when she cheered, stutter-stepping and dipping, flashing one hand high and one hand low, shaking her fingers as though she were on fire, the muscles in her calves tightening. At least half the players had girlfriends who were cheerleaders; and when Linda clapped her hands in rapid succession twice, Mary Jean Trivalia came out on the floor, bobbing and dipping for Larry. The cheerleaders looked at each other knowingly whenever a boyfriend was involved; the words for the cheers took on double meanings.

The players formed three lines at half-court, facing the basket for layup drills. We wore silver satin warmup suits that shimmered in the light as though they were made of foil. We looked like liquid metal, but we were not allowed to clap or show emotion; we concentrated on the intricate weave of the three lines braiding in and out, passing, rebounding, shooting. Perhaps we pranced a bit as we ran to the end of the line, but only subtly. The excitement of the gym was only hinted at, like the occasional squeak of our sneakers on the maple floor—a brief, thin, shrill cry that pierced the air. No one stood up tall and touched the floor with both hands or called attention to himself by stretching. At best, a boy would kneel down to tie his white Converse sneakers. In the spirit of denial which controlled us, I did not dare to look over at Linda directly, although I stole glances whenever I could. During basketball season the coach regarded girls as a necessary evil, but during a game they did not exist.

After the game it was a different story. The girls sat bunched on the bleachers in the semi-dark, dutifully subdued if we had lost or ecstatic if we had won. One by one the players ambled out of the locker room casually, just as we had ambled into the gym: our hands jammed in our pockets, each with a towel tucked under one elbow, one eye cocked. After a game, win or lose, certain rules were suspended: after practicing all week we were free for the night. We strutted diagonally across the full length of the court without the least concern for the red out-of-bounds line which surrounded it, taking the long walk slowly, reliving for a moment the glory of having been out there in uniform.

One by one the girls fell in step with their boyfriends, joining them near the darkly lustrous circle at mid-court. In the beginning of the season Linda had walked slightly behind me, but toward the end of the season, her face flushed from the glow of the EXIT sign, she crooked her arm in mine and rested her head against my arm.

Cold and clear, the snow crunched under our boots as we walked toward my mother's old Plymouth, the stars bright enough to light the entire playing field. "Good game," she always said as soon as we closed the doors, no matter how I had played.

After the car warmed up, Linda cocked the rearview mirror so she could put on lipstick, smacking and blotting her lips, laughing and moving deftly, anxious to be beautiful. Brushing her hair, she let her mouth fall open just slightly, provocatively tilting her head to the side. I had learned in Spanish that Linda meant "pretty."

"You're beautiful," I said, and she lowered her eyes, sometimes stretching up to kiss me on the cheek as though I were an older man. I did not know why exactly, but I liked to drive away without responding after she kissed me, as though we had known each other forever and didn't need to rush, pretending we would live forever.

"Second shift," Mr. Barry said as soon as we arrived at her house; he and his wife had their coats on and were waiting by the door. On Friday night they went dancing at the Italian-American Club. Linda's grandfather had shortened his name from Barcello to Barry, but they ate spaghetti and still went to the club.

"Suzie's down," Mrs. Barry said. "I just changed her." Mrs. Barry moved quickly, racing back into the bedroom to grab her purse. Mr. Barry shouted from outside, "There's beer in the fridge."

I sat on the sofa waiting for Linda to come in from the kitchen where she was starting to make popcorn. "Aren't you starving?" she asked. I didn't answer. Except for the lights from the Christmas tree, the living room was dark. Mrs. Barry loved Christmas and hung mistletoe over the door into the dining room. Year after year the branches of the artificial tree collapsed back into the main trunk. Like the house, the tree would last forever. Mr. Barry always bought the latest inventions, and he had bought the second Lustron Home in town. Peach-colored in and out, the porcelain enamel panel walls never had to be scraped and painted. All that was needed was a bucket of warm water, a sponge, and some soap. Mr. Barry said the house was steel-framed, fire-proof, termite-proof, rat-proof, and decay-proof. "Want to hang a picture?" he once asked proudly. "Let me show you." He took an adhesive pad containing a hook, pressed it against the wall, and hung a picture of a Spanish dancer which might have come with the house as a "decorative option." A few minutes later it crashed to the asphalt tile floor. He laughed, shook his head, and swept up the glass. "The house may last forever, but I don't know about the bullfighter."

I looked up and saw Linda standing in the doorway; the light from the kitchen was on her hair. "Don't you want some popcorn?" she asked.

"Sure," I said, but I never understood why she wanted to waste time when her parents left the house. "Can I get a beer?"

"Dad said you could."

"How about you?" I asked.

"I'd rather have a Coke."

"What's the matter?"

Her eyes grew sad. "I don't see how we can expect to get married someday and not get along."

I looked over her shoulder at the glass cookie jar on top of the refrigerator. It was full of red cellophane cigarette tabs, the ones used around the top of the packages. Mr. Barry saved them because he had heard that, if he could get fifty thousand of them, the cirgarette company would buy a seeing eye dog for a well-deserving blind person.

"What do you mean not get along?" I asked, choosing the easier part of the sentence.

"Don't you like my mother and father?" she asked.

"Sure I do. Why do you say that?"

The popcorn had started to pop; Linda skipped the pot back and forth across the burner with fury. "You hardly said . . . hello to them . . . that's why!"

"I did say hello! When we came in! Your father was . . . they were out the door before we stepped inside the house!"

Linda pushed a red button on the stove; the entire kitchen came with General Electric appliances. She sprinkled salt on the popcorn and skidded it across the formica table. She was smiling now, eating popcorn as though famished. Her moods were hard to follow. I read through the phone book looking for funny names.

"Do you still want to get married?" she asked.

"Here's one," I said. "Cowlick. Maynard Cowlick."

"Thanks a lot," she said, pouting.

But I wasn't sure. Love was new to me. I loved Linda and I loved being with her, but I was almost as happy when we were not together—except at school. Without her, I could not have gotten through the day in school. Every morning we met to check our schedules, plotting out schemes to pass each other in the hall between classes, checking times and routes so we'd have a chance to smile at each other at least once on the back stairs. We also met before and after lunch beside her locker, opening the narrow door, hiding and whispering in its shadow.

"I don't know," I said. "Not for a long time anyway." Whenever we made love we promised one another we would love each other forever, but still I did not know the answer to her question. Linda's eyes grew sad and narrow. I wanted her to tilt her head to the side and brush her hair back so she would look the way she had looked in the car.

"I know," she said. "Me, too. I want to wait, too. Sometimes I think we should wait on everything." I knew she meant we should not make love anymore until we got married. I grabbed her leg under the table and smiled. We first made love in the back seat of the car one night behind a pile of cinders left by the State Highway Department, and now there was no stopping us. She was still pouting. I could not figure out what had gotten into her.

I got up from the table.

"Sometimes I think you're conceited," she said.

"Conceited?"

"Sometimes you think you're better than anyone else. You think you can do anything you want. Other kids say you're conceited, too."

"What other kids?" I did not think I was better than anyone else, but I did think I should be able to do whatever I wanted. At least, I thought, I should be able to do whatever the rich kids could do, and deep down I knew I could not.

"Don't you like me anymore?" I asked, avoiding the word "love."

She did not answer for a while, then she said, "yes," softly, inexplicably crying; neither of us knew what we were talking about.

I went over and put my arm around her shoulder, standing there like a statue, not knowing what else to do. She took my hand, and we walked into the living room, stumbling as we kissed under a sprig of mistletoe. I sat on the sofa while she turned on the television. We did not have television at home, but I had no interest in watching. After a basketball game, one beer made me feel lightheaded.

"Mom will get worried if she drives up and doesn't see at least one light on," she explained, turning off the sound.

"I'm not worried about it," I said after she sat down. The blue light of television made the porcelain walls look soft and quilted.

"Me neither. I'm not worried about it."

I kissed the butter and salt off her lips, timing myself with her breathing, waiting for the right moment to put my hand under her blouse.

"You make everything so hard," she whispered in a troubled voice.

"No," I said in mock seriousness. "You do."

"Oh, Dave," she laughed. "I love you."

"I love you, too," I whispered, and she did not ask how much.

CHAPTER 18

Work

Before picking up Jim on Saturday night I swung over to the other side of town to a filling station on the top of Mill Street to buy a pack of safeties. Mr. Gill sold gas, oil, and groceries, and he kept a cigarbox of Trojans under the counter. "Quarter each, four for a dollar. You want me to wrap 'em for ya?" I pretended he was funny and said good-bye.

After I picked up Jim, we went down to the Emery Hotel for a shine. Mr. Henry shined shoes across from the Gold Room. He also handed out towels, soap, and hair tonic for the men's room. I knew Mr. Henry from the African Methodist Episcopal Zion Church, but we pretended we only knew each other on Saturday nights when we listened to the top ten tunes on the radio together. Mr. Henry's room had a marble floor, marble walls, and just enough space for two mahogany chairs with two brass footrests. Mr. Henry wedged his radio, a cream-colored Motorola with a round brown dial, on a triangular shelf in the corner behind the door. Mr. Henry hummed as he worked, rubbing in the polish, front and back. I could feel his fingers through the leather on my feet. I didn't feel hypocritical asking him to shine my oxblood wing tips, but I thought about it. I would have shined his shoes for a dime too, but he never asked me.

"What's your favorite?" Mr. Henry asked.

" 'Earth Angel,' " I answered quickly.

"Mine, too," he said, smiling. "Mine, too. But what about 'Stranger in Paradise'?"

"Yeah. I like that, too."

Mr. Henry hummed one note deep in his throat, letting it simmer down there until it erupted as "Take my hand; I'm a stranger in Paradise." We both laughed. "Damn!" he said.

Mr. Henry played sax in the best jazz band around town. Some said he played in Olean, Jamestown, and all the way to Buffalo. I liked Mr. Henry because he could joke with us without looking down at us.

The smell of shoe polish carried out into the street as Jim and I pushed through the revolving lobby door. The polish had a new, clean smell, the only perfume I wore. After we got our shoes shined, we stood out under the marquee feeling important and watching cars make the loop around Veteran's Square. Jim said hello to people as they entered the hotel, and sometimes I thought he said hello whether he knew them or not. Once he pointed out Mr. Satterwhite to me, the *S* in WESB. The Emery was where the rich people ate, drank, and bought their clothes. Jim said that the oil men inside the Gold Room drank a cocktail called a "Black-Eyed Susan," a martini and an olive with a thin film of oil floating on top.

Jim was riding high. He sang along with Billie Eckstein to "Ebb Tide" in the car, twisting his face into a proper expression of romantic anguish, his eyes closed. Jim smiled and tried to whistle as he rang the bell to pick up Jan, rocking back and forth on his heels like an excited salesman. Jan was tall and quiet. She got into the back seat and said hello formally. Jim put his arm around her as though she were cold, talking softly.

When I stopped for Linda, I could tell she was anxious to get going. She had been taking care of Suzie all day, and her mother had been riding her. She sighed in relief, and we laughed at our shyness with one another. Every time we dressed up to go to a picture show, we looked like strangers to each other. I opened the door on her side of the car, and she said thank you. I felt uneasy going to the movies and holding hands; actually, all four of us were just waiting for the movie to end so we could drive out into the countryside under the stars. The night was darker than the inside of the theater, and whatever we did was more exciting than watching a picture show. It was pitch-black alongside the road to Rock City, and we all stared up at the sky. The stars were crisp and low in the sky.

The Ho-Sta-Gah was a bar and lounge just over the New York state line, a Seneca name for "Up on the Rocks." I shifted into second gear as the Plymouth struggled up the hill. We were relieved if there were only a few cars in the parking lot; Jim checked the cars for Pennsylvania license plates. I backed in under a hemlock, tucking the car in up close to the tree so no one could see our plate. Once inside Jim turned up the collar of his father's blue overcoat, unbuttoning the front and jamming his hands into his pockets. He looked jaunty that way, as though he was wearing a cape. Acting as maître d', he seated us near the fireplace. When the waitress came to our table, Jim lowered his voice and asked the girls, "What is your pleasure?" Linda giggled and ordered a 7 & 7, then Jan said she would like one as well. Jim ordered a Carlings, and I ordered an Ox-Cart, a local beer out of Rochester, the cheapest on the menu. The Ho-Sta-Gah was expensive.

After one beer Jim nuzzled up to Jan and lowered his voice. "You can't see it now," he said, "but out that window on a clear day you can see . . . I don't know. How far can you see, Jan?" Jan smiled and didn't answer.

"Forty miles to Holland," I said, glancing at Linda. On good days we either drove to Thunder Rocks or here, to Rock City. "On top of Signal Rock you can see a thousand miles of river valley." Rock City had a network of fissures through the rocks like streets, the rocks themselves as big as buildings.

"The man with the cane told us we could see Holland," Linda explained. Jim looked mystified, as though we were trying to pull something over on him.

"Holland," I repeated in an effort to explain. "This little town up by East Aurora. Almost to Buffalo."

"The old man pointed out towns and everything with his cane," Linda said with excitement. "Remember?" We both liked high places and that was why we liked the Ho-Sta-Gah. There was a saying over the fireplace inscribed in stone which made us blush: "Sweet is the union of kindred souls."

After we had two drinks and dropped Jan and Jim off, Linda and I went to the Lustron Home to make love in the blue light of television. Her parents were asleep, but she kept her dress on because they might wake up to go to the bathroom. The door to their bedroom was right down the hall off the living room, so we had to be careful. One night Mr. Barry stumbled out into the hallway in his pajamas while we made love ten feet away. Linda sat in my lap backward with her skirt spread over her knees, her underpants dangling from one foot. Mr. Barry asked us in a groggy voice how it was going. "Fine," Linda answered; she tried to make her voice cheery, but it sounded thick and husky.

"You live too high off the hog," my mother said when I asked her if I could borrow a couple of dollars. "If you're going to play basketball all day and carouse all night, you've got to work like the rest of the world."

Going with Linda was expensive. Even when Mom allowed me to borrow the car I had to pay for the gas, and then she complained that I drove all over God's Creation.

Although I needed more money, I never considered quitting school. People often said I looked as though I belonged to the country club, took tap dance lessons, and belonged to the Episcopal Church of the Ascension. Sometimes my looks caused resentment, like the day one of the assistant football coaches stopped me in the hall.

"Hey, McKain," he said, his hand heavy on my shoulder. "Guess what. If you're lucky, good looks and a dime'll get you a cup of coffee." I had been chosen as one of the three "best looking boys" in my class, and he spoke close to my face, furious. But whatever he or my teachers thought, I did not think I was better than anyone else nor was I, at least consciously, a rebel. I rebelled spontaneously, out of some vague sense of moral outrage I could not define. On the surface I only wanted to earn enough money to buy a pink shirt, charcoal slacks, and saddle shoes. I did not want to leave town. I only wanted a job, and, unlike my father, I felt lucky.

If I wanted to double-bank the eight ball into the side pocket badly enough, the ball dropped—at least if I expressed enough humility to show God I knew Who really made the shot. I no longer attended church, but I still prayed, and that was how I got my job delivering the *Bradford Era*. I prayed to God for a paper route and He delivered.

It was, I thought, the best job in town. I liked getting up at five-thirty in the morning and I went out to meet the town as I had done when we had lived on Amm Street, as though the town were a person. I liked the stillness of the hour, the promise, and the distant pumping of the donkey-jacks on the hills. The streetlights glowed. Men stood in shadows, waiting for their rides to work; they stood ordered in their space, almost painterly—part of a dark composition of purple light on snow. As I walked by them I breathed in the rich odors of gun-oil and wet wool, of tobacco and coffee on their breath. The smell of pure, raw crude oil was strongest in the morning, an odor of paraffin and shale belched up from deep inside the bowels of the earth.

Trapped inside the narrow alley behind the *Era*, a gust of wind rose up at my feet, carrying another early morning smell, that of printer's ink and newspulp—a wet smell, something like charred wood and rain. But the smell was even more pungent in the printer's room where we picked up our papers. We waited inside a cage made out of a heavy-gauge screen that ran from the top of the counter to the ceiling, a braze of two-inch diamonds. When we waited for the rain to stop or when we were feeling lazy, we folded our papers inside the cage and talked.

Puffy and white, the three printers smoked cigars in their undershirts, lighting up and chatting as they broke down the presses and cleaned and oiled them. Pale and sallow, they looked like poker players in the early green light. They scratched their bellies and yawned, leaning against poles that supported the ceiling. Then, in an exaggerated pantomime of civility, each man put on a clean grey work shirt, elegantly buttoning his cuffs and tipping an imaginary hat to say good-bye.

My route started across the street from the *Era* at the Bradford Filling Station and the Congress Street Diner, then ran along the west side of Congress to the city limits. The route included seven small side streets that veined up the foot of Quintuple Mountain. I loved the easy iambics of the hills, the rhythm of the donkey-jacks.

But most of my one hundred customers lived in houses perched on top of a steep flight of stairs. During the winter the steps were hard to climb because of the ice. In three easy folds and a tuck, I could toss a paper so that it landed on the edge of the porch, skidded smoothly to the door, then fell open with a whisper to the headlines. But if I wanted to whack someone's front door for spite, I threw with all my might, banging the sleeping house with a paper rolled as tight as a boomerang. Sometimes I did this just for fun, watching the dark house brighten in yellow rectangles: first a light in the front bedroom, a light in the hall, and then a light on the porch—but by that time I was gone. After an all-night rain, the street smelled of wet hedges and trees, of black earth and bloated earthworms on the sidewalk. I could smell my way through my route. I knew where soggy papers lay rotting under porches, smelling of black earth and Indian pipe, and where people left their garbage in the snow to rot— the sharp sweet smell of kitchen midden, of purple onions and grapefruit rinds.

Alone in the morning mist, I made up my own rules. I let some houses sleep and woke up others according to whim. During the winter, when I was first to break the snow, for however long a stretch I could walk without taking a breath or running I owned all the houses I passed. I owned every brick in the sidewalk, I owned the cars, and I owned the street—owned everything, until I gasped and sputtered, sucking in the dry, cold air and coughing.

I enjoyed work more than school—the excitement, the freedom, the money. When I heard about the possibility of another job and of earning even more money, I walked across town to look into it. A reconverted meat-packing plant, the Alpine Ice Cream Company sat in the shadow of the pole and transformer where Honey Myers had been electrocuted in second grade, on the wrong side of Davis Street. I was no longer afraid, I said to myself, and I wouldn't run.

I climbed the tile stairs to the office and listened to the gruff voices on the other side of the closed door. I knocked timidly and said hello.

"Ohhh," someone trilled in falsetto, "do come in!" Half a dozen men in tattered clothes sat in beat-up wooden chairs tipped against the wall. I glanced from face to face. A couple of the men half-smiled.

"Close the goddamn door!" someone shouted. "You born in a barn?" The man jumped up from his chair and brushed by me. "Come on," he muttered, slamming the door after me as we walked out into the hall.

"Yeah?" he said out of the corner of his mouth, looking me up and down. "What do you want?"

"Lee McKinley said there might be an opening for a job loading trucks," I said as evenly as possible.

"Lee, huh? Lee's full a shit. I'm the boss here. I'm the foreman." A short man, he backed away with his hands on his hips, wary and defiant at once. He wiped doughnut crumbs from his twisted mouth and walked in small, troubled circles without speaking.

"Tell you what I'll do, kid," he said finally, his back turned. "Tomorrow morning. Come in tomorrow morning. We'll see what we got." He turned and glanced at my shoulder. "Tomorrow," he repeated, pointing a finger in my chest. "And my name's Paul. Paul Pascarella."

During the next few weeks I began to wonder if I had made the right choice. Red, Tony, Harry, and Bob made ice cream in their shirt sleeves. The rest of us were bundled up in layers of old shirts, sweaters, jackets, and coats—a ragtag ensemble of whatever we could find to keep warm. The temperature in the hardening rooms was kept a few degrees below freezing. A series of fans blew the frigid air up under my cuffs and through my clothes, no matter how warmly I dressed. I moved quickly from aisle to aisle, brushing the frost from the containers with a stiff glove so I could read the labels. Every twenty minutes we had to take a break, huddling around the potbellied stove on the open dock to thaw out. The stove sizzled from the ice on our gloves and from the snow that howled in off the street.

Each order was scribbled in pencil on a damp slip of paper which froze into a wrinkle after two minutes in the hardening room. A big order could take five minutes: seventy-two gallons of vanilla, sixty gallons of chocolate, thirty-six gallons of fudge ripple, twelve gallons of strawberry, cherry, and butter pecan, and on down through the novelties. Each tray was the same length, width, and height as a long flower box, a basket with tabs on the corners that held the trays intact. Six trays high, the stack stood over seven feet tall. Stacked that high, one single order weighed over two hundred and fifty pounds.

Given my skinny frame, I could hardly budge it; it felt like a ton. We filled the orders inside the hardening room, then dragged them out with an iron hook attached to the bottom tray. The hook was three feet long, and to get the stack going, I had to bend my knees and squat to the ground, throwing myself backwards, the hook engaged. Sometimes the stack did not move at all, and I had to get a push. I worked there a month before I was strong enough to drag a full stack of trays across the hardening room floor by myself, and even then I would slip and skate on the frost. Coming around the corner once I tipped an entire order, spilling bricks of ice cream in Paul's path.

"Jesus Christ!" he screamed. "Get the hell out of here! Get the hell out of here!" Together we put the ice cream back in the trays. "What did I just tell you?" he asked, his hands fisted on his hips. "Go on. Git. You're gonna be late for school." That was the first time I realized that Paul had a tender side. The man actually liked me. Ever so faintly, he smiled with his eyes.

The time clock where we punched in and out hung on the tile wall at the top of the stairs. All the walls were tile inside the factory so that Bob Kuda could hose them down at the end of the day. Although I only worked an hour before school, I worked a twelve-hour shift on Saturday. At ninety cents an hour, I sometimes made ten or twelve dollars a week after taxes and deductions. Every morning I hid in the toilet to gain a couple of minutes on the clock. My ear to the bathroom door, I listened for the minute hand to clack forward, timing my check-out for 7:38, fattening my paycheck by an extra fifty cents a month.

Some mornings, if I finished my paper route early, I ran across town to sit with the men upstairs in the factory office and drink coffee. These men were like the men who waited in the cold for their rides to work and, I thought, we shared the knowledge and promise of morning. Among other things, we were first to know what had happened in town and around the world the night before. I usually brought an extra paper, and a couple of men read the headlines. But, more importantly, we had watched the crack over the roof-tops turn colors—purple, orange, yellow, gray—and, I was sure, that made all the difference. Together, we had seen the world begin.

A wooden sign hung on the wall over the boss's desk: "I complained when I had no shoes, then I saw a man with no feet." At first I was moved by the message, but then I wondered who put it there and why. I asked Kuda if he thought the boss put it there to keep us from complaining.

"What's the matter, you unhappy?" Kuda asked, laughing. I knew he felt the same way I did, but it didn't matter. "All right. Come on, McKain. You going to work or what?" Paul said I daydreamed and talked too much, but I did everything he told me to do. "Come on, kid. You got a good deal and you're pissing in your own playpen. Wise up."

On Saturdays, after the trucks were loaded, I worked in the ice cream room folding waxed cardboard sheets into half-gallon containers. It was a relief to get out of the hardening rooms. The ice cream room was just large enough for two stainless steel vats, an overhead system of stainless steel pipes, and the four men who worked around a stainless steel card table, plus me; I stood in the corner folding cartons and watching. Oozing out of a stainless steel nozzle into the containers, the ice cream had the consistency of soft dough; Jack Harrison called it "shit." Harry sat on a red stool filling containers and yelling at Bob to change the mix.

"Come on, you Kuda!" he shouted with a lisp. "This shit's too soft!"

"Hey Harry! For Christ's sake, knock it off," Paul said as he barged through the stainless steel door. Paul patrolled the dock and the ice cream room, appearing out of nowhere. He barked out of the side of his mouth.

"Hey kid! What are you staring at? Come on. Give Harry a hand. You wanna work in here where it's nice and warm or what? I'm tellin ya. You're shittin' in your own playpen."

Red laughed and shook his head, as though I were hopeless. I was glad none of the men knew that my high school nickname was Dummy. Red was always telling stories, making fun of people. As soon as Paul left the room he nodded for me to come closer.

"Let me ask you something," he began. "How come we're doing this shit anyhow. You know why? I'll bet you don't know. Here we are breakin' our balls for nothing and you don't even know why."

He paused and looked around at the faces at the table, shaking his head as though he was sorry for us. Harry was pretending he was not paying attention, standing there with his mouth open, looking down. Harry and Red had traded places; now Red was filling. Tony made circles with his finger around his ear, looking disgusted. Bob was smiling, watching me.

"Tell you what. Since none of you jerks know the answer, I'll tell you. Here's what happened. God made the world and he made smart guys and dumb guys. Am I right? I mean really dumb guys. Dumb assholes like Harry here. Is that right, Harry? Hey Harry, do me a favor and tell Dave how dumb you are.

"Harry's so fuckin' dumb he screwed his mother-in-law one night. He thought she was his old lady. But it's not Harry's fault he's dumb. It's not your fault neither. You're stupid, too, or you wouldn't be here. Me? I think I'm smart.

"Big deal. God made us this way 'cause we screwed up. We sinned. We did somethin' wrong. That's how come we're doing this shit right now. Hey Tony, tell Dave. Am I right?"

"Yes, Red," Tony said in a hollow voice. He rolled his eyes in mock disgust. "Asshole," he added. "You're nuttier 'n poor Harry."

Harry looked at Tony and scowled.

"Don't make no difference," Red said. "We're all sinners. That's how come we're workin' here."

Red cleared his throat and held up his finger, signaling for attention. The men at the table stood in readiness for his performance, still weighing, stamping, and bagging half-gallon containers of ice cream, exchanging glances.

"Oh, Lord!" Red howled, his arms shaking over his head. "I done wrong. All my life I done wrong! I drank beer and whiskey and fucked slow. My wife, Harry's wife. It don't matter none. I drink beer and whiskey and jerk off in the Fudge-Ripple! Oh, Lord Jesus forgive me! All I want to do is drink and fuck!" Red ranted in high-pitched sentences.

I wore a frozen smile, folding cartons with my head down. I was finding it difficult not to run away from the table. Red was terrifying.

"Hey you guys," he said confidentially. "When I'm going on about Harry's wife you're supposed to say, 'Oh, Lord' or something. You know what I mean? I mean this just isn't me up here. It's you too. We're all in this thing together. We're all fuckin' sinners."

Red smiled and bounced up and down on his stool as though he was riding a horse on a merry-go-round, hooting like a circus calliope, lifting and falling in his saddle, his tongue lolling out of the side of his mouth.

Harry took his fingers out of his ears and Kuda shook his head in disgust. Tony smiled lewdly. "You Fuckin' Asshole Aitner," he said.

Red dropped his jaw and grinned, his right hand polishing an invisible shaft six inches over his fly.

By the end of the day on Saturday my arms trembled as I walked up Main Street carrying my black lunch bucket and waving to the passing cars. Saturday was the best day of all; everyone could see for themselves I had a tough and dirty job, and the more ragged and tired I looked the better I felt. After the first couple of months I enjoyed the work, dragging a full stack of trays across the dock, shouldering a hundred-pound bag of sugar up the stairs, aching until my legs shook. In Bradford's terms, at least in the only terms I could see and understand, I was learning to become a man. On some days I skipped school to work, but I was wearing thin from working two jobs and trying to play basketball at the same time. I had grown another inch or so, but I had also lost weight. My friends called me "Spear" because when I took a jump shot, from the side, they said I looked like one. Paul called me a long drink of water and wrapped his hand around the muscle in my arm. He joked about how puny I was, but I could tell he was concerned. "Okay, kid," he said one day. "No more workin' during school."

School was a breeze. I never took any books home. I never studied. Some teachers, including Miss Rufus, resorted to insult. "David doesn't have to work. He's so bright he knows the material without reading it. He picks it up by osmosis." When she asked me in class which battle was fought before Brandywine, or what treaty followed the Crimean War, nine times out of ten I didn't know the answer, and then she would gloat. She would take off her wire glasses and smile pointedly, shooting off small arrows of sarcasm. I noticed she never asked anyone else such hard questions, but I pretended that nothing she said could touch me. As I had done for years, I guarded my inner life by observing what was going on around me. As long as I knew, or felt I knew, what was happening, I felt secure inside, untouchable. Despite what my teachers thought, I was interested in school; only they had treated me with such disdain for so long I wasn't about to show it. I slouched in class and listened. I had gone beyond caring what they gave me for a grade.

We called the coach "Duke." An All-American football player from Ohio, he carried the hit-and-grunt psychology of football into basketball. He demanded what he called "hard, tough, basic ball." Practice was an exercise in wooden thought. He insisted we shoot foul shots underhanded, shoot two-handed set shots, and shoot all layups going straight in off the wooden backboard. Limited to a half-court offense, we practiced the same plays over and over until it seemed that the X's and the O's from the blackboard had been superimposed onto the court. In a game we were afraid to drive for the basket without first setting up, looking for the X's. White spittle glued to his lips, the Duke screamed, "Don't anticipate! Don't anticipate!" Strange advice for a game of intuition.

One day at practice I stood on the sidelines and held my chest. We were not allowed to sit, but I felt so weak and dizzy I thought I would collapse. I wanted to lean over with my hands on my knees, but the pain in my chest intensified as I bent over. I rested my head on my shoulder with my hands on my hips, shifting foot to foot like a chicken.

"McKain!" the coach screamed. Don Devoe threw me his soggy shirt, and I shivered as the dampness slapped against my bare arm. The wet shirt felt heavy as I lifted it over my head and began to shake. The other players on the court floated off into yellow light; I could barely make out the muffled sound of the distant whistle. The next thing I knew the ball was in the hands of the man in front of me, and, as though I had gone to the fountain, he turned and drove right by me, scoring an easy two.

"McKain!" the coach screamed. "Get the lead out! Cover that guy when he breaks across the key! Let's go!" I wanted to tell him that my shirt was too heavy and that the lights were fading, but I knew he would not listen.

Now we had the ball. The point guard tossed it to me from out of bounds, stepped in, and clapped for me to toss it back so he could bring it up the floor. Instead I dribbled away from him because I did not want him to see the tears in my eyes. The other team was pressing, and I dribbled by two defenders and across the ten-second line, fired by pain and rage. I kept dribbling, cutting in with my shoulder low, challenging the middle of the back line to stop me at the foul line, faking left, then driving straight up the middle for a one-on-five fast break, jumping higher than I had ever jumped, my fingers releasing the ball over the front of the rim for a poor man's dunk.

We played another half hour and the coach slapped my butt as I went into the locker room to take a shower.

"That's more like it," he said. "You play like that every day and you could be All-State."

His words comforted me as I drifted the mile and a half home through the late-afternoon darkness and snow, the cold air like a compress on my head. But when I stepped inside the apartment, the euphoria of pain was gone. My mother was not at home, the house dark. I could hardly breathe. I stretched out on the couch with my coat on and closed my eyes.

The next day I woke up in the hospital. The sun was glaring on the bruised snow outside my window. My mother was sitting at the foot of my bed smiling. She put a finger to her lips, and I closed my eyes. I fell asleep, and the following morning a nurse woke me up.

"Well," she said, "going to stay with us awhile?"

My eyes ached and I tried to smile.

"Yeah," she said cheerily. "I bet you don't know it, but you almost died last night. You've got double pneumonia."

CHAPTER 19

God's Plan

L ying in bed in the hospital gave me a chance to think, and I thought about my father. Just after the Good Friday flood, I remembered, he wove back and forth, then grabbed the wall and swooned, a thin smile on his lips. As a cough wracked his body he spit into his handkerchief, examining the yellow sputum at arm's length, muttering, shaking his head and grimacing as though he had swallowed poison.

"TB," he announced. "TB, bronchitis, and pneumonia. All three. Just one, any one, of them would kill most men." He shook his head and smiled pitifully, looking up at heaven. Whatever the illness, each "bout" ended in victory, proof that God was in his corner. The Lord had given him the strength every day to open the Pet Shop, and for that he was grateful. During the ten years he had the shop in Bradford, he had never missed a day. "Who would turn up the heat?" he asked rhetorically. "Who would feed and clean the birds and fish?"

"All I need is a hat and a scarf," he boasted, walking out into the cold. Winter and summer he wore the jacket he had worn thirty years before as basketball coach of Avalon High: a maroon jacket with yellow leather piping around the pockets and down the front. At night he applied an Indian poultice to his chest and slept with the window open. During the day he took 4-Way tablets and sucked on coughdrops by the boxful. "I like winter," he repeated, rubbing his hands together and making his own heat. The rest was up to God.

Dad dealt with illness and the surprises of his life in his own way. An ex-basketball player, he had unusual powers of peripheral vision. He caught sight of things out of the corner of his eye: a ricochet of light, a pigeon shaking its feathers on a ledge behind us. Actions no one else seemed to notice made him flinch.

He held up one to five fingers behind my ear, then asked me to count the number out loud with my eyes straight ahead. We practiced. I became nearly as good as he was in sensing the periphery of things. Sometimes he held the fingers up behind my back so that I could not see at all. Then he encouraged me to guess. "Come on," he said seriously, "you can tell. You know." He called it "fly-vision."

Gradually I did develop his wariness, particularly in watching for his scowl and for his eyes to glaze over and roll, ready for the fall. I had learned to sidestep and move with him, keeping my eye on the edges of the room for a sign the world was about to collapse: a lamp smash, a glass shatter, a table break apart. Sometimes when his breathing muscles tightened, he screamed before he fell, a high-pitched note like a rabbit in the claws of a hawk. Then he lost consciousness and bounced off the earth as though he had been dropped from the sky.

As he lay there his body stiffened, and we were surrounded by a protective space. Standing over him, I felt like a dog with its stricken master, but I also felt safe and secure, as though we were wrapped inside a halo of forgiveness. A breath of air blew upward from the earth, covering us both.

Then his breathing stopped, and he would start to turn faintly blue. This was my biggest test: learning to trust that he would come back. My mother had said, "Don't believe everything he tells you. He'll lie 'til he's blue in the face." And then, despite myself, I would get angry, especially when he wet his trousers as though he did not care, lying in a stain on the sidewalk, our lives soiled for all the town to see.

When he came out of it he jerked forward and grabbed his knees as though they were something other than himself, trying to get up too fast, staggering, bumping into things. Unsteadily he yawned and smiled, frowning at the same time. "My head is splitting," he said, and there was a deep gash to prove it. Then he undid his shirt as though it was time for bed. "Hey, Dave," he said groggily, "have you seen my pajamas?" I did not know how to tell him that it was not time for bed. Smiling in bewilderment, he blamed the linoleum or the wet leaves on the street, and, whatever my faith, it turned to anger and hate. Let him turn blue in the face, I sometimes thought. The next day his lying got worse; he boasted. He called it courage, but it was boasting, and he spent it wantonly, the way a rich man squanders his money: "Not many men have been through what I have been through in life. . . . Most men would have quit long ago. . . . Sometimes I wonder if I can go on living. . . . I pray to God and He gives me strength. . . . God must be on my side or I would have been dead long ago."

After I got out of the hospital I felt shaky; sometimes I felt feverish, sometimes cold. But lying around in bed had given me a chance to think, and I wanted to know as much about falling sickness as I could. It was, according to a pamphlet in the Carnegie Public Library, "the disease of artists and kings . . . a special infliction of the gods." The pamphlet also stated that it was "an illness which strikes the rich as well as the poor, the colored man as well as the white." My father would have loved that, I thought. The pamphlet did not help. The librarian suggested that I check the contents listed under "Psychology" for each book in the card catalog, and that was when I stumbled on Freud. We have, Freud wrote, only two primitive fears with which we are born: the fear of noise and the fear of falling. All other fears have to be learned: fear of love, fear of hate, fear of water, and even fear of death. I thought that the sound of a human head hitting the pavement was the most fearful noise I had ever heard, but there it was—both fears bound together in a single spell. In some ways the silence following the splat was even worse. That was why my mother prayed: to fill the horrible silence with God. God, she believed, soothed the pain of fear. I closed my eyes and turned away when he fell, not looking back until the silence had gone away.

Freud called the disease "daemonic" and wrote that it "belongs to all that is terrible." He argued that "the uncanny effect of epilepsy and of madness have the same origin. The ordinary person sees in them the workings of forces hitherto unsuspected in his fellow-man but which at the same time he is dimly aware of in a remote corner of his own being. The Middle Ages quite consistently ascribed all such maladies to daemonic influences, and in this their psychology was not so far out."

On this particular subject Freud sounded a bit like my grandmother. Her assumption was nearly the same as the one I read in the book: that the more severe the seizure, the more serious the sin behind it. The fact that no one could name or understand the sin only made it worse. Grandmother McKain called it a spell: an interlude in the midst of all that was normal, an inexplicable pause in the world of sense. In an effort to lighten the burden of the mystery, my father called his seizures a spill, as though the long arm of God had reached across the Alleghenies for salt, brushed the tall man, and knocked him from the table to the ground, spilling his blood.

Spell or spill, I knew he could fall any time or anywhere. When he fell he crashed as a tree in the forest, without warning. That was how my mother and father responded to each fall—as though it had occurred in the middle of the woods with no one present to hear the crash. They wiped up the blood and looked off into space, praying in silence.

One day while I was shooting baskets in the alley, the ball my father had given me hit a sharp ridge of ice and blew into a bubble, blistering and popping overnight. The deflated ball caved in like a Halloween pumpkin left on the porch to rot. In the morning I woke and found it sagging by my bed.

Playing basketball was a way of staying connected, a long, thin cord to school. My father never asked me about the games or even if I played, but I wanted to believe he cared. The Saturday after I left the hospital, I hitchhiked to Olean to see him. He smiled for a moment when he saw me coming into the shop, a quick smile, as though I had just stepped in out of the next room, but I could tell he was glad to see me.

"How's school?" he asked.

"Good," I answered.

"That's good," he said. "Always do your best."

Then we didn't say anything for a while, and he went back to his crossword puzzles. Later in the afternoon he stuck a "Back in 10 Minutes" sign on the door so we could go out for a bottle of pop, but we rushed back in five minutes.

"I've never missed a day of work in my life," he said.

"Never?" I asked tentatively.

"Never," he insisted. "Not unless I had the heart block. Then I get so sick sometimes I can't see straight." He squinted and massaged his temples, rubbing out the pain.

On another visit, two sheets of plywood were nailed across the front window of the shop. At first I thought the place had been boarded up and closed, but an OPEN sign was scrawled on a cardboard box inside the other window. Dad sat inside, his chrome chair back a little farther than usual, in shadow. His head was taped and bandaged in a turban, his lips raspberry.

"Did you read the clipping?" he asked as I came in. "It's on the door. The *Olean Times*."

I went back outside and closed the door so there would be no draft on the birds. The clipping was taped to the lower left-hand corner of the plate glass so that I had to stoop to read it:

CUT BY GLASS AT PET SHOP

Charles V. McKain, about 50, proprietor of the McKain Pet Shop, 303 W. State St., was severely cut in an accident at the store about 9:15 a.m. today. It was reported that he was cleaning bird cages in a display window, when he fell against the glass, which broke. He suffered a severe laceration on the back of his head, and a deep laceration over his left eye.

Both the Fire Department ambulance and the Empire Ambulance Service were called, together with a police prowl car. Mr. McKain was taken by the Empire Service to the Olean General Hospital where several stitches were taken. He lives at the New Central Hotel.

"Well, Pal," he said, "yesterday I almost got killed. For the first time in a year the heart block attacked me. I flew right through the plate glass." He smiled as he spoke, his hand taking off like a bird into the air. "You should have seen them at the hospital. I have fourteen stitches right here." He reached back and touched the bandage on the back of his head; the bump stuck out farther than he realized, and he winced. He pointed to his forehead and smiled proudly. "I have another five stitches right here. The doctor that sewed me up said he never saw anyone so brave." He tightened his arm and turned his wrist. "I didn't make a peep. Not a peep. God must have a future planned for me still. Don't you think, Pal? I would have been killed by now if He didn't. I know that. You know that, too." He smiled as a show of his strength, but I did not know anything about God's plan.

The Pet Shop was losing money. While he went out to do some errands, I rummaged through the papers on his desk and copied the clipping from the *Olean Times*. There were threatening bills from suppliers and an overdue notice from his landlord. There were also two letters from his father, handwritten on legal stationery: MCKAIN, OHL & SWAN- NER / Law Offices. In the first letter my grandfather ex- plained banking procedures. Dad must have claimed that he had lost money through a bank error. Grandfather wrote: "Let us get this bank situation straightened out. A bank rarely makes a mistake. It employs trained personnel. It uses adding machines: bookkeeping transactions daily. There is no excuse for a customer not being able at any time to prove the amount of the balance by the bank's own record. . . . There is nothing but simple addition and subtraction to it."

In the second letter he wrote:

Dear Charles:
If you will give me authority to deal with your bank and turn over to me your records I will come to Olean and straighten out your bank tangle.

I have spent many thousands of dollars helping you during the years past. No part of this, except one check for $25.00, has ever been repaid. I still hold a number of your checks which I shall immediately destroy. Your first duty is to make your business pay so that it can support you.

I have turned our house over to a realtor today. My doctor will not allow me to do any work and your mother cannot keep up the house without help.

You have never paid the slightest attention to my ad- vice concerning either your business or domestic affairs.

A marriage is a life partnership in which both parties bind themselves to support each other in sickness or in health. In your situation you have broken this agreement. Otherwise in your present financial difficulties your wife is earning plenty of money to temporarily tide you over. You have lost David and made it harder for him to live an upright life. Your divorce has brought shame and sorrow to your parents. If possible the situation should be rectified.

Awaiting your request on my bank suggestion, I am

Your

Dad

My father's reply began, "Dearest dad, If I hadn't had the 13 to 15 thousands loss due to a fire and 2 Robberies I would be O.K. . . . " That was as far as he had gotten: the single sentence took up half a page. I kept an eye on the door and copied down my grandfather's letters as quickly as I could.

It wasn't that I was lost to my father, nor he to me. He was just difficult to keep track of, that was all. He rarely stayed in one place, and that made him difficult to find. Why should my father's latest moves surprise anybody? By the time I had entered junior high school he had moved his Pet Shop seven times since I was born, and we had lived in six different houses and apartments. There was a war on. Not many people were buying lovebirds and angel fish. He moved, my father explained, to make ends meet. I accepted the many changes as one accepts the weather.

But I did not understand what my grandfather had meant by "You have lost David. . . . " I had not felt lost until I read his letter. Then, the more I thought about it, I realized he was probably right. I was lost. By the beginning of my senior year, work and school and basketball had begun to blur. If I sharpened my pencil, punched in on time, and shot my foul shots underhanded I would graduate. I hoped for nothing more. After graduation I would get married, make union wages pouring cement, and, I hoped, play basketball for Fishkin Clothiers—City Champs of the Men's Industrial League. I didn't think much about my future at all. Once in awhile I wished I could fill out college applications like other kids, but with only a few months of school to go there wasn't much I could do about it. Miss Fox, the guidance counselor, had recommended I join the Army.

I went back to Olean the next Saturday to prove my grandfather wrong: I was not lost to my father, nor he to me. As I walked into the shop, the new dressing wrapped around his head made him look like a thin Indian prince, a pale guru sitting in a chrome chair, slight and gray. He smoked quietly and burned incense, sitting in one spot to avoid the pain of moving.

After I swept up the birdseed and mopped the floor, he said he was not feeling well and wanted to close early. He smiled wanly and asked me if I could stay and carry his groceries. It was rare for him to ask anybody's help for anything, and we shopped in silence.

He had moved from the YMCA to a front room in the New Central Hotel on Union Street, Olean's main street. The dark green blinds were shut, letting in random pinholes of light. The room had a metal dresser and a matching metal closet painted honey-maple. I put the sack of groceries on the bed.

"Thanks, Pal," he said, pressing a coin in my hand at the door. "It's getting dark. You'd better get back."

He had given me a fifty-cent piece, and I flipped it spinning to the ceiling half a dozen steps in front of me as I bounded down the stairs. A half-dollar meant a lot to him then, and I knew he had given me the money with love.

Coach Wilson insisted we squat at the foul line and shoot free throws underhanded. One day he brought Bunny Levitt to school to put on a demonstration. Bunny Levitt, the world champion, shot foul shots underhand, and so should we. He had made five hundred foul shots in a row, and no one else

had come close. Now he stood in front of an all-school assembly at Bradford High School bouncing a basketball. He
dribbled from one end of the court to the other, pretending
that he was examining the exact height of the basket. He was
short and had a pug nose which did not twitch.

In a high nasal voice he said he was honored to be in Bradford, "a town with a great basketball tradition." A few people
in the crowd snickered. It was true that Bradford teams had
been great under Coach Harold Brace, but the best teams in
town had always played football. Bunny smiled at those who
had snickered and walked to the foul line. As he raised his
right hand, a hush fell over the gym.

"I spread my feet just far enough to feel comfortable, each
Spalding sneaker planted parallel with the natural drop of
my shoulders." He took a deep breath and bent his knees. "It
also helps to use a Spalding ball," he said, and he interrupted
his demonstration by parading around the gym with a brand-
new leather ball, balancing it shoulder high on the palm of
his hand like a waiter carrying a tray.

He imitated various ways not to shoot fouls, including my
own shot, the one-hander. He heaved the ball at the front of
the rim, then shot it so soft it dropped halfway to the basket.
Some of the students in the wooden bleachers cheered, kicking the floor in unison until Mr. Fretz, the assistant principal, lumbered toward the bleachers, pointing a stout finger
as a warning. The banging stopped.

After Bunny stopped clowning, he squared himself at the
line and swung his whistle around to the back of his neck.
The basketball team sat together in the front row so we
could study his technique. After he had made thirty in a row,
we exchanged glances and shook our heads in disbelief. After
he made forty-five, Reeder Huff muttered, "Miss, you little
asshole." On the next shot the ball grazed the front of the
rim and rolled out. The audience groaned, then applauded.
Reeder and I whooped and cheered.

"Okay," Bunny said after the noise died down. "I didn't make five hundred this time. I only made forty-two or forty-three."

"Forty-six! Forty-six!" the Duke shouted.

"Well then, forty-six. That's better than forty-two. Thank you. Does anyone want to come forward and make forty-seven?" Bunny exaggerated his smugness, tucking the ball under his elbow, hitching up his sweatpants. We whooped and hollered some more, and the assembly was dismissed.

I had wanted to go forward to take up Bunny's challenge but, in front of the whole school, I had not dared. The next day, Coach Wilson praised Bunny at practice. He told us he expected us to work on our foul shots so we would be as good as Bunny someday. As a mocking challenge to those who wanted to shoot one-handed, he promised that if we could better Bunny's Bradford mark we could shoot however we wanted. After the team practice, I went down to the Y to practice alone.

The gym rats were home for supper, so I had the place to myself. I held the ball high, then flicked it up with one hand, all wrist, just aiming over the front of the rim. I knew that shooting one-handed was more accurate than shooting underhanded. The ball simply started closer to the basket. After I had been practicing for half an hour with perfect concentration, I decided to keep count, shooting and whistling, weaving back and forth from the foul line to the basket to retrieve my shot as the ball kept dropping.

"How many is that?" a voice asked out of the hollow of the silence. Coach Wilson stood on the sidelines smiling, his hands in his pockets. He hardly ever came to the Y. "Come on. Let's see how many you can make. I'll feed you."

He took off his brown hat and stood under the basket. I took two deep breaths, bounced the ball twice, looked up over the rim, and scratched the first one in. I was surprised it had touched the rim at all. I concentrated and swished the second one. I liked that sound better. I did not bounce the ball between shots. I hardly took my eye off the basket. The Duke started counting and the shots kept dropping. The greater his surprise, the more confident I became. When I let the ball go, I knew each shot would be good.

The coach bounced the ball back with the same deliberate precision each time. At first I thought he was being helpful, then I wondered if he was giving me a perfect bounce so I would not have an excuse if I missed. At forty-three he smiled. At forty-four he counted more loudly. I smiled back a little myself, but I knew all the others would go in as well. I was doing nothing to stop them. I was on a roll. I swished forty-five, forty-six, forty-seven, and the next two shots to forty-nine.

"Forty-nine!" the coach shouted. "Forty-nine!"

I made fifty and laughed. Mr. Wilson nodded and smiled, shaking his head. The ball came back waist high. Fifty, I thought: that's a nice round number. I had broken my concentration. Fifty-one hit the back of the rim and rolled off.

"Four more than Bunny," the coach said in a controlled monotone. "Four more than Bunny." He smiled and shot an imaginary ball one-handed, permission granted. I could shoot however I wanted.

After the next mid-week basketball class, Coach Wilson leaned over the lectern to read some basketball scores from around the nation, games won or lost by a single point, games that proved the importance of making foul shots and of squatting at the line.

"Bunny Levitt has been an inspiration to all of us," he began haltingly. "We are lucky to have had him come to Bradford." The coach shuffled back and forth in front of the blackboard, his hands in his pockets, pondering what to say next.

"I'm sure McKain has told everyone in the school by now.

But I was there. I was at the Y when he did it. He made fifty foul shots in a row without missing." He raised his right hand and flicked his wrist, shooting a one-hander. He smiled and looked at me quickly, then turned back to the board.

"Okay then. Any questions about the 2–1–2? You all know your assignments against Dubois Friday night? Any questions at all?" He touched the board with his chalk but no one had any questions.

I dug my fingernails into the palms of my hands and stared at the floor. I had not told anyone about making the foul shots, nor would I have told anyone. The Duke must have known that. He must have known that braggarts at our school were tormented to silence.

"Wow!" Larry Gildersleeve said in the hall. "I didn't know you and the Duke were buddies. You guys go down to the Y a lot together?"

At the first sign of snow I had stopped hitchhiking to see my father. We did not exchange letters, and he did not have a phone. A phone would not have helped anyway: no one made long-distance calls unless it was an emergency. I carried his picture. When he became a minister he had had his photograph put on the front of a postcard. I trimmed it down to fit my wallet. When I asked my mother to tell me about his life before he became a preacher, she said I knew as much as she did.

But one night she came in and sat down on the edge of my bed. "Are you still interested in your father's past?" she asked. I nodded that I was, and she brushed my hair back with her fingers.

"Here," she said, "you might enjoy looking through these. These are his College of Wooster yearbooks." She had put little scraps of paper in the pages with his picture. The year-books were called *The Index*, and there were two of them. In the 1923 *Index*, they wrote:

CHARLES V. MCKAIN

Isn't that pose simply grand? No, we aren't discussing bathing beauties: just watching Chas. shoot baskets. He is one of '23's standbys on the floor. His interests are confined chiefly to Boy Scouts, 500, and a victrola. An "A" student in History, yet he doesn't specialize in dates. "There's a reason." Watch him Post 'em.

Ouija says:—"A good scout—forever."

In 1924, his senior year, there was this entry:

CHARLES VAN KIRK MCKAIN

"The world is good, and the people are good.
And we're all good fellows together."

That was all it said. I looked at his picture again. Mom said he looked like Tyrone Power. Grandma McKain said that as a boy he had had too much of everything—that he was too rich, too smart, and too good-looking. In his college pictures he did look handsome: he had a long face and a high forehead with deep-set eyes. He looked as though he were brooding, as though he were searching for some way to save the world.

"What happened to him?" I asked. "How did he get this way?"

Absently she closed the book and smoothed the cover as though it were cloth. "Oh, Dave," she said wistfully, "Lord only knows."

CHAPTER 20

Graduation

eel-to-toe, half a dozen students fidgeted outside the principal's office waiting to learn their rank in the 1955 graduating class. I got in at the end of the line hoping someone would fall in behind me so I would feel less conspicuous. The girl's hair in front of me lay flat against her neck in sticky little ringlets. Her skin was blotchey and damp, as though she had just come from gym class. As she shifted from one foot to the other, the hem of her dress brushed against my leg. It was hot. Mr. Bell stood in the hall to keep order. He wore a bow tie and swung his arms and clicked his fingers at his side self-consciously. The girls in the line looked at each other and giggled to show him how much they enjoyed his performance. Mr. Bell looked over at me, and I flashed a smile to satisfy him. The last week of school, I was on my best behavior.

The nervous girl in front of me struggled as she tried to open the heavy door with an armful of books. Mr. Bell and I reached over to help her at the same time and nearly collided. Only four students were allowed inside the office at once. The massive door whispered to a close and clicked emphatically. The girl with the sticky hair and I went in together.

"Name?" a woman behind the counter asked without looking up. She wore pink glasses and stabbed a red pencil through her hair. Line by line, she slid an amber ruler down a mimeographed list of names, jotting down numbers and screening the paper with the wall of her hand.

The line moved quickly. Lynn Stead beamed as she turned from the counter and flashed her rank at Joyce Simons: eighteen. Mark Rosen had to repeat his name, the back of his ears turning red. "Rosen," he mumbled. "Rosen." The girl with the damp hair peeked at the wrinkled paper cupped in her hand and cried.

As I pronounced my name, the secretary looked up and paused knowingly. "Oh, yes, McKain."

I tried to make the effort of opening the massive door look easy. I did not look at my rank until I got out into the hall. My real fear was that the school would ask me to repeat my senior year. I walked on the balls of my feet as though walking on air. Reeder Huff was waiting outside in the hall leaning against the fire alarm. We had made a bet, and he was grinning.

"Whats ya got?" he asked.

I glanced at the scrap of pink paper crumpled in my fist. "Two eighty-five," I said casually.

"I beat you, you bastard, I beat you!" He slapped me on the back and put his arm around my shoulder, laughing his Woody Woodpecker laugh. "Pay up, buddy, pay up! I'm two ninety-four!"

There were three hundred in the senior class. Reeder and I had made the bet to flaunt our indifference, but both of us knew how the other felt. We had been feeding each other lines to save face since we had met in the fifth grade. Deep down we were both just glad to graduate.

The day after Commencement I went back to the Alpine Ice Cream Company. I had tried to find other work, but no other jobs in town were available. The head of the local hod-carriers union shrugged his shoulders and laughed when I applied for membership. "Who do you know?" he asked. "You gotta know somebody." All the high-paying jobs in construction went to friends and relatives.

My mother and I didn't see much of each other. I left the

house for work in the morning before she got up, and when I got home she was halfway out the door heading to choir practice or to a meeting. As president of the McKean County Teachers Association, she had to drive "from one neck of the woods to the other" giving speeches. She had also joined the Civic Music Association, Delta Kappa Gamma, the American Association of University Women, and the board of the Visiting Nurses Association. She continued to play the organ for the First Baptist Church, teach Sunday school, and conduct the senior choir. "Some days," she joked, "I feel like I'm running around like a chicken with my head cut off," but I thought she was only saying that to hint of her success and to suggest that there were others who could not do without her.

One day when I came home sticky from syrup and milk and my joints numb, I filled the bathtub with the hottest water I could stand. Suspending myself by holding onto the sides, I hovered over the steam and lowered myself into the water inch by inch, my legs and bottom burning. No sooner had I finally gotten myself submerged than Mom walked in, closed the toilet lid, sat down, and started filing her nails. She looked tired.

"I have a rehearsal in ten minutes," she said. "I can't play the organ with a broken nail."

"I didn't say anything," I said. "Have a seat."

"No. But I know what you were thinking."

I scrunched down into the tub, covering myself with the washcloth. The bath water was brown with chocolate and dirt, so I knew she couldn't see anything; but I didn't like her in there anyway.

"Well, Dave," she said with a sigh, "you graduated from high school three weeks ago. What are you going to do with yourself?"

"I thought you had broken a nail?"

"I did, but I still want to know what you're going to do with yourself."

"What does that mean?"

"Just what I said. What are you going to do with yourself?"

"Well, let's see. After I take a bath I'm going to put on clean clothes, eat a hamburger at the Congress Street Diner, then see a movie or something."

"I don't mean tonight, and you know it. The rest of your life. What are you going to do with yourself?"

I ducked under the water to rinse my hair and to give myself time to think. The urgency of her question caught me off guard. She had never pressured me about the future before; no one had. I had simply taken the future for granted, like the rising of the sun. I did not pretend to understand God's gift to me of well-being, but my belief in that gift was strong. My mother's anxiety was uncalled-for, out of place. Her concern meant no more to me than the radio commercials I had heard on the radio urging young men "to join the future of America" by becoming engineers. Although I attended church spottily, I had heard the word "faith" all my life, and my belief in God was such that any concern I might show for my future seemed an act of heresy. My so-called conceit and self-confidence were nothing more than a belief in God's gift of well-being. I sat up in the tub and shook my hair.

"I would like a decent answer," she said coolly.

"What?" I asked, poking a finger in my ear to free the water. If she had to repeat herself, she might realize she had no business asking me such a question in the first place.

"I want a decent answer to my question," she said matter-of-factly. Nothing expressed her exasperation more forcefully than her matter-of-factness: the dramatic pause between her words, the theatrical patience in her voice.

"I don't know," I answered finally, honestly. "Besides, I don't feel very decent right now." I buried my face in my washcloth, hoping she would go away.

"I'm not going to be put off like this. I've asked a civil question and I want a civil answer." She spoke slowly, forcing herself to remain in control. "What about college? Are you going to go to college?"

"I told you before. Coach said the only two schools interested said no when they looked at my record." I wanted to remind her that college had been her idea from the start, but I could not handle an argument. She knew that I had not applied anywhere and that, despite the rumors, no one had contacted me.

"You don't have to go to Cornell or Penn State to go to college," she said. "You don't have to play basketball either. There are schools that would give you a chance. If you only showed you cared about something. Anything!" She got up and brushed her teeth as she spoke, spitting mouthwash into the sink as though she was spitting out a fire.

"Can you at least look at me when we talk?"

"I did. My eyes burn," I said evenly. "There's ammonia at work all day. Besides, I'm not doing the talking; you are."

She slammed the door as she left, widening the crack made by my father with his fist.

"I hope you are happy," she said in the kitchen, "because I am not."

The two worst things my father ever had said about my mother were that she griped about little things and that she was an ingrate. He hadn't said much about her being an ingrate because that was the more serious of the two charges—devastating even to suggest—and besides, it was the griping that drove him crazy. She had griped about his socks on the floor, the mess in the bathroom, his ashes in the sink. In turn, he complained that she had made "a mountain out of a molehill," for it seemed he loved to say the words "gripe" and "ingrate." "Gripe!" he would shout; "ingrate!" he would curse. Sometimes he did forget to lift the toilet seat, but when she mentioned it he called her "a calamity howler." He rested his foot up on the bathtub while he shaved, and his shoe left scuff marks. "Dutch Cleanser won't even take it off this time," she'd fussed as she scrubbed behind the door. Dad had been standing at the kitchen sink running water over the end of a lit cigarette. After he'd stepped on the trash bucket pedal and tossed the butt inside, he turned and faced the door. An anger that looked like pain crossed his face: without a word, he hauled off and smacked it so hard the wood split.

I knew their squabbles and storms by heart, and since my father wasn't there to say his lines and act out his part, I found myself taking over for him. He had complained that his wife spent all her time doing things for others and escaping from her responsibilities at home. That was not the final word on her civic-mindedness, but I saw that there was some truth in it. I remembered the sign that had hung at the top of the back stairs in Clarion, the words of Frances E. Willard, the founder of the Woman's Christian Temperance Union: "Do Everything." My mother tried to obey the challenge.

The next morning I was not surprised to see my mother sitting at the kitchen table at five-thirty when I got up to go to work. She looked up pleasantly, but I knew that we were still locked in battle and that I had to be aware. "Hi," I said after I had splashed water on my face and sat down to eat a bowl of Shredded Wheat.

"I have some good news," she began with a smile. "Now that you've graduated, I'm going back to school to get my master's degree." A bottle of camphor and two aspirins lay in front of her on the table. She waited for my reaction, but I had none. I sensed that there was more to come and that she was holding back. In her usual manner of releasing information slowly, she asked me to reach over and hand her her pocketbook. The pocketbook was sitting on the floor by her bed. I tipped my chair back, hooked the handle with my spoon, and lowered it onto the table like a crane operator dangling a sewer pipe over the river. She wiped off the bottom of the purse with her napkin and placed it squarely on her lap. She opened it and placed a new emery board in front of her on the table.

"Where?" I asked, before she started filing her nails.

"To Columbia," she answered enthusiastically. "Columbia University in New York. I can hardly wait. I have a job playing the organ at the second largest colored church in New York. The Church of the Master." She was beaming now, a joy I recognized as unstoppable. "I've always wanted to work with the people in Harlem," she added. "This is a chance I can't pass up."

She filed the emery board back and forth in a flurry of carefree sweeps: then, flinching, she dropped the board in her lap and put the tip of her thumb to her mouth. She wrapped her thumb inside her hand like a wounded bird; a drop of blood showed above the nail.

"What about me?" I asked.

"Well, I'll tell you one thing. You won't have to go back to that horrible ice cream plant anymore," she said, holding her cut finger mid-air and smiling. "I've already worked it out with your Uncle Walter. You can spend the summer in Connecticut."

I did not let her know how I felt, but her plans were fine so long as I could get out of the Alpine. Working at the ice cream factory for the past three weeks had left me exhausted. I had become so tired I didn't even see much of Linda. "You tired again?" she would ask sarcastically when I yawned at ten o'clock; but if I stayed out much later than that, the next day I could hardly stand up. The constant banter and the vulgarity drove me wild. Red and the others would get on me for being too sensitive. "Careful, Harry," Red would jeer. "Davie had a late night. He doesn't feel too good today. You don't want to hurt his feelings, do you?"

Linda and I argued about how much I loved her. Even though I tried, I couldn't assure her of anything, then, after awhile, I wasn't sure how I felt. "You're right," I said painfully one night. "Maybe I only care about myself. Maybe we should stop seeing each other."

I had not wanted to tell her I was going to Connecticut, but after I did I felt greatly relieved. I had told her the truth, and I put my arm around her to comfort her. She seemed far away to me then, small and unreachable, as though I was comforting somebody I hardly knew. Hunched over, her face buried in her hands, she wouldn't stop sobbing. I slid away from her to roll down the car window and stayed there. "You should try to see things the way I do," I said without irony. "You may be right about how selfish I am, but at least I'm happy."

The following payday I told Paul I was leaving.

"Come again?" he said, sneering, his hand cupped to his ear.

"I'm leaving."

"In the middle of the goddamn ice cream season, and you're leaving?"

I told him I had no choice, hiding behind my mother's plans.

Disgusted, Paul swore under his breath and turned away as though I no longer existed. But I was not sorry. After listening to Red Aitner for ten hours a day, my brains felt soft and warm. I wanted to shout I was glad to leave at Paul's back, but he turned and walked back toward me, his hand extended. "Get the hell out of here, kid," he said out of the corner of his mouth. "And good luck. You're going to need it."

CHAPTER 21

The Man Who Looked Like My Father

The man who looked like my father stood under the clock at Grand Central Station wearing a tan seersucker jacket, a pair of baggy khaki trousers, and a pair of brown cloth shoes with crepe soles. He had a newspaper stuffed under one arm and a paperback book in each pocket. My Uncle Walter was an inch or so shorter than my father, and his shoulders were a bit wider, but he had the same overall shape, lanky and athletic, like a country pitcher who could throw a wicked curve. Both men had large heads, long faces, small mouths, and deep-set eyes. Still, I did not recognize him until he smiled. I had not seen that almost shy McKain smile since I had last seen my father, and I had not seen my uncle since he and my aunt had visited us on North Center Street. I had been nine or ten at the time, and we'd walked around the block so they could stretch their legs after the long drive, my mother apologizing for the "sights" in the neighborhood nearly every step of the way. They did not spend the night.

"Dave!" Uncle Walter said enthusiastically in greeting. "Boy, you're taller than I am!" That was not quite true, but I did not care. I laughed in the presence of the big friendly man, glad in his easy calm and strength.

I studied him closely as we rode the train to Hartford. He wore a wrinkled jacket and the knuckles of his toes pushed up against the soft canvas of his shoes. I knew only that he was my father's youngest brother and a professor of rural sociology at the University of Connecticut. Even though he and my Aunt Elizabeth hardly knew me, they had invited me to their house to spend the rest of the summer. I was a stranger, and they were taking me in.

I did not know what to expect. I had never met any of my cousins, and I was curious, even apprehensive. Uncle Walter told me their names and ages. "We have three boys and two girls. Richard, who is eighteen. Nancy, who is sixteen. Let's see . . . Woody. Woody's fifteen. Doug's eleven, and little Susan, uh . . . Susan is three." He laughed that they had so many children he almost forgot their ages. He tried to tell me a little about each of them, but I did not know how I felt about other children in the house. Uncle Walter sensed my apprehension and said, "Oh, you'll get along fine with all of them."

During my first week in Storrs I did not let my uncle out of my sight. I followed him around as he gathered eggs and fed the chickens, I followed him to the garden to pick corn and tomatoes for supper, and I tagged along beside him as he mowed the lawn. I even squatted near him under the chestnut tree as he listened to a baseball game or read a book.

In the evening, the family played canasta, bridge, blackjack, gin rummy, or solitaire. I slept on the side porch, a small room enclosed with glass windows and a glass door that led to the living room. I left the door wide open so I wouldn't miss anything. Most nights, after everyone else had gone to bed, my uncle stayed downstairs and read awhile. I fought off sleep to listen as he talked to his book. "Hey, Dave," he would sometimes call, "listen to this!" and then he'd read a sentence or two out loud and laugh.

When I asked him what rural sociology was, he said it was the science of counting mail boxes along the dirt roads of America. Mac, as his friends called him, liked his job and his life. He wore clothes that mirrored his indifference to anything but the essentials: khaki work pants, colored cotton T-shirts, and socks that got sucked down inside his shoes when he walked.

One night when the house was still he called me into the living room to talk. I joined him gladly, sitting down on the couch, watching his eyes dart back and forth across the page, waiting for him to read out loud. I liked to watch him read in the same way that I had enjoyed watching my father read, but Uncle Walter read more than just the paper and mysteries. That particular summer he was reading *The Kinsey Report* and a dime-store novel with a half-naked farm girl on the cover. Even though I never shared my mother's piety, I was mildly shocked that my uncle read such books. Smiling, he claimed he had to read bad novels in order to keep up with his field.

"What was my father like as a boy?" I asked.

"Gee, Dave, I really don't know. I was pretty small when he was still in the house."

I hung on during the silence, hoping he would remember.

"Wait," he said, aware of my disappointment. "I do remember a couple of stories. But I don't know how true they are. Neither of them is very flattering, though. I know that. Do you still want to hear them?"

I nodded.

"Well, your father was something of a troublemaker. He and some of his friends used to get together and eat horse-radish and beans. They'd have contests to see who could eat the most. Three, four cans of beans and a jar of horseradish." Walter stopped and shook his head in mock disapproval, giving himself a chance to frame the next sentence. "You know what they'd do then?" he asked, still shaking his head. "They'd take a match and chase each other around lighting their rear ends. The gas would shoot out behind them just like a rocket!"

"Didn't they get burned?"

"I don't know," he answered thoughtfully. "But when he

was smaller, he'd round up all the stray cats in the neighborhood and put turpentine on their rear ends. Those cats would go crazy! They'd run around in circles until they dropped. I guess your dad liked that, too." He made circles in the air with his hand, stirring an invisible stew. "They'd run round and round, just howling."

He looked at me closely, unsure how I would respond, but I didn't really care about the stories. The room fell silent, and I just felt good being with him. I listened to the peepers singing through the open windows. After a moment or so he looked at me with a serious expression and then he looked back down. "What are you going to do this fall?"

"I don't know," I answered warily. I suspected that he had been talking with my mother.

He laughed good-naturedly as though I had made a joke. I did not know why he laughed, but his laughter was infectious. "I spoke to Mr. Richards about you today," he said. "The dean of admissions. He said you could go over and take an exam. Mr. Greer said something, too. I don't know. Some exam to see if you can get in."

Mr. Greer was the head basketball coach, a white-haired gentleman who looked like a senator. Uncle Walter said he never raised his voice during a game and that was why people called him a gentleman. The coach had asked me over to scrimmage one Saturday on the court outside his house. We had played three-on-three, and I had guarded Richie Kiernon, last year's starting varsity guard. Richie had hair in the hollow of his neck below his Adam's apple and he wore a St. Christopher's medal. The other five players were on the varsity, too, a team that had finished the previous season among the top twenty in the country. Each of the players wore a ring with NIT in gold letters across a ruby. After we scrimmaged, Coach Greer shook my hand and said I had played well. He said he would be in touch.

"What kind of exam?" I asked my uncle.

"A special exam to see if you can do college-level work. It's tomorrow at one o'clock if you want to take it. You can take the car." He turned the book over on his lap, took off his glasses, and looked at me. "This is sort of a second chance, you know. You want it, don't you?"

"Yes," I said cheerfully, not wanting to appear ungrateful, but I was not sure what I wanted.

The car he let me drive was a 1928 Ford, a jalopy everyone in the family called the "Putt-Bang." Since the car had no top, chickens hopped in at night and roosted under the dashboard; and if no one had used the car earlier, the chickens were still there after lunch. They squawked and flapped their wings when I opened the door, lifting themselves just high enough to clear the rumble seat, then thudding back to earth, bouncing like huge cabbages with wings in the dirt.

Dean Richards sat behind a stack of neat papers and smiled through the heatwave, in control. His fingernails were manicured and he wore a freshly ironed shirt, a narrow bow tie, and a light gray suit. Short and trim, he made me nervous.

"How is the basketball team going to fare next year?" he asked dutifully.

"I don't know," I said with an embarrassed smile.

"I've heard good things about your game, David," he said, but it was obvious he did not care much about basketball.

He glanced at his pocket watch. "Well, I have ten after. Let's find an empty room."

We walked up three flights of stairs to a cubbyhole just wide enough for a desk and a chair: Mr. Richards handed me a packet of papers wrapped in plastic. He looked at his watch again, handed me two freshly sharpened pencils, and said he would be back at 3:15.

Without air-conditioning and on the top floor, the small room was stifling. As soon as he was gone I opened the window and leaned out over a parking lot. The sun clanged off the chrome bumpers and the windshields: the heat and glare made me dizzy. A man stood in front of his car with his hands on his hips and kicked the gravel. His hood was up, his engine steaming. Beyond were cornfields, a meadow, and a long slope called Horse Barn Hill. A mustard haze hung over everything and, to my surprise, I began to cry.

For the first time I realized how much I did not want to pour cement and get married right away, whether I passed the exam or not—and I did not want to play basketball in the City League either, not even for Fishkin Clothiers, the city champs. I blew my nose, broke open the seal of the exam, straightened my chair, and did not look up until the dean rapped at the door two hours later.

I had been lucky. The next day I learned I had scored in the top five percent of those in the nation who had taken the exam, an exam that measured potential rather than performance. The score meant a great deal to me. I was not a "dummy." Dean Richards called it "a calculated risk for all concerned," but I would be attending the University of Connecticut on a basketball scholarship. At first I did not believe it; then I felt oddly guilty. I felt as though I were running out on my friends back home, leaving the men behind at the ice cream factory, abandoning my father. Mom, I felt, could take care of herself; she had her friends, her music, her church. But I imagined Dad's entire head wrapped in a tulip bandage with a hole just large enough for him to smoke and to dribble coffee down his chin: each time he fell he hurt himself more. I also thought of Grandpa McKain's letter and the sentence, "You have lost David and made it harder for him to live an upright life."

A week before school opened, Coach Greer introduced me to the other members of the team. The varsity was made up of older guys who had been in the Korean War. At twenty-six Gordon Ruddy was nine years older than I. The other members of the team were all in their twenties. Gordon said that, according to the *New York Times*, we had the best freshman basketball team in the country.

"In the country?" I asked in disbelief.

"Sure, that's what it said. But don't forget, that's only freshman. When you play us, it's all over." Gordon smiled menacingly, then became quite friendly again, gentle. "I was only kiddin'," he said. We were all standing around joking, but I could not get rid of the nagging thought that I did not belong on the best freshman basketball team in the country. Other guys from Bradford played better ball than I did, and yet there I was living next to Marco Malone, one of the stars on the varsity. With his soft, deft hands, Marco could make shots from all over the court. Except for a bed and a forty-five rpm record player, his room was empty. At night he lay on his cot, drank beer, and smoked, joining in when the chorus sang "Oh-Oh" in "Kisses Sweeter than Wine." That was the only record he owned. He bragged about never doing any work and promised to show me the ropes. When he wasn't in his room drinking beer and listening to "Kisses Sweeter than Wine," he was out with the vets drinking beer.

Basketball at Connecticut was really like a full-time job. Practice lasted most of the afternoon, from three o'clock right on through supper. Only the most disciplined students were able to stay in school and play basketball at the same time. I was at a disadvantage. I did not know where to begin. I was trying to learn how to study while everyone else was actually studying. Sometimes I stared at an open book for hours, too embarrassed to ask for help. I did not want people to know that my uncle taught at the university because they would think that was the only reason I got in. And they would be right: at least it was thanks to him that I was given a chance to take the exam at all. But I was not ready to think about anything. I was in over my head, and I knew it. I wasn't ready for college, and after a month of agonizing, I joined a fraternity.

At Connecticut anyone who did not belong to a fraternity went home for the weekend. The fraternity provided a great escape. I felt as though I was back in high school. Most of the fall term I managed to get along with four or five hours of sleep, but by the start of Christmas vacation I felt weak. I had overdone it. The least bit of light made me feel dizzy. My head split. One doctor at the school infirmary said I had a relatively new disease called mononucleosis. Another doctor called it the kissing disease, smiling knowingly. Together they decided what I needed was a couple of months of rest, so they sent me back home to Bradford.

CHAPTER 22

Balls and Strikes

I kneeled and buried my head under both pillows in bed like an ostrich, pinning the corners to the mattress, squeezing tight with both hands. The thinnest light made my head throb, and I could not close my eyes tight enough to screen out the gray brightness that seeped through the shades on a winter day. Now I understood what my father had meant when he said his head split so badly that he could hardly see straight. For the first two weeks I was home I rocked back and forth on my knees like a Mohammedan at prayer, wailing and moaning softly.

I lived on Empirin, one of my mother's favorite painkillers. Waving camphor in front of my nose didn't help. The stuff smelled like tansy, a plant Grandma Crawford used to grow by the back door to keep away ants; my mother thought camphor worked quiet miracles. At night, to take away the pain, she rubbed it on my forehead with the tips of her fingers. She spoke soothingly, the gentleness of her voice a balm. After a couple of weeks the headaches stopped, and in the weeks that followed I discovered reading. Though I was still weak, I propped myself up in bed and tried to prepare myself for the five final exams I had missed.

"It's a blessing in disguise," Mom said as she came into my room with the thermometer and a glass of orange juice. "I'm glad to see you finally reading. What's it about?"

"It's about the coal mines," I answered faintly. I turned the book over on the bed so she could see the title. *Sons and*

Lovers. Actually, as I read the book, I thought it was written about the two of us, our lives of passion and confusion. I was beginning to see myself in most everything I read, but I was too embarrassed to talk about it to anyone.

"If you want a really good book about coal miners," she said enthusiastically, "read *How Green Was My Valley.* That's the book. It's beautiful. The theme picks you right up off your feet! What about Mr. Lawrence's book? Can you say that about Mr. Lawrence's book?"

"I don't know. Does a book have to be inspirational? There are a dozen different themes in this book."

"Yes," she said, "I think a book should offer a direction. The world needs courage and love. Anybody can find fault. That doesn't take much gumption. A little gall maybe, but not much gumption. Llewellyn's people pray to the Lord and mean it. Every night the children of the Welsh coal miners pray before they go to sleep." She looked at me hard and blew a strand of wayward hair from her face, as if to suggest that's more than we can say about some people.

"Lawrence knows about prayer, too, but there's more to life than . . ."

"You'd better watch yourself," she warned playfully. "One of these days you'll get so broad-minded you'll go flat." She picked up the brush on my dresser and dusted the flat of her hand across the top. "If you don't believe in something one of these days, you'll just go flat!"

I laughed quickly. "Maybe you just like Welsh coal miners more than English coal miners," I said, knowing her Scotch disapproval of anything English.

"Maybe," she said, smiling, and she left the room to watch television with Strut. I could hear the metallic laughter of comedy through the wall. My father was gone, Strut had ducked out of marriage, and that left me. *Sons and Lovers:* the title must have frightened her more than she could admit. She was, I felt, afraid she might lose me as well.

I did not want to talk to her or to anybody about the real

reasons I liked Lawrence, but when I read him I could feel the moonlight outside the coal miners' cottages; I could see the "queer mounds and little black places among the cornfields and meadows"; I could feel Paul's anger and his love, his mother's fear, his father's drunken rage; I was drawn to his every word because he understood why people fell apart. He understood the coal miners of Nottinghamshire and, through him, I felt I was beginning to understand the oil workers of Bradford and my own family as well—the people who had shaped my life. It did not matter that the bravado of the miners' struggle was often pathetic and that their escapes were futile; their lives were filled with courage, and that was what moved me, both in the book and in the town. Broken and dying, the tormented had more passion to their lives than those protected by wealth. The rich used money to insulate themselves from history and experience, but nothing cut off the poor from pain and suffering.

My mother called it fiction.

By the middle of February, my temperature dropped. Mom made a joke about my "kissing disease" ending on Valentine's Day. I was beginning to need less sleep; it was time to go back to Connecticut. The second semester had already begun; I wasn't looking forward to adding five new courses while I was still making up five finals from the first semester, but I was glad to be able to get out of the house, to put on a pair of shoes, and to walk around town. Prickly-skinned and dizzy, I walked down the hill to the Congress Street Diner for a piece of homemade pie. I needed to emerge from the darkness of my room into some kind of recognition that I was alive. A few of the regulars at the diner teased and greeted me, and their warmth was enough.

Linda called that night. "I hear you're feeling well enough to be walking all over town," she said critically.

I had seen her once during the entire six weeks I had been home. She had come to the house and stood just inside the bedroom door. I was in the early phase of the illness then, moaning on my knees with two pillows over my head, the blinds pulled. We had tried to talk a couple of times on the phone, but I grew tired quickly. I felt too weak to take up with her again, too confused and unsure. It wasn't her fault. She was still in high school. I tried to explain Paul's relationship with Miriam in *Sons and Lovers*, but all I could do was talk about Paul's love for flowers and his anger. "Well," Linda said distantly, "Happy Valentine's Day."

I slept on the bus nearly all the way to Connecticut. Feverish, I hitchhiked the last twenty-five miles from Hartford to Storrs and rang the infirmary night-bell. The next day the doctor who had originally sent me home entered my room with a clipboard, shaking his head. The tests showed that my white blood cells were still eating the red cells, and according to the disappointed doctor I would not be able to play basketball for the rest of the season. I lowered my head as expected and accepted the doctor's sympathies, but I wasn't sure if I wanted to play basketball anymore or not. If I didn't play, I wouldn't wear myself out, and I wouldn't have to agonize on the bench waiting to be called into the game. Basketball didn't mean as much to me as it once did. It had become more work than fun, and I wanted to read. Even though I wasn't very good at it yet, I wanted to study and to learn.

In two days I was out of the infirmary, busy making up my first-semester finals and switching from the School of Business Administration to the College of Arts and Sciences. For the first time ever, I looked forward to signing up for courses. I wanted to take as many philosophy and literature courses as I could. Then, a month or so into the new semester, Uncle Walter called me into his office and closed the door. He sat down on the edge of his swivel chair and rubbed a pencil between his palms, clicking it against his ring.

"Dave," he said after a long, uncomfortable silence. "I don't want you to worry about this, but I think you should know. Your father's in the hospital. They want to give him some tests, and he needs a chance to rest. I don't know how long he'll be there. He's been through a lot." He looked up at me and added, "You know better than I do."

I had not thought about my father for months. Even while reading *Sons and Lovers* I had thought more about myself and my mother than I had about him. He was as distant and erratic a figure as Paul's father had been: at the edge of the action though the cause of much of it. While Mac talked, it occurred to me that I had been lying in bed in Bradford while my father was being taken to the hospital. He had been only eighteen miles away, and no one had said a word. But who would know to tell us?

"Gowanda," Mac said, "is a good hospital. I've been out there a couple of times and everything's provided for. The store, the birds . . . I'm sure he'll get good care." He stopped talking and looked at me closely, finding it difficult to talk. He smiled gently and reached into the middle drawer of his desk. "Here," he said, "take this. I've written to your grandfather about what happened. You're old enough to know how to handle it. There's no reason you shouldn't know."

Mac handed me a six-page single-spaced letter written in blue ink. I read bits and pieces of it, slowly. My father had been sentenced to the hospital by the court for writing threatening letters to the chief of police and for threatening his landlady (a Mrs. Waltzer) with a gun. Mac had driven the five hundred miles to Olean to take care of his things and clear up his debts. He had traded four birds (value, $1.25 apiece) and six turtles to the SPCA in exchange for their "disposal."

I kept my head down and pretended to continue reading. The particularity of the letter had staggered me. About my father's clothes, Mac had written, ". . . about one half of it was so unpleasantly dirty I put it in a box and gave it to a mission house to be used as they saw fit." I did not want to think of the baggy gabardines and soiled shirts, the spotted neckties and the gold cardigan with its pockets stretched out—half of what he had worn, jammed into a box.

"What's a homeopathic hospital?" I asked, forcing myself to say something.

"A homeopathic hospital? A way of treatment. It's a good hospital, I know that. They give patients small doses of certain medicines—certain medicines that in large doses would cause symptoms of the disease itself."

"They give him medicine to make him fall?" I asked. We had never talked about my father's illness, and neither of us had ever mentioned the word *epilepsy*. I had never talked to anyone about my father falling.

"I doubt that," Mac said, "I really doubt it." His eyes darted from side to side, searching the far corner of the room for answers. "Who knows," he said reassuringly, "he could be out in a couple of months. He could get a lot better."

When I got up to leave, Mac got up too. He reached into the pocket of his jacket and handed me a slip of paper with my father's address on it.

"I'm sure he'd like to hear from you," he said. "Sometimes hospitals can be pretty lonely."

"I might have known," Mom said when I got home for summer vacation and told her about Dad being in Gowanda. "As usual, I'm the last one to hear about anything. Well, let's go up and see him. See if there's anything he needs." The next morning she got a permanent, and that afternoon we drove to Gowanda. She did not ask me why I had waited almost two months to tell her, but I knew she wouldn't have gone to see him without me anyway. "Close the window, Dave," she said, frowning and ducking away from the wind. She wanted her hair to look nice.

"Fine," I said, rolling up the window. I knew we would be exhausted by the visit and I wanted to save as much emotional strength as possible. I turned my attention to the long drive through the Seneca Indian Reservation. The land was flat in the river valley, spread out and open. Trees were clear cut from the berm on both sides of the road, and we drove in a straight line into the haze and shimmer. The Indians grew corn and tomatoes in their front yards and left their old cars to rust in the Queen Anne's lace and mustard grass.

"There's poverty everywhere you look," Mom said. "The men drive up to Tonawanda or Buffalo to the foundries and the railroad. It's a long haul. And every day? It would test a person's sanity."

We passed a particularly shabby place with shredded tar paper on the roof. Green shades hung in the windows up-stairs and down, tattered and torn. A cement mixer sat hope-lessly next to the porch; an old maroon Packard poked up through the weeds.

"It's a shame," she added abstractly. "Nobody seems to care anything about the Indians anymore."

I did not join in on the conversation. Her concern had more to do with going to Gowanda than it did with the Indi-ans. She was, I knew, thinking about my father, working her-self into a state of exhaustion that would keep her from doing anything. I continued to look out the window, drawn to the desolation. The unpainted houses and rotting cars filled me with peace.

I did not think of Gowanda again until we pulled up in front of the visitor's entrance, a nineteenth-century red brick building as massive and ugly as an armory. I recognized the place from a postcard I had found in one of the psychol-ogy books at the Carnegie Public Library. The caption below the main gate read: "The State Hospital for the Insane—at Gowanda."

Mom sat in the car and looked straight ahead, burrowing down into her seat. She stared at a fly caught in the grid at the base of the window. Patients strolled across the grounds in front of us. One man paced back and forth between two elms, touching the bark, then pushing off, doing determined laps. Another man stood with his arms hanging slack at his sides, his ear on his shoulder as though his neck had been snapped by a rope. A third man dragged his toe in a wedding shuffle, stopping every few feet, then starting up again. I glanced at my mother.

"It's okay, Mom," I said. "He's not out there," and I moved around to her side of the car to open the door.

"I'm staying right here," she announced in a spent voice.

"Okay," I said easily. I did not blame her. She had not seen my father for five years, not since he had pushed her into the Christmas tree.

The attendant at the main desk would not give me clearance to go inside to visit because I wasn't twenty-one. He said I would have to see a Dr. Prokosch, and he nodded across the hall to a small office with the door open. A man sat at his desk in a tan cotton jacket and a red tie. When I introduced myself, he said, "Oh, yes. Your father has been with us for a couple of months now." He looked up at me closely, then glanced at his watch. Still seated at his desk, he gave me the feeling that he expected me to raise informed questions, but I simply asked him what was wrong with my father. Whatever it was, I wanted a name. Dr. Prokosch looked at me closely and said he was not well. He asked me if I could come back another time.

"I don't have another time," I lied. "I'm leaving for Wyoming tomorrow morning."

"Please, then," he said, standing. "Won't you sit down." Again, he looked at me as though I might have specific questions. I fixed my gaze on him to show my concern. "Your father has been quite upset lately," he said finally. "He did not come here of his own free will. Do you understand?"

"I don't understand," I said. My mouth was dry, and I wished I was back in the car with my mother heading home.

The doctor held up his finger and pushed his chair back from his desk to a small file cabinet behind him.

"Okay," he said, "I'll try to explain. Page . . . page . . . ah! Here we are. Let me read you some of the proceedings. On

January 6, 1956, Judge William L. McDermott of the Cattaragus County Court and two psychiatrists appointed by said court found in accordance with criminal procedures that Charles V. McKain be admitted to Gowanda State Homeopathic Hospital, Gowanda Psychiatric Center, Helmuth, New York." Dr. Prokosch looked up. "Do you know why?" he asked.

"No."

"Because Judge McDermott ruled he was incapable of comprehending the charges brought against him." The doctor spoke with emphasis, as though the judge's ruling explained more than I could understand. "Now, then," he continued, "your father said, 'I will spend one million dollars to fight this case. One million dollars!' Of course he was brought here. He had to be." Dr. Prokosch looked up and paused, anticipating my questions. Afraid he might decide I was too young to make sense of the report, I remained silent.

"What had he done?" The doctor asked rhetorically. "He smeared his feces on the walls of the Olean YMCA and flooded their bathroom. He threatened the manager of the Y, the landlady of a boarding house, and the chief of police. Because of these threats the FBI was brought in. From Jamestown, New York. It has to be a serious matter to bring in the FBI."

He paused again and looked at me searchingly, but I didn't know what to say. I did not care about the FBI and the law, but I was afraid to say that.

"Your father was obsessed by money matters. Simply obsessed. When he came here he said his father had sent him fifty thousand dollars from Hawaii which he had given away to the poor. In fact, over and over he said he had money problems because he gave his money to the poor. And then he would contradict himself by saying he had lots of money. That his father was a millionaire and all he had to do was ask. The report says that he snapped his fingers when he said that. They keep very accurate reports here. Every little ges-

ture that might mean something. Look at this." Dr. Prokosch held up a weekly log-report filled in from top to bottom, by hand. The report looked as though it had been
completed by a fastidious grade-school teacher.

"What's wrong with him?" I blurted out.

"What's wrong? Well, to start with, he is a violent man.
He is dangerous to himself as well as others. Let's see . . . ah,
yes. It says when he arrived he spontaneously produced rent
receipts to prove his innocence. Spontaneously. No one
asked him. He did not know where he was. He was disori-
ented, and he was still trying to prove that he was innocent.
To a court of law. But this is no law court. The admitting
officer said there was nothing he could do, and that's when it
happened. Your father became outraged. He was belligerent
and demanding. Arrogant. Threatening. We had to put him
in seclusion for his own good. At first he would not eat so we
fed him through the veins. To prevent dehydration as much
as starvation. People think it is for the food, but it's the dehydration. In seclusion, he unscrewed the electric plate on
the wall with the handle of his spoon. What for? He could
have electrocuted himself."

I could see my father kneeling by the baseboard unscrew-
ing the outlet plate; but however foolish or dangerous he appeared to others, I did not find him so. The report was simply incomplete. It merely mentioned a series of bizarre
events without ever seeming to realize that my father felt
threatened by the police and the hospital, desperately so. No
one seemed to understand him at all. I wanted to tell the
doctor about all the years he sat in the Pet Shop working
crossword puzzles without harming a soul, but the doctor
leaned closer across his desk.

"He is a desperately sick man," the doctor said urgently.
"To give you some idea . . . He denied he had epilepsy. He
even denied he had convulsions and blackouts! Listen.

" 'Well then,' one of the doctors asked, 'how did you fall
then?' And your father answered, 'It was nothing. I slipped

on the filthy floor.' And yet, the doctor notes, at other times he would say, 'It was just a spill.' Just a spill! Sometimes he fell so hard he almost killed himself.

"To calm him during these episodes of violence, we give him electric shock treatments. That makes him relax. He becomes calm after that."

The doctor became calmer as well. He took his elbows off the desk and leaned back in his swivel chair.

"So, David," he continued, "that's about it. I'm sorry I don't have better news for you. Do you still want to see him? We never know . . ."

"Yes," I interrupted, "I want to see him."

Without saying a word the guard led me through three separate buildings and six steel doors. After opening one door he would pause to let me pass in front of him, then he would drop back and relock it while I waited for him to move ahead of me and lead the way to the next door. He wore a pistol on his belt and would not look at me or answer questions. The sixth door opened up on a room that smelled of sour milk, a gray cavernous hall that looked like an airplane hangar. Dimly lit, the scale of the place overwhelmed me; the ceiling was fifteen feet tall. I felt small, insignificant. The beams and flying joists were covered with grease and gray fur from the kitchen.

Sitting alone and waiting at a table with twelve empty chairs, Dad snuffed out a cigarette when he saw me; he smiled and stood up to shake hands as though it had been yesterday. He did not open his arms to me, and I did not open my arms to him. That was the way he had taught me. Just act natural, as though everything is all right.

His skin was as white as talcum. His pale blue eyes had lost their lustre, his hair was as gray as a dustball. He coughed and spit a gob of yellow mucus into his handkerchief, cursing through a thread of phlegm.

"Get me out of here, Dave," he said. "This place is killing

me." These were his first words. He spoke urgently. I realized he had never asked me for anything important before in my life. I shook my head no gently and smiled. He lit another cigarette and smiled back, accepting my impotence without judgment, letting me know by his smile that he understood that, in the face of whatever madness seized him, we were both helpless. He wore a look of composed anxiety and pain.

"I have an appointment with the mayor of Gowanda," he said desperately. "I want him and the entire town to know what's happening here. How we're treated. Like cat dirt. You wouldn't believe it. The filth! In the halls, under the beds!" He grew angrier as he spoke, his eyes watering. "They defecate in the halls . . . they relieve themselves in the yard." He stopped himself and smiled helplessly, switching immediately from fury to pity. "But you can't blame them. They can't help it. These poor people can't help it."

Love swam in his eyes as well as anger and pain, the old and familiar triad. Then he grew serene: the same expression which came over his face as he gave out gum and candy—a beatific look, unhinged, holy, dangling. I said nothing. When he started up again, the anger took over.

"Even the umpiring," he said venomously. "The officiating at the softball games is lousy. Last night they let a run come in from first on a ground-rule double! One minute the strike zone's a keyhole, the next it's a barn door!" Overwhelmed by disgust, he could not continue. He stood up, smiled, and held out his hand, the grip as firm as the old days.

"They need somebody here who can call balls and strikes," he said, speaking toward the guard. "Isn't that right, Al?" Dad winked at me, and we both smiled. "No. Al's all right. Al's a good guy. You like baseball, don't you, Al?" My father wasn't making fun of the guard, but I didn't know if the guard knew that or not. Al lit a cigarette and looked suspiciously at the floor.

"Well," Dad said to me casually, crossing the floor as if we were walking across the living room to the kitchen for a dish of ice cream. "Be good." Al unlocked the door and folded his hands officially behind his back. Dad turned and cupped his hands so the guard would not hear. "Take care, Pal," he mouthed in secret. "Take care."

When I returned to the car, Mom was reading Dr. Elton Trueblood, *An Alternative to Futility.* She read all of Dr. Trueblood's books and the books of Catherine Marshall and Norman Vincent Peale as well. I got in and turned on the radio to country and western, a weepy song sung by a man who drank "licker in the mornin'."

"How is he?" she asked.

"Good," I said. I rolled down the window and stuck my face in the wind as I backed up. Mom turned off the radio. "Do you mind?"

"No," I said, "I don't mind."

"How did he look?"

"Good. He looked good," I answered; then we didn't say anything for several miles. My focus blurred; heat rippled off the tar.

"When he gets better . . ." I started to say. "I mean when he really does get better, do you think he could come back home and live with us?"

"Oh . . . I don't know," she answered vaguely.

"It wouldn't be too bad," I said cautiously. "He'll be okay. I bet he'd mostly sit in his chair and read, as he always did. You know, at the Pet Shop . . . no one hardly ever comes in. He'd be okay in there all day. Just doing crosswords and burning incense. He wouldn't be any trouble."

She didn't answer. Her permanent lay flat and heavy against her forehead. "Did he say anything about me?" she asked as we crossed the reservation.

"No," I said a bit sharply.

"Oh, well," she sighed, "I wish things could have been different."

"Yeah," I said resignedly. "He should have been an umpire."

"Please, Dave," she said in an overly patient voice. "Don't *yeah* me when we're talking about things that hurt."

For the next ten years my father and I exchanged letters irregularly. Dad's letters always began "Dear Pal," then he complained about the hell-hole of Gowanda, outlined fuzzy escape plans to Ottawa, and concluded with a summary: "I am nothing but a prisoner here, held against my will. If it was not for my Mother and Dad, and for the strength given me by Jesus Christ, I don't think I could stand it another day. They treat us all like cat dirt. God Bless You and Keep You, Pal. Love, Your 'Dad.' "

My letters were brief. During baseball season I recapped the career of Ewell Blackwell, my father's favorite pitcher and the ace of the 1947 Cincinnati Reds. Blackwell had won twenty-two games, and Dad had gloated over it as though they had been friends. Once, while closing up the Pet Shop for lunch, he stopped right in the middle of the sidewalk on Mechanic Street, kicked his leg up over his head, reared back, and uncorked a fastball. "The Whip!" he shouted with a leer, unleashing Blackwell's nickname from the back of his throat to the tip of his tongue so that the final *p* popped into the catcher's mitt sixty feet away. I had never seen him happier; his blue eyes burned as the ball left his hand, gaining speed as it caught the outside corner of the plate for a called third strike, winning the game.

CHAPTER 23

Shoe Box

Ten and a half years passed before I went back to Gowanda to see him. It was December 29, 1966, the day after my twenty-ninth birthday. Mac called me to meet him at the hospital the following day. My father was dying. My wife and I were spending Christmas with my mother in Bradford, and we had planned on driving back to Connecticut before New Year's. Sharon was expecting our first child in February.

"Go ahead, then," Mom said resignedly when I got off the phone. "Before the storm. You have to see him through this, too." At first she had seemed rather businesslike about his dying; then later in the day she said she wasn't hungry. By evening she had collapsed on the couch, breathing camphor, the lights dim, a wet washcloth on her forehead.

During the past decade I had devoted myself to books as an editor for McGraw-Hill and as a professor of English at the University of Connecticut. My mother called my change of fortune "miraculous," but neither she nor anyone knew much about me. She called my interest in literature "downright baffling." "But I like stories," I protested. "Dad read me the Bible every day before school, and you, you told me stories all the time, too. Don't you remember?" I put my arm around her to show that I was grateful.

"It's over my head," she responded shyly. "But, then, so is just about everything else."

"No," I said easily, "I won't let you get away with that. You just want praise and pity."

She looked at me cautiously, not sure how I had meant it. I smiled and hugged her. "Be careful on these roads," she said, shaking her head. "It's starting to snow already."

Mac was smoking his corncob pipe in the lobby, leaning up against a wall near the elevator. He said he had been waiting only a few minutes, and we took the elevator up to the third floor in silence. In Room 314 Dad was bent in the middle, cranked up in a hospital bed—a man tipped to an audience, framed inside a doorway, on display. Tubes hung from upside-down bottles on either side of him, and a floor-length curtain separated him from the man in the next bed who wheezed erratically, as though air were escaping from a child's balloon. When he looked up and saw me he opened his mouth to smile, sliding his hand across the white sheet and wiggling his fingers, his strength nearly gone. His right hand was smooth and dry, as though he had rubbed it with talcum, ready to shoot a game of pool. His teeth, on the nightstand beside him, bubbled up slowly in a glass of water, leaving a stutter of circles on the Bible.

"Hi, Pal," he rasped, a pinprick of light deep in his eyes. A catheter snaked up under the sheets from the side of the bed. Although his skin was yellow and he looked older, he had also stayed the same. He still had the harried look of a man who never knew when he would collapse, of a man who never knew what had hit him. I began slipping back into the old world of both his constant fear and mine, hoping he would offer me a stick of gum or a piece of candy.

Mac broke the silence. In an everyday voice he said, "Hey, Charles, how are you doing?"

"Not bad, Wally," he rasped again. "Medicine has my voice." He clutched at his neck and puckered his lips in disgust. All his life he had made a face taking medicines. Indian doctors gave him Salamanca Salve, unguents, and herb balms; white doctors prescribed belladonna and bromides. Mac told me he drank bromides in the bathroom as a boy, hiding the blue bottles under his bed. I also had seen the blue bottles, two or three empty bottles of Bromo Seltzer in the trash every week. "Bromo," Dad called it bitterly. "Greek for bad smell. I hate the stuff." He'd laugh and pucker up his lips as though he had chewed on a lemon, but the Bromo lifted his spirits. Someone had told him it would help cure his spells.

I looked from one man to the other for traces of family resemblance. Mac and my father looked less alike than I had first thought, but I did not want to concentrate on the differences. All three of us had large heads, I decided. The three of us had long faces with deep-set eyes.

"Dave's doing real well at Connecticut," Mac said. "He's a poet and an assistant professor."

Dad smiled serenely, his lips white and cracked. "Dave," he whispered, "how about getting me a dish of ice cream?" He tried to lift himself up in bed to locate his trousers. He was thin now; under his johnnies his collarbone jutted forward like a hollow shelf.

"That's okay," I said, patting my pocket. "I've got money. Chocolate?"

He smiled as if to say "of course, chocolate," pleased I had remembered. I did not stop at the desk for directions. I ran as I had run as a boy, hurling myself down the back stairs five or six at a time, bouncing off each step like a boulder bounding down a hill. The booming of my boots in the empty stairwell somehow calmed me. As fast as I could run, I hurdled snowbanks and sprinted across the network of parking lots toward the snack bar, or at least toward where I thought the snack bar would be. As I had done as a child, I pushed headlong into the world as though the wind would hold me. My voice came in waves as I howled and half-chanted, my tears drying quickly in the cold. I ran with my eyes closed as I continued to wail. Blind faith: so long as it provided comfort, I did not try to understand. There it was. Without breaking stride, I opened my eyes and jumped a snowbank in front of the snack bar.

When I got back with the ice cream, Dad was gazing up at the ceiling and at heaven, his hands folded softly, still smiling. I knew he was gazing up at heaven because I had seen him do it many times. He narrowed his eyes and smiled faintly: a subtle smile, at peace, holy. Pain created a serenity of its own, and dying promised no more than a pause, a brief interlude like one of his spells—a moment between a cup of ice cream and eternal life. I quickly peeled back the cardboard top of the dixie cup, guiding his thin wrist that held the wooden spoon. No matter how careful I tried to be, ice cream dribbled down his chin. A person can make a mess at the end, I thought, and it doesn't matter. The room was hot, and my face stung. I fixed my eyes on the wooden spoon; it was wide on top and narrow at the heel like a shoe.

The next day Mac flew back to Connecticut, and I stayed at Gowanda to take care of details. My father had died alone in the middle of the night. Fire-white, the sun glared off the snow like a naked bulb hanging over a bathtub. After a partial thaw, the top layer of snow had frozen into a porcelain glaze. The young nurse from Records wore a cranberry sweater over her uniform. "Sure," she said, "I'll draw you a map." She turned over a used envelope and drew a long shed and a smokestack. She laughed at her primitive drawing and added a long curl of smoke to the chimney. Her fingernails were lacquered red. "Might as well make it look good," she said. We pretended the smokestack was not phallic, but the loops of smoke had made it worse—like graffiti in a bus station. "Physical plant," she said nervously. "And there, just beyond, what we call the barracks. You can't miss the barracks," she laughed. "They look like chicken coops."

The frozen snow made the world sharp and clear, linking the hospital grounds with the distant farms. The crust of ice broke as I waded through the soft powder underneath toward the smokestack and the barracks. The snow concealed boundaries, shrinking distance and space. When I got there, my face stung and my back felt prickly with sweat. A wall of icicles hung to the ground, blocking the cheap, warped door; the eave of the barracks was eye-level. I held onto the side of the building so I wouldn't fall. After yanking the frozen door open, I stood dazed for a moment inside the narrow hall, blinking, with spots before my eyes.

Three men sagged against a broken sheet-rock wall, their chins on their knees as they hunkered down, their gray shirts buttoned to their necks. The childhood scars on their scalps looked pink in the overhead light of the EXIT sign. They had been shorn nearly bald. Tapping my boots lightly, I tried to make myself small, but my coat brushed against the walls as I shook off the snow. All the dials of energy had been turned down except mine, and every slight noise was a violation of their quiet dying. My chest heaved as I filled my lungs with stale air. One of the sagging men covered his ears at the sound of my breathing.

The man in charge of my father's belongings sat inside a cage smoking a dead pipe and watching television. He was short and bulky and wore a green visor like an old-fashioned dispatcher for the railroad. I handed him the slip the nurse had given me, and when he spoke he seemed to shout.

"Hey," he said, holding the voucher in two hands, "take anything you want. Whatever belongs to him, it's yours now. But anything you don't want, we'll take. It goes right down to our recycle shop. The other patients, some of them don't have no family. You know what I mean?"

"Is this where my father lived?" I asked, picking up some of his twang.

"Right here," he said. "Six-D. And everybody liked him. He got along good with people. Knew his sports, I'll tell you that. Couple of years ago he did a little coaching. Softball, baseball. Everybody liked Charlie."

He flattened my voucher on the metal counter and handed me a ball-point. My father's son and sole heir, I was entitled to what the slip called his "personal effects." I had never heard anyone call my father "Charlie" before. I wondered if he had winced when they called him that. I signed our name carefully so people could read it, putting a ditto mark under the *c* in "M⸍Kain," lifting it up the way he would have done, making it special.

The man in charge put the old Philco table radio and a shoe box on the counter. I wanted to stay for a while and talk. I wanted to get to know the man as well as I thought he must have known my father. He had seen him every day. He had seen him light cigarettes and eat candy. He had seen him lean against the wall behind me. He had listened to him talk.

"You knew him pretty well?" I asked.

"Oh, yeah. I knew him as good as anybody. He come in here every day. He always had a nice word. He stood right there where you are. He'd come in and talk . . . you know, baseball, basketball. You name it. Charlie was a good guy."

The man stopped and looked away. There was a slowness in his eyes under the visor I had not noticed. He held the voucher up against the light as though looking for a secret code. "By law," he said, "any of this stuff is yours." He directed my attention back to the items on the counter: I was asking too many questions. I left the radio and thanked him. He waved the voucher in the air and nodded. "Any time," he said, "and thanks for the radio. The guys can listen to the ball games in the summer. Hey, just like your dad did."

The funeral was in three days. My mother sat on the couch looking small and forlorn, as though she was trying to understand what had gone wrong. I did not allow myself to understand why she mourned; I did not have her memories. I did not want her to see the shoe box, so I smuggled it into my room and closed the door, emptying the contents on the bed. A ring spilled out, a packet of letters, and my father's working Bible. I had never seen him wear a wedding ring, only this particular ring with the chipped translucent stone, pale blue, the color of his eyes. He had boasted that the ring was platinum, "worth a fortune."

I glanced inside the cover of the Bible at my grandmother's inscription: "To Charles, from Mother and Dad, May 14, 1937." Little flecks of leather crumpled on the bedspread. It was "The New Chain-Reference Bible," containing "Thompson's Original and Complete System of Bible Study, Chain References, Text Cyclopedia, Analyses of Books, Outline Studies of Characters, and Unique Charts." The book had the familiar smell of molted feathers and dander, incense and tobacco. He had read from it to me a thousand times. Now the spine was broken, the cover stained with water rings from the hospital.

His wallet did not bulge with bills as it once had, but I opened it eagerly, searching for clues. Inside, three quarters were scotch-taped to the lining where the glue had melted, the tape yellow and brittle. There were also three soft and faded dollar bills, a 1932 Pennsylvania driver's license, and a business card advertising:

BIG LEVEL INN
8 Miles east of Kane
Junction routes 219 and 6
Clean Rest Rooms
Phone Mt. Jewett 3821

I could not make connections. The card meant nothing. Perhaps just another temporary room where he might have once stayed. I didn't know. His license was thirty-four years old.

I carefully untied the butcher's string around the letters.

Some of the envelopes were addressed to my father and others he had addressed and never mailed. I arranged them according to postmark; most of them were from the Olean years, 1951 to 1955. The first letter was a brief typed note from John C. O'Hara, General Secretary, Young Men's Christian Association, Olean, New York.

Dear Mr. McKain,
I have wanted to see you personally but since our paths haven't crossed I will make use of this means of saying that because of difficulties which are apparent in the dormitory, you are hereby asked to leave by the end of the period to which you are paid—namely Tuesday morning, September 13, 1955.

My father wrote Mr. O'Hara the next day:

Dear Sir:
I am more than at a loss to understand request.
  If it has to do with towels put in rinse basin I have never put one in. In fact I have shut it off when it was running over or about to, 10 times at least.
  I speak to everyone, am friendly to all. Is not this supposed to be a YMCA?
  My father was on Board of Directors of YMCA College at Youngstown, Ohio and I have directed some of the largest Boy Scout and Y Camps in America.
  Please, elucidate for me on this matter, reason for it or it will go much higher.
  I have been as friendly and cooperative as I know how. But an action like this is slander, plus.
  Please give me any reasons. Room 6.
    Sincerely,
    Rev. McKain

When Mr. O'Hara did not reply, Dad sent another letter, this time threatening to sue him for $10,000. "You will," he

wrote, "be ousted from the Y, for which you are clearly un-
fit. As I said before it is Unchristian as well as ungentle-
manly for you to act this way. May God pity you."

He wrote yet a third letter on the following day:

Dear Sir:
Are you not man enough to tell me why I am evicted
from a place where more profanity is used than regular
English?

I think I know reason. There is a crippled fellow that
from night I came here will not speak to me. I know not
why . . . Two Sundays ago I told him that the C in
YMCA stood for Christian and asked him what I had
ever done to him. He didn't even speak . . .

On 6 or 7 occasions I shut off water he had left running in that big sink. Maybe he didn't put the towels in.
I do not know.

You will have my prayers, if you know what prayer is
but you cooked your goose.

The above letter was scribbled in a grand and sweeping
manner covering three sheets of stationery. In a fourth letter,
in a cramped hand, he wrote:

I have had a severe cold, temperature 101 at times so
until I can find a nice room may I stay here?

Ask the young Italian boy operated on recently for
Hernia what he thinks of me. He is best fellow around.

Finally, not a fifth letter but a postcard, unmistakably
written by my father with his left hand:

Hon Sec ???
Send the Electric Vibrator, Slippers and Shirts hanging
in room 6 to our best friend Rev. McCain at 138 N. 1st
St. at once. I suppose you want them out.

He was our best friend. We are leaving soon and you will be going too, soon.

Several of Rev. McCain's best friends.

Dated July 4, 1955, there was a single receipt from the New Central Hotel. He had moved to the hotel after being evicted from the dormitory at the Y, but he did not stay at the hotel long. Mac told me that he had been asked to leave because he had set fire to his room. No one could be certain if he had started the fires deliberately, but he had started them twice. The second fire had to be put out by the fire department, and the police were asked to investigate. That must have been the beginning of his problems with Chief Hand and the FBI.

In the fall he had moved again, this time to a room in a boarding house run by Mrs. Waltzer. He had kept her pink rental receipts inside a blank envelope, the same receipts, according to Dr. Prokosch, he'd brandished at Gowanda to prove his innocence. Mac had written to his father: "Mrs. Waltzer probably had a very difficult and harrowing experience with Charles. She was very much afraid of him." Mac had been more direct with me; he told me my father had threatened her with a gun, and she had called the police. In a matter of weeks, he was back in court.

There were other letters as well, all of them dead; they had been written by my father to his parents and never sent. In his last letter he wrote:

Dearest dad and mother

Thanks a lot for the candy. It tastes like more.

It has been raining here for several days. But yesterday, the place was filled with visitors. Only about 4 of us didn't have any.

Please see that I get out of here right away. It is no place for God's Servant and your eldest son. I want to get busy and prove to you that your many kindnesses to me have not been in vain.

Write when you can, but *please* see that I am out of here soon.

Lots of love,
"Charles"

P.S. I weighed 147 pounds, Saturday night. A gain of 22 pounds. But I must get busy and making my own way.

The day of the funeral the roads were icy. Mom wore a dark blue suit and a matching hat with a veil that dropped to within a quarter of an inch of her eyes. She looked down at her lap and massaged the gold clasp on her blue vinyl purse. We had wanted to limit the service to the three of us, but when we arrived at the funeral home we had to park the car a block down the street. Mac crooked his elbow for my mother on the icy sidewalk and up the icy steps. Mourners stood inside the small foyer, old people with their coats on. I did not recognize any of the faces in the room or any of the names in the red leather sign-in book.

A sprite of an old woman came over and patted my hand to tell me that she remembered my father well. He was, she said, especially good with children. "He always had something for them, even back in the Depression. A lollipop, a gumdrop. Always something sweet."

The only person who did not know my father was Reverend Donner, the minister in charge of the service. He smiled gladly and held up his arms in rejoicing. I sat in the front row of folding chairs facing the closed coffin. I remembered when my father had weighed two hundred pounds without looking heavy. Reverend Donner spoke with confidence and joy. He said we should not view death as the end but rather as the beginning. "The words of Reverend McKain," he went on, "brought solace to all in dark times . . ."—but I closed my eyes and stopped listening.

"Oh my, no," Mom exclaimed when the funeral director asked us if we wanted to go to the Cambridge Springs Cemetery. She smoothed out the front of her dress and put on her gloves. "I've had enough." Back home I sat in the living room listening to the rub of polyester on nylon as she changed clothes behind her bedroom door. She wanted, now, only to rest: to wrap her hands around a cup of coffee, her eyes half-closed, breathing in the steam.

"I have been doing things for others all my life," she said. "Now I would like to do a few things for myself." When she came into the living room she wore an ankle-length house-coat that whispered as she walked, the folds of her turquoise robe billowing like silk. Strut had given her the housecoat for Christmas. "It's just like silk," he had said proudly.

On a small scale, ever since Dad had first moved to Olean, my mother's life had changed. She had thrown away the hollyhock slipcover and reupholstered the chair in a demure beige with needlepoint flowers; and, on installment time, for the living room she had bought a hide-a-bed sofa and an imitation Italian marble coffee table with a bowl of plastic fruit. Instead of Grandma Crawford's handpainted fruit bowl, now an 8 × 10 photograph sat on top of the piano. In Ektachrome, the color brilliant, almost metallic, a new woman leaned back comfortably in a newly upholstered chair, smiling in a turquoise housecoat, light-hearted, gay at last.

CHAPTER 24

In Everything
Give Thanks

M y mother's smile did not last long. Even the happy Ektachrome snapshot faded. Now, wearing diapers, she sleeps with her knees tucked up under her chin in the flex-burial position. No one understands why she sleeps in this position, but I take it as a sign of her refusal to roll over and die. The doctors no longer call her illness "hardening of the arteries," but the senility is the same, the self-prophecy fulfilled. Unable to feed herself, she has become "just like Grandma." Either she sleeps most of the day, or she slouches in a gerry-chair.

My friends say the nursing home is the best place for her, but I have my doubts. I don't believe that old people should be put away just because they make us change our lives. Even after she had been at the Mystic Manor for a year, I continued to search for a private home or for a person willing to spend the day at our house. I advertised and called ministers, but no one in New London County in Connecticut came forth with home care. I considered taking care of her myself, but I could not afford to give up my job. I guess that was the way everyone else felt. Still, I was troubled— you don't walk away from people who need you, I said to myself. You don't sign a check to have somebody else clean up the mess. After I said these things to myself, I realized it was my mother talking.

What would she have done? I wondered, but the minute I asked the question I knew the answer. She would have said you should not worry about your life. By heart, she would have quoted Jesus: "Therefore I tell you, do not be anxious about your life, what you shall eat or what you shall drink, nor about your body, what you shall wear. Is not life more than food, and the body more than clothing? Consider the lilies of the field, how they grow; they neither toil nor spin; yet I tell you even Solomon in all his glory was not arrayed like one of these. . . . O men of little faith . . . do not be anxious." That would have been the message: do nothing, so God has room to operate. We lived our lives as though there had been a terrible accident, and we needed to get out of the way to make room for the Heavenly Healer, the Ghost with blankets and hot soup, the Lord with stretchers, bandages, and salvation.

It is my mother talking and I try to stop it, but I can't. I don't like the idea of people living in institutions. A doctor pokes his head into her room once every two weeks. One of the doctors admits that they don't even know what is wrong with her.

"It's terrible," her favorite nurse says, touching my arm. "You probably don't want to hear this, but I've seen her CAT scans. In profile, there are hollow spots all through the brain. The ventricles open up and there are these big holes in there. Like Swiss cheese. All through the brain."

I give up trying to find a private home in Connecticut and decide to try the Alleghenies. There might be hope back there. The Alleghenies are still cut off from the rest of the country, frozen in time. I tell one of my mother's Bradford friends I'd like to find a place for her and she says, "You could do a whole lot worse. The hills out here might be good for drainage, but they're even better for the human soul." The friend promises to pray for both of us, and within a month I stumble on an advertisement in the *Mountain Peddler:* "Wanted: Older woman to take care of in my home."

For a moment I don't believe it, but I answer the ad quickly. The woman on the other end of the phone has a difficult time giving me directions.

"I don't know if there's a name on the mailbox out front or not," she says slowly, "never looked." She yells to her husband to see if he knows; he does. They live in an old white farmhouse on Eleven Mile Road, just outside of Shinglehouse. I look for the Chrystal Baptist Church and a farmhouse on the right about half a mile beyond it with the name Dailey on the mailbox. If there's a front door, I can't find it. The house sits back fifty yards from the road. Chickens, ducks, hogs, and cows roam the yard and two dogs bark. I get out of the car warily, a voice from the shadows of the house shouts that the dogs won't harm me.

A man who turns out to be Mr. Dailey wears denim work pants, a gray work shirt, and a baseball cap; he stands with his large arms folded, his legs apart, like an umpire or a third-base coach. Mrs. Dailey wears a faded paisley cotton dress under a Christmas apron; her glasses are crooked, the lenses are smudged from spatter and flour. In their late fifties, they are warm and wary at the same time.

Three or four flies buzz in the middle of the high ceiling of the large kitchen. Surfaces have been scrubbed and scoured to the point where they are worn. The porcelain on the sink has been rubbed down to cast iron, the nickle-plated faucets down to brass. Even the pearl-gray of the formica table has been bleached out from rubbing, and black patches show through the linoleum in front of the stove and the sink. My mother would have smiled and said the house looks lived in.

"After we get the room fixed up, she'd be in here," Mrs. Dailey says as we walk through the kitchen to a room off the dining room. Her voice is slow, sing-song.

"How do you mean 'fixed up'?" I ask. A plastic bauble dangles from a light fixture hanging by a wire from the ceiling.

"Well. We'd paint first, then put down the wall-to-wall

rug. All we're doin' is waitin' for someone to come." Mrs. Dailey sings more and more as she speaks, her voice lilting but hoarse, as though she smokes heavily. Jim holds a cigarette behind his back, leaning against the doorjamb.

"Have you ever taken care of a patient who needs to be changed and fed?" I ask.

"Well, let's see," Mrs. Dailey answers vaguely, as though she is trying to think of someone. She speaks even more slowly than I had realized on the phone, as though time meant nothing to either of us. "Yes," she finally answers, "I guess I have. There was Jim's aunt a few years back. And now there's Fanny. Fanny's out back." Her laughter leads to a coughing attack. I don't know why she is laughing, but I imagine it has something to do with Fanny. "You haven't met Fanny yet," she beams. "Fanny's my aunt."

I walk out into the dining room. There are pink and band-aid colored pictures of children of all ages hanging from the walls and propped up on the tables, on the bookcase, and on the Victorian organ. One of the children, a girl, is black. Her picture is on the walnut organ above a hymnal opened to "I Walk in the Garden Alone." No one is watching the midday game show on television in the living room.

"My mother played the organ for years at the Baptist church in Bradford."

"Oh!" Mrs. Dailey exclaims, and I wait for her to add something else.

"Ruth plays, too," Mr. Dailey finally says.

"Here?" I ask, pointing down the road toward the Chrystal Baptist Church.

"No. Down to the Millport Methodist Church." The "no" is pronounced so slowly it seems to have two syllables.

We move to the living room and sit in large, overstuffed 1930s chairs and sofas, but no one turns off the television. A sleek new Pontiac roars around a curve to the jingle, "We build excitement. . . ." A gun rack hangs over the couch and black ridges run up and down the linoleum where the floorboards have worn through. We are separated from one another by the volume. I stay for the commercial, then get up and walk back into the dining room, looking for some positive sign that this would be the best place for my mother. The Daileys follow as though it were perfectly all right for me to wander through their house on my own.

"Why do you want to take care of somebody?" I ask Ruth.

"Well," Mrs. Dailey answers slowly. "So we can keep the farm. We can't hardly meet our taxes now, and we need the extra money. If we don't find someone we'll have to sell."

"We got the For Sale sign out front. Did you see it?" Jim asks.

I shake my head no, disarmed by their candor. I had hoped for a more standard reply, something more encouraging, but I realize I've picked up the often false and cheery professionalism of the nursing home.

"How can I find out about you people?" I ask. "I want to be sure, you know, before bringing my mother back five hundred miles."

"Sure you do," Ruth says thoughtfully. "Well. Let me tell you. I've lived in this house all my life. We've taken care of people all our lives, haven't we, Jim?" Jim nods and Ruth laughs. I have not caught onto their sense of humor yet; I recognize it, but I don't understand how people on the verge of losing their farm can laugh so often. "We have five boys of our own and two girls. Three, counting Debbie. She's adopted, but one of our own. That's her picture on the organ." She points to the picture of the black girl with the pale blue glasses. I'm sure she must have been the only black girl in all of Shinglehouse.

"Who are all these other kids?" I ask.

"Those are ours, too," Ruth says. "Our foster children. We raised thirty foster children. Didn't we, Jim?"

Jim nods.

"Thirty?" I ask skeptically.

"Thirty," Mrs. Dailey answers, shaking her head. "One

year I put seventeen kids on the school bus every day and still had two at home." Ruth leans back and laughs her great husky laugh.

"And now you farm?" I ask.

It's Jim's turn to laugh; he laughs quietly and shakes his head. "No. Should have been a farmer. Worked out all my life." By "worked out" I realize he means he worked for someone else. He says this in hushed tones, with the intonation of a humble man. In speaking about himself, unless asked directly, he drops the first person singular.

"What do you do for a living?" I ask.

"A logger. The cows, hogs . . . we sell a few every year, but not enough. We had sheep up to a couple of years ago. But they never amounted to much. We have over three hundred acres."

"And, we take in hunters," Ruth adds slowly. "One time we had fifty-nine of 'em all at once. But I'll never do that again. Gangsters, some of 'em. From New Jersey. All they did was drink whiskey and shoot whatever moved out there. I won't have 'em back. But some of the hunters is just like family. Been coming twenty years."

It's hot. I'm not sure why I'm standing here talking to these people. I promise Mrs. Dailey I'll phone her, then I drive up the road where I had seen a sign for maple syrup. I want to ask the neighbors what they think of the Daileys. A man and a woman are sitting out on the shade of their porch. The house is freshly painted, the lawn clipped and edged. The two of them appear to be retired. They wave as I approach the house, and before I have a chance to introduce myself, they ask me to pull up a chair. I tell them about the Daileys' ad and that I am considering having my mother stay with them.

"Don't be thrown off by the house," Mr. Kemp says. "It'll always be warm and there'll be plenty to eat. What they lack in material comfort, they make up for—they more than make up for it—with love." He continues to look at me earnestly. "Did you feel it? Did you feel the love in the house? They raised so many kids and done so much for people. And Jim will help too. They share everything. I wouldn't hesitate if it was my mother."

"I wouldn't either," his wife adds.

The Daileys had said little to enhance themselves, but their neighbors are making up for it. I thank them, but Mr. Kemp won't let me leave until I follow him out to the garden where he loads me down with tomatoes, lettuce, squash, and a sack full of odd-looking potatoes he calls blue. I buy a gallon of maple syrup. He says if I don't like it, just bring it back.

I keep thinking about the Swiss cheese holes Mickey mentioned in my mother's brain. There are potholes in the road and holes in the universe. Black holes, they say, are just stars with such gravitational force that light cannot escape, as though the pull of a thing back on itself leads to darkness. I drive out of town to the hills that surround it, moving all over God's Country with no destination. People are scarce. An old man keeps his eye on the tall grass beside the road, pushing a supermarket basket that glints in the sun. There are bottle gatherers everywhere—people of all ages carrying burlap sacks slung over their shoulders picking up glass and aluminum. I see a dozen or so after driving around for a couple of hours. I wonder if the Daileys would ever have to go out and pick up bottles along Eleven Mile Road. A man my age on foot waves as I drive by. Hesitantly, I wave back.

I struggle with the decision about what is best for my mother, but I come to the conclusion that I need to have more trust in people. I was brought up to trust people. What has happened? I remember what my mother once said, and I smile. She warned that I was becoming so broad-minded I ran the risk of going flat.

On balance, I look back over the years and feel lucky growing up as I did. The demands placed on my parents to pay the

rent and to cope with my father's spells gave me the freedom
of the gypsies. I don't want to overstate this, but there are
blessings in having grown up in certain kinds of poverty. No
doubt my kind of freedom had its price, but I would always
choose bad teeth and an occasional well-meaning bowl of
stewed tomatoes if I could grow up wandering in and out of
school, down by the Tuna Creek, along the tracks out of
town, and up into the woods.

I trusted people then; I decide to trust people now. I even
convince myself that my mother will feel at home with the
Daileys. I double back to Shinglehouse to tell them. When I
get there, a wash of white sheets is dancing like a choir of
angels in the sun. Ruth is standing at the kitchen sink. I can
see her through the window that opens out onto the back
porch. She smiles when I tell her that I hope they get along
with my mother.

"I was thinking after you left," she sings. "Thinking about
nice days when your mother can sit out on the porch. Jim
called the VFW and they'll give us a wheelchair for her. Then
she can sit right out there. Right outside my window."

The cows, chickens, hogs, ducks, geese, and dogs use the
house as a windbreak. Ruth laughs and says that sometimes
they get up on the porch too. She bangs a wooden spoon on
the window over the sink, and the cows and the hogs jump
off. "Your mother doesn't mind company, does she?" Ruth
asks and laughs. I think of my father talking to his lovebirds
and canaries all those years, and how, in a few days, my
mother will be talking to birds and animals, too.

There's an hour left in the day so I drive the back dirt roads
over Clara Hill and through more state game lands to Port
Allegany—all over God's Creation, my mother would say.
Wandering runs in the family. People who have lost their
minds wander in an effort to find them, as though the mind
were a misplaced wallet or a missing ring. I have lived in Big
Sur, New York, Mexico, San Francisco, Greece, and maybe
fifty other places. All these strange and temporary shelters

have seemed little more than bad leads, dead ends. My father used to remind me that his first name, Charles, meant "Strong," and his middle name, Van Kirk, meant "Son of the Church." He did not say that our surname made us wanderers, sons of Cain. During the thousands of times he read me the Bible before school, he never read me the story in which Cain, a marked man, is sent out from the presence of the Lord to wander over the face of the earth.

I drive up Two Mile Road, one of the hollows, park my car, and leave it unlocked. The hill is steep, and I climb bent double, my hands on my knees. Up on top, facing west, I look out over Two Mile Creek, Open Brook, and thousands of acres of farms and forests to the Allegheny River. From the hillfarm I can see Prospect Peak, the highest point of land in a straight line from the Atlantic Ocean to the Rockies. I sit and stare, watching the sun set behind it.

The late-afternoon light is gold. I watch the mountains roll over one another in endless waves like the ocean, folding in on each other. I can see why the Indians called them "the Endless Mountains," but the illusion doesn't last. After awhile, one ridge resembles the next ridge, sharing features and contours common to the entire range; but the mountains are not endless, nor are they like the ocean. Geologists say that the Alleghenies are like a suture of earth, an "uplifting erosion" where great masses of land festered and knitted, like scars, healing over, growing stronger. One day I will spread my mother's ashes from the top of one of these mountains, and the wind will catch them and take them, just as she had wanted.